Gunboat on the Yangtze

Gunboat on the Yangtze

The Diary of Captain Glenn F. Howell of the USS Palos, 1920–1921

by Glenn F. Howell

edited by Dennis L. Noble

McFarland & Company, Inc., Publishers
Jefferson, North Carolina, and London

Library of Congress Cataloguing-in-Publication Data

Howell, Glenn, 1891–1973
    Gunboat on the Yangtze : the diary of Captain Glenn F.
Howell of the USS *Palos*, 1920–1921 / by Glenn F. Howell ; edited
by Dennis L. Noble.
        p.   cm.
    Includes bibliographical references and index.

    ISBN 0-7864-1232-1 (softcover : 50# alkaline paper) ∞

    1. China—History—19th century.   2. United States—Relations—China.
    3.   China—Relations—United States.   4. Howell, Glenn, 1888–   I. Title:
Diary of Captain Glenn F. Howell of the USS *Palos*, 1920–1921.   II. Noble,
Dennis L.   III. Title.
DS755.2.H68   2002
951'.033—dc21   2002009158

British Library cataloguing data are available

Cover photographs: USS *Palos* (1921);
Glenn F. Howell aboard the *Palos* (1920)

Manufactured in the United States of America

McFarland & Company, Inc., Publishers
  Box 611, Jefferson, North Carolina 28640
    www.mcfarlandpub.com

This book is for Therese, Kathleen and Patrick.
They helped make twenty years of service easier.

ACKNOWLEDGMENTS

I especially want to thank someone who has crossed the bar. Adm. Kemp Tolley, the dean of the historians of the Yangtze River Patrol, offered encouragement and advice throughout the long period it took to bring the diary into publication. Earlier in his career Admiral Tolley served on the Yangtze River Patrol and readers can do no wrong by reading his classic *Yangtze Patrol: The U.S. Navy in China*. Adm. Kemp Tolley was an outstanding example of what the old term "an officer and gentleman" represented. He will be sorely missed.

I wish to thank Dr. Dean C. Allard, now retired, but at the time I began this project, head of the Naval Operational Archives, and eventually head of the U.S. Naval Historical Center, for his support and encouragement. Bernard F. Cavalcante, Head of the Naval Operational Archives, Naval Historical Center, and his staff, assisted me quickly and efficiently in my many requests. The U.S. Naval Historical Center awarded me an Admiral Edwin Hooper Grant that allowed me to spend time at the center.

Loren A. Noble helped me finish the work quickly by typing a large portion of the manuscript. Peggy Norris once again read and checked the manuscript for inconsistencies and my many misspellings. Tom Beard read the manuscript and offered helpful suggestions. Dr. Robert M. Browning, Jr., helped me in understanding the old steam navy. Readers will thank Susan Browning for her work on the maps illustrating the locations that played a part in this diary about a sailor in China.

I wish to thank Professor Emeritus Leonard H. D. Gordon, of Purdue University, for his great abilities to teach an ex-sailor something of Chinese history, culture and language.

I wish to thank the family of Glenn F. Howell for permission to publish the diary and the use of photographs contained within it.

And finally I wish to thank the editor of *Shipmates* for the use of Vice Admiral T.G. Settle, "The Last Cruise of the *Palos*," *Shipmates: U.S. Naval Academy Alumni Association*, 24, No. 4 (April 1961): 2–6.

—D.L.N.

TABLE OF CONTENTS

PREFACE

While working on a book dealing with the U.S. military in China from 1901 to 1937, I soon discovered, as have many researchers before me, the lack of personal observations from those who served in the peacetime military. Then I visited the Naval Operational Archives in the U.S. Naval Historical Center, Washington, D.C. The staff at the archives introduced me to the diaries of Capt. Glenn F. Howell, U.S. Navy. Howell kept a journal, or as he put it a log, of his activities for sixty-two years, in 202 leather bound volumes. To my knowledge, portions of the 202 volumes contain the largest single source of a military man's observation of service in China during that huge country's struggle to throw off one power and come to grips with a new one. I felt the years of Howell's service as a skipper of a Yangtze River gunboat, the USS *Palos*, contained valuable and interesting material on a number of topics, so I set about editing the journals for this particular period, 1920–1921.

Glenn F. Howell proved to be a very articulate officer, thus making the editing much easier than some personal observations. In general, I have edited the diary entries very lightly. Many of Howell's paragraphs consisted of a single sentence and, where possible, I brought together a number of these to form longer paragraphs. Where I did edit heavily was in the constant refrain of parties attended. I left in those that were important or had something interesting to offer to the flow of the narrative of the diary. Howell had a propensity for the use of dashes in his manuscript and I have left them as he recorded them. Howell did not set off ship's names in any way, so I followed normal custom in this matter.

There have been many attempts at the Romanization of the Chinese language over the years and the matter can be confusing even to those who have studied China for many years. I will use the older Wade-Giles

method, as it was in use during the period Howell served in China. Howell, however, appears to have used his own system, probably trying to pro-
nounce and write the names to the best of his abilities, thus making the
identification even more difficult. The names of places and people are as
they are recorded in the diary. I have added the current system of *Pinyin*
for the location, or for Chinese names, the first time it is used in brackets after the word, thereafter it is left as recorded. Thus, Canton
[Guangzhou] and Peking [Beijing]. Howell would at times phonically
spell a Chinese name, Lee for Li, and I have left them as he recorded
them. I suspect he did this also for Westerners he met. Where I could
learn the proper name, I have placed it in brackets following the name.

In Howell's diary are some entries dealing with cases of courts martial and an officer transferred from a gunboat in disgrace. As the events
in the diary are of relatively recent history, I do not think history is hurt
by my not including the names of the people involved. I have therefore
left a line _____ to represent the names.

Very few Americans realize their country's armed forces served in
China before and immediately after World War II. Furthermore, most
Americans have only a vague idea of China and the Chinese. Because of
this, many of Howell's entries may not be understandable to readers of
today. Instead of placing an excessive amount of explanatory footnotes in
the diary entries, I have arranged this book with an introduction that
includes a brief biography of Howell, a brief history of China from 1800
to 1920, and a brief history of the United States military in China for the
same period of time. The sections on China and the military are not
meant to be exhaustive essays, only an overview of the subjects so readers may better understand what the diary represents.

After the introduction, to make the actual diary entries more understandable, I have divided the diary into three sections. At the beginning
of each section I have written comments on some of the aspects in the
section. In the first section, covering from June 6, 1920, to November 8,
1920, for example, Howell's entries have a number of remarks on Chinese junks, and I discuss some aspects of junks and other Chinese craft
on the Yangtze River. Again, the introductions are not meant to be the
final word on any subject, only an overview. Within each of the sections
of the diary are notes concerning people who I could identify and other
aspects of the entries.

The epilogue comments on the importance of the diary. So that the
reader may see how another naval officer viewed the *Palos*, I have included
as an appendix an article by Vice Admiral T.G.W. Settle , USN (Ret.),
about the gunboat's last cruise up the mighty Yangtze River.

The recognized expert on the Chinese junks and sampans of the Yangtze River, G.R.G. Worcester, wrote in his book on the subject, "Some Chinese mythical legends have found their way into these pages. Many, of course, sound trivial and cannot always be regarded with uniform gravity; but they cannot be excluded, for they are, taken as a whole, so important a part of the junkman's life and throw a valuable light on his mental attitude.

"Modern young China is scornful of these stories and dismisses them contemptuously as superstitious nonsense; but, apart from the interest and pleasure entailed in collecting them and associating them with the locality where they originated, there is the satisfaction of conserving these interesting legends and superstitions of the old-time junkmen lest they too pass away unrecorded."

Some myths have also crept into this work and, like Worcester, I feel it important to leave them as they are, for they are a part of the story of the U.S. Navy on the Yangtze River. One of the values of Glenn F. Howell's diaries is it allows readers to be transported back to an era and a place that is little-known. The stories, both real and imaginary, including those surrounding the events in the diary, help in this journey back in time.

—D.L.N.

INTRODUCTION

1. Glenn F. Howell

The Yangtze River, at 3,964 miles, or 10,000 Chinese *li*, is the world's third longest, surpassed only by the Nile and the Amazon.[1] It is called by the Chinese the *Chang Jing*—the Long River, or simply *The River*. It begins in Tibet and makes its way southward heading for Vietnam and the Gulf of Tonkin until northern Yunnan Province in China where it makes an extremely sharp bend near Shigu, which causes it to flow through China and into the East China Sea. The diversion is caused by a geo-morphological feature known as river capture. Chinese legend, however, says that over four thousand years ago the river flowed out of China in what is now Yunnan Province taking with it all of China's soil to the Annamese. The emperor known as Yu the Great became so angry that he set a large mountain down at Shigu and blocked the river, thus causing it to flow through China. The hill Da Yu chose is called *Yuan Ling*, Cloud Mountain.[2]

The *Chang Jing* pours 1.2 million cubic feet of water at its mouth every second, with the number doubling in August and September when the snowfields have melted and after the summer rains. The river has over seven hundred tributaries that help push out a total of 244 cubic miles of water into the East China Sea.

The Yangtze is sometimes used as the dividing line to explain the people of China. Those who live north of the river are usually paler, tall, wheat-eating, Mandarin-speaking, reclusive and conservative. Those living to the south are stocky, darker, more flamboyant, rice-eating, and speak in coastal dialects.

The population that lives in the river's valley is huge. The writer

Simon Winchester notes that "[o]ut of all the people of the world, one in twelve lives in the river's watershed." The Yangtze watershed contains the world's second largest population, with only India having more people. Most importantly, the river "is the symbolic heart of the country, and at the very center, both literally and figuratively and spiritually, of the country which it so ponderously and so hugely flows."[3]

The Yangtze is also a highway for the transportation of goods and, much to the dismay of the emperors, one of the ways foreigners penetrated China. In 1854, the first United States warship, the USS *Susquehanna*, cruised up the *Chang Jing*, thus beginning what would become known to U.S. sailors as the Yangtze River Patrol, or simply the Yangtze Patrol. America's naval force actually began service in Asian water fifty-four years earlier.[4]

Sixty-one years after the *Susquehanna* began her slow cruise up the mighty Yangtze River, a young U.S. Navy officer, Glenn Fletcher Howell, visited Peking [Beijing] on official duty as aide to the Commander, Asiatic Fleet. Howell would return in 1920 as the commanding officer of the USS *Palos*, a gunboat on the Yangtze River, and then again from 1925–1927 to serve on the staff of the Yangtze River Patrol.

Glenn F. Howell was born February 5, 1891, at Woodhull, Illinois, the son of Silvanus White and Sara Black Howell. After graduating from the Woodhull public schools, he applied to the U.S. Naval Academy, Annapolis, Maryland. Howell graduated from the academy in 1911 and commissioned an ensign. Promoted to lieutenant in 1915, he became the personal aide to the Commander in Chief, Asiatic Fleet in 1915–1916. His next promotion, to lieutenant commander, came in 1918. During World War I, Howell saw action as the executive officer of the USS *Schurz*, an unprotected German cruiser seized by the United States. He received a Letter of Commendation for taking command of the ship when the captain suffered injuries during a collision.

From 1920–1921, Howell commanded the gunboat *Palos*. His next duty assignment took him to the U.S. embassy in Rio de Janeiro as naval attache from 1922 to 1925. After this tour of duty, Howell again returned to China as the Chief of Staff to the Commander, Yangtze River Patrol. After this assignment, he became the Executive Officer aboard the USS *Henderson*. Howell was retired in 1932 for physical disability, due to tuberculosis, and bought a ranch near Lowman, Idaho.

Howell first entered public life when elected mayor of Caldwell, Idaho, and then, in 1941, he became an Idaho State Senator from Boise. Recalled to active duty in 1942, Howell's assignment took him to liaison duty with the Canadian armed forces and a promotion to captain the same year. He then became the naval attache in Ottawa, Canada, from 1943 to 1946. Howell's active duty ended in 1946, and he returned to Idaho.

After returning from active duty, he became executive secretary to Gov. C. A. Robbins from 1947 to 1948. Continuing in public office, Howell was elected mayor of McCall, Idaho, from 1948–1949. Glenn F. Howell died on February 6, 1973, at Boise, Idaho.[5]

The above brief description of Glenn F. Howell indicates a moderately interesting naval career, but nothing of great note, followed by a varied career in public office equal to, or surpassing, his U.S. Navy record. An obituary chose to note Howell as a "prominent Idaho political figure" rather than stress his military record.[6]

Despite first appearances, this little-known officer is important in understanding the U.S. Navy's role in China prior to World War II. In his day, Howell saw a part of China relatively few Westerners even ventured into. Even today, some of the areas he observed are still only slightly known by people in the United States. Furthermore, the *Palos*, the gunboat Howell commanded on the Yangtze River, was a part of the old steam navy. Like most aspects of the peace time military, very little has been written on those who served in the steam navy.

Howell's importance is as a diarist. To say he was prolific is to understate on the grand scale. From 1911 to 1973, the naval officer—"political figure"—kept an incredible series of journals. Some diarists are content to enter the weather and a few cryptic remarks. Not so Howell. Some of his hand-written entries run to ten pages in length. In total, he filled 202 leather bound volumes.

Howell proved to be a keen observer of his surroundings and very articulate. His entries are a treasure trove for those who are interested in naval history, social naval history, twentieth century Chinese history, and especially the interactions of two very different cultures in the early twentieth century. With the building of the Three Gorges dam by the People's Republic of China, Howell's description of the region takes on a new significance, as it describes the life of an area still little-known to Westerners that will soon be lost to rising waters.

The sheer volume of material present in the Howell diaries is daunting. Some of the most interesting material within the leather bound volumes, however, is on the naval officer's time in China. One of the mental images people of today have of America's rise to world power is of U.S. gunboats enforcing the thrust of the eagle in distant regions of the globe. It is not uncommon to hear the term "gunboat diplomacy" bandied about during arguments and discussions of the period. This edited version of

Glenn F. Howell (left) and G.H. Cassidy aboard the *Palos* in 1920. Gunboat-men had a relaxed manner in the wearing of uniforms. (Photograph found in Glenn F. Howell's diary.)

Howell's diaries will shed light on one of the gunboats in what Westerners then would define as a very remote area of the world.

There were, of course, other naval officers serving in East Asian gunboats and some probably did more than Glenn F. Howell. What sets Howell apart from his brother officers are the diaries. Howell's entries contains the largest amount of contemporary, articulate material by an American military man in China.[7]

2. China from 1839 to 1920

After the Chinese defeat at the hands of the British during the Opium War (1839–1841), the Treaty of Nanking [Nanjing], on August 29, 1842, supplemented by the Treaty of the Bogue (October 1, 1843), laid the foundation for China's relations with the West for almost one hundred years.

The two treaties provided an indemnity of $21,000,000, which included $6,000,000 as compensation for the opium destroyed by the Chinese, $12,000,000 for war costs, and $3,000,000 for debts owed to British merchants. The island of Hong Kong [Xiangang] was ceded to Great Britain in perpetuity and the ports of Amoy, Canton [Guangzhou], Foochow [Fuzhou], Ningbo and Shanghai were opened to foreign trade and consular service. China agreed to a uniform tariff fixed at 5 percent ad valorem, to be changed only by mutual agreement. In the Treaty of the Bogue, the full privilege of extraterritoriality (the exemption of foreigners from Chinese legal jurisdiction) was obtained for British subjects, and Britain received most favored nation status. This insured that any right, privilege, or concession extended in the future to any other nation would automatically accrue to Great Britain. Furthermore, the Chinese agreed to set aside, in each of the newly opened treaty ports, areas where foreigners could reside. These would eventually constitute foreign cities under foreign governments at all important points throughout China.[8]

Great Britain was the first nation to force China into submission, but it was not the only nation to take advantage of the war. In short order, the United States and other major powers began to seek advantages. In 1842, after the signing of the Treaty of Nanking, Commo. Lawrence Kearny, commanding a naval squadron sent to the Far East at the outbreak of the war, approached Chinese officials and formally expressed the hope that American merchants would be put on the same basis as those from Great Britain. Subsequently, the United States received most favored nation status. The United States did not force this right. The Chinese

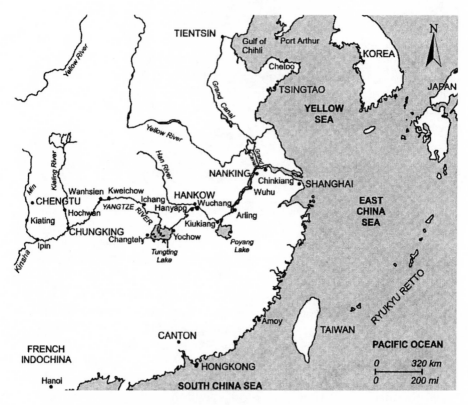

Glenn F. Howell's China. (Map by Susan Browning.)

granted it. This was a calculated move on the part of the Imperial government, which believed that safety might be found in playing off one Western nation against the other.[9]

The emphasis on trade by Kearny reflects the perceived importance of commerce between the United States and China. One student of early Chinese-American relations has noted that the "China trade was a vital factor in U.S. capital formation during the nineteenth century." As early as 1784, goods from New England were being traded at Canton, mainly for tea. Importation of Chinese tea rose steadily. In 1790, for example, three million pounds were shipped; within twenty years, the amount rose to eight million pounds. By 1812, there was a brisk triangular trade which brought goods from the East Coast to barter for furs from the West Coast, which then were traded for goods in Canton to be shipped to the United States. This triangular fur trade produced its first millionaire, John Jacob Astor.[10]

The trade between the United States and China boomed until the

American Civil War. Following the war, it slowed, reflecting this country's preoccupation with internal matters. Nathaniel Peffer has pointed out, however, the most favored nation status "became one of the fixed points in American foreign policy." The United States was second only to Great Britain in gaining advantages from the opening of China. A treaty following the same lines as the one between Great Britain and the Middle Kingdom was signed on July 3, 1844.[11]

Matters concerning opium, the coolie trade, the humiliation over defeat, and other grievances continued to fester and cause unrest in China. In the American and French treaties with China, a provision had been made for revision in twelve years. As the date approached, Great Britain demanded a review. The British wanted additional concessions; one of the most important was the right to navigate the Yangtze River. The Chinese refused to negotiate. Tensions rose.

In 1856, a Chinese ship under British registry, the *Arrow*, was boarded by the Chinese, who claimed the vessel was harboring pirates. Twelve crewmen were taken prisoner and the British flag hauled down. Britain demanded an apology and the release of the sailors. The men were returned, but Viceroy Yeh Ming-Chien [Ye Mingchen] refused to apologize. The Royal Navy bombarded the Canton forts and Yeh called upon the Chinese to crush the British. In the Arrow War (1856–1858) the British had the support of the French, who were angered about the torture and killing of a French missionary in Kwangzi [Guangxi] Province.[12]

The lopsided Western victory brought about demands for settlement in Peking. Britain and France had been joined in their demands by representatives of Russia and the United States. The emperor told the Chinese negotiators to deal with the officials in Canton. The Western powers refused this arrangement, and an expedition started toward the capital. An Anglo-French force took Shanghai and then moved to the port of Tientsin [Tianjin], the traditional gateway to Peking. After the capture of the port, negotiations again took place, with all four powers signing a treaty in June 1858. This did not end the hostilities. The treaty was to be ratified in Peking, but problems arose. The American minister John E. Ward, for example, left the capital when he learned he had to perform the kowtow. (Prostrating oneself in front of the emperor.) In 1860, in retaliation for the imprisonment and killing of a British and French delegation at Peking, a strong Anglo-French expedition burned and looted the Imperial Summer Palace. The Chinese at last were forced to submit.[13]

Britain, France, Russia and the United States won the right to maintain diplomatic representation in Peking. Citizens of the four powers could now travel anywhere in the interior of China, under the protection of extraterritoriality; ten more ports were opened along the coast and up the Yangtze River to Hankow [Hangzhou], and foreign ships were permitted to navigate the Yangtze. Opium was legalized, and the right of missionaries to preach Christianity and to own property anywhere in the interior was recognized. While foreigners could travel to the interior, only missionaries could live there.[14]

At the same time the Arrow War was being waged, China was racked by a domestic uprising known as the Taiping Rebellion. The rebellion is a major watershed in modern Chinese history and cost millions of lives. It was basically an uprising of peasants who were converts to their own forms of Christianity. The rebellion was a mixture of anti–Manchu revolution and a religious crusade, with the rebels at times receiving help from the West. In the main, however, it was in the best interests of the West to have a strong central government that stood by its treaties. By the end of the rebellion, the Western powers were giving arms, naval support and advice to the Manchus. This aid came with strings attached, in the form of greater demands for more influence in China.[15]

The effects of the Taiping Rebellion were huge. It changed the political situation in China by weakening the central government. Another result of the rebellion was a "shift in control of the military and political power from the central government to local governments." The Taiping Rebellion also had an important influence on China's modernization. Many thoughtful Chinese could see the problems arising from Western intervention during the rebellion. These Chinese began to try to rely on themselves. One of the projects they undertook was the modernization of their army and navy. "There is do doubt that the Taiping Rebellion greatly stimulated China's westernization."[16]

As the nineteenth century drew to a close, many Chinese were frustrated and the cause of their unrest centered on the foreigner. Anti-foreigner feelings were a strong admixture of anti–Christianity, anger over imperialism and resentment of foreign economic domination. China had also experienced a series of natural disasters and the despair brought on by these calamities added fuel to a very charged *fin de siècle*. All of the frustrations eventually became a part of the Boxer Uprising of 1900.[17]

The spark that eventually led to bloodshed in 1900 came from a secret society called the I-ho chu'an, or the "Righteous and Harmonious Fists," after their calisthenics. In the West they were known as the "Boxers."

The Boxers began as an anti–Ching secret society and helped in the White Lotus Rebellion. By the late 1890s, the anti-dynastic society was xenophobic, vowing to kill foreigners and their collaborators. The Boxers used magic, claiming that after one hundred days of work with their society, one would be immune to bullets and, if new members worked for four hundred days, they would be able to fly. As an anti-foreign secret society, the Boxers felt that the use of firearms was not correct and preferred swords and lances.

The Boxers gained a great deal of favor in the Imperial Court. In 1900, Tzu Hsi [Zi Xi], the dowager empress, had the leader of the Boxers demonstrate to her his invulnerability to bullets. Tzu Hsi was convinced that the demonstration "proved" the Boxer's claims and she ordered court attendants to learn boxing. At least half of the government's troops joined the Boxers. Meanwhile, Westerners were beginning to feel uneasy as anti-foreign feelings, coupled with the boxing craze, spread throughout the areas where they resided. Western diplomats requested guards for their legations in Peking. The Boxers, feeling they had the support of the court, cut the railway line from Peking to Tientsin. Foreign diplomats felt a blood bath was in the offing and called for military assistance. The events of the Boxer Uprising were now set into motion.[18]

The Boxer Uprising was quickly put down by a coalition of troops from Great Britain, France, Germany, Japan and the United States. The entire action took less than two months. The long-term results of this short action, however, were large. The shadow of the Boxers always hung over the Westerners living in China, especially anytime crowds of Chinese gathered.

3. The U.S. Military in China, 1800–1920

In the pre–World War II United States military, one duty station was held to be the ideal. Stories passed among old salts and soldiers about the fabled China Station. Barracks tales and sea stories circulated that all the onerous duties of garrison duty, such as KP, mess cooking, or fatigue details, were eliminated because American servicemen were replaced by Chinese for these mundane duties. Charles G. Finney, an enlisted man who served with the Fifteenth Infantry at Tientsin during the 1920s, recalls when he signed on for the China Station, he managed to find two old China Hands and asked them about the duty.

"There ain't any duty to speak of. You catch guard every nine days. But you don't do any fatigue, and you don't do any KP, you hire coolies to do it for you. You don't even make your own bed; you don't shine your own shoes; you don't fill your own canteen; you don't shave yourself; the Chink coolies do it for you. You get waited on hand and foot."[19]

The American military prior to World War II was largely confined
to the contiguous United States. How then did American servicemen
come to be stationed in a country that was so little known by people in
their own country?

The first American military force in China came from U.S. Navy
ships that made nine separate deployments to Asia between 1800 and
1839. In 1835, the senior officer present was authorized to fly the pennant
of a commodore. This marks the beginning of the East India Squadron,
although it was not until 1845 that the squadron was organized in regular form.[20]

The purpose of the East India Squadron was to protect American
lives, property, and commerce and to assist in increasing commercial interests in China. During the time the U.S. armed forces remained in China,
the protection of lives and property of U.S. citizens eventually became
the primary missions of the services. The area of responsibility stretched
from west of the Hawaiian Islands to the east coast of Africa. In the early
years this huge area was patrolled by a squadron consisting of only two
or three ships. The flagship was usually a frigate of fifty-four guns or a
sloop-of-war mounting eighteen guns. The squadron increased during
Commo. Matthew C. Perry's mission to Japan (1853–54), but then
reverted to normal size after the mission.

The squadron existed more on paper than in a tactical sense. Its ships
made individual cruises, and it was unusual for more than one ship to be
in the same port. By the nature of their patrol area, the ships logged many
miles and visited a number of Chinese ports. In addition, some vessels
penetrated part of the Chinese river system. The *Susquehanna*, as mentioned earlier, sailed the Yangtze River. The navy continued to be the only
American military force in China until the beginning of the twentieth
century.[21]

The purpose of the American military forces in China changed over
the years. In the nineteenth century, the navy best served diplomats.
Diplomatic relations opened ports that allowed naval ships to move freely
along the coasts and rivers. Charles T. Hanson, Jr., has pointed out that
"movement is the key word in discussing the naval-diplomatic association." Warships provided diplomats with independent mobility in China
and, in fact, provided an outward sign of style and dignity appropriate to
their rank. In other words, it was more impressive for an official to arrive
in a warship than a mere merchantman. Further, navy ships usually were
the means of transportation for diplomatic personnel from the United
States to East Asia. "Navy vessels probably rendered their greatest service as floating legations."[22]

The officers of the navy did play a role in Chinese-American relations prior to the Boxer Uprising. Commodore Kearny, as pointed out earlier, helped to gain a most favored nation treaty for the United States. During the same period, the Chinese hired an American lieutenant from the USS *Constellation* to demonstrate explosives. Kearny and his officers demonstrated the art of Western shipbuilding and armament. The navy also played a role in trying to suppress the coolie trade. In one action, for example, a navy ship intercepted and freed 423 Chinese aboard an American merchantman. James M. Merrill, however, has pointed out that the "customary attitude of American officers, who looked upon Orientals as inferior beings, whose territory could be used with impunity by their men-of-war whenever the situation warranted" canceled many of the chances of gaining goodwill and respect.[23]

Officially, the East Asian Squadron remained neutral during the Opium and Arrow wars and the long years of the Taiping Rebellion. Commo. Cornelius K. Stribling, when ordering a ship to Foochow in 1860 to protect American interests informed the captain: "In all your intercourse with the Chinese you are to act with kindness. Force must not be resorted to except upon being satisfied no other means at your command will be effectual. [I]t is of utmost importance that we should in our intercourse with the allies and Chinese evince our neutral position with perfect impartiality."[24] In reality, however, "perfect impartiality" was almost impossible, given the racial attitudes of the time. Probably the best example of how American forces could become involved in the hostilities in China occurred during the British and French bombardment of the Taku forts, near Tientsin, in 1858. The allied gunboats could make little headway against a strong current and stood in danger of receiving heavy casualties. Commo. Joseph Tattnal, the American East India Squadron Commander, ordered a rented vessel to tow the gunboats out of range. "Blood is thicker than water!" is the traditional recorded reply given by the commodore for his actions. One of Tattnal's lieutenants, however, said the commodore remarked that "he'd be damned if he'd stand by and see white men butchered before his eyes."[25] Apparently, Washington felt Tattnal correct, for he received no reprimand. All in all, for a neutral power, American naval forces kept busy in matters concerning force. The U.S. Marine Corps, for example, recorded a total of twenty-two landings, from 1854 to 1899, in China. A total of twelve sailors and marines were killed during the operations and twenty-nine were wounded.[26]

The navy played a small role in the Taiping Rebellion. During the early years of the uprising, Commodore Perry's sympathies were clearly on the side of the rebels. When merchants and Commissioner Humphrey

Marshall requested additional help in protecting American businesses from the rebels, the commodore replied that no command of his would be used against "an organized revolutionary army gallantly fighting for a more liberal and enlightened religious and political position."[27] It is important to understand, however, that to Perry his most important duty was in Japan and that "his determination not to permit any interference with it" helped to govern his actions toward China.[28] As the years passed, the Taiping Rebellion had less diplomatic importance than the treaty revision with the Manchus. Hanson has observed that by the end of 1854, the "navy was obliged to operate within the framework" of State Department policy regarding the Chinese civil war; this policy, as noted, was one of neutrality. Furthermore, the "squadron commanders did this without complaint, despite their obvious sympathies for the Taiping cause."[29] Lastly, the squadron simply could not muster enough ships to play a very large role, even if it wanted to, in the affairs of the rebellion.

The American Civil War marked a major change for the East India Squadron, as well as for the U.S. Navy in general. The federal blockade of Southern ports required the navy to recall as many ships as possible from foreign stations. By September 1862, only a pair of ships remained in the Far East. After the war, the navy began to return units back to the foreign stations and simultaneously renamed all the distant stations. The East India Squadron became the Asiatic Squadron in 1865.[30]

After the American Civil War the navy was allowed to degenerate. Dudley W. Knox has aptly labeled the period from after the war to the late 1800s as "the maritime eclipse of the United States," and naval historians recognize the period as the nadir of the navy.[31] Instead of carrying out the innovations in steam and armament introduced in the Civil War, the service actually regressed. Rather than joining the other world powers in converting to steel and steam warships, the United States clung tenaciously to wood and sail. Following traditional practice in America, the navy shrank rapidly after the cessation of hostilities. During the Civil War, for example, the Federal Navy mustered 58,296 officers and men. By 1889, only 9,921 men were carried on the active rolls. The ships statistics for the Asiatic Squadron graphically demonstrate the cutbacks. In 1876, the squadron consisted of thirteen ships, but twenty-two years later, in 1889, there remained only three units, little better than when the squadron was first formed.[32]

The navy continued with wooden ships and sail for a number of reasons. The nation was isolationist and had no desire to compete with Europeans. Most policy-makers felt that the Atlantic and Pacific Oceans protected the United States from any invasion and that the traditional role of the navy, that of single-ship commerce raiding and coastal defense, was sufficient. Single-ship commerce raiding required distant stations to protect American shipping, and this led to the establishment of such stations prior to the Civil War. If the United States shifted to a steel and steam navy, it would need overseas coaling stations, which the country did not possess. In other words, the United States needed only sailing ships to maintain distant stations. Policy makers, as already noted, did not care to become involved with European affairs and instead shifted their interests to the Latin American and Asian areas. In these regions, even obsolete U.S. ships were better armed than those of the surrounding areas. Lastly, navy line officers, led by Adm. David D. Porter, fought with engineering officers to keep navy ships in sail. In short, national policy and a conflict within the navy combined to cause the U.S. Navy to become obsolete.

Nearing the end of the nineteenth century, the navy made a complete reversal to become a world class force. The "Naval Revolution," from the late 1800s to the Spanish-American War, saw the demise of the "Old Navy" and the advent of steel and steam ship force, with first class battleships. The genesis of this revolution is attributed to changes both in national policy and from within the navy.[33]

The diplomatic historian Samuel Flagg Bemis notes that prior to the Spanish-American War and the acquisition of the Philippines, which he describes as a "great national blunder," the United States had committed no serious mistakes and made few errors in international relations. This was due largely to the European concern for a balance of power in Europe and Asia and the United States' isolated position. The main foreign policy objectives of this country were freedom, peace, and fair trade, all of which were compatible with its national security. The blunder of the Spanish-American War, according to Bemis, led to increasing involvement in the political affairs of Europe and Asia and to a "long row of further diplomatic blunders."[34]

Revisionist historians, however, believe economic forces are the key to understanding the commercial and territorial expansion of the United States. William A. Williams, for example, points out that as early as 1860 agricultural interests were convinced their economic welfare depended upon an overseas expansionist policy, and it was their urging and support that helped to produce a strong navy to help in overseas expansion.[35]

Historian Walter LaFeber also favors an economic interpretation of American diplomacy in the late nineteenth century. LaFeber notes that by the 1890s the industrial sector of the United States had produced a large surplus of goods, as well as a severe depression and growing labor unrest. With the economic panic and following the depression of 1893,

American decision-makers felt the only way out of the current domestic problem was through the establishment of an overseas commercial empire, which again called for the building of a strong navy.[36]

No matter which explanation one chooses to support, the changing emphasis of national policy meshed with internal naval developments. Young officers lobbied for modernization and, beginning in 1882, under sympathetic secretaries of the navy and presidents, the service began to rebuild. Most naval historians recognize the large role two men played in forming the "new navy."

Capt. Alfred Thayer Mahan, son of army officer Dennis Mahan, who was professor of Engineering at the U.S. military academy, entered the naval academy against his father's wishes in 1859. His career was uneventful for the next twenty-five years, although he soon found that he cared little for the sea and wished to make his mark in intellectual pursuits. In 1884, after writing a history of the civil war navy, Alfred Mahan was invited to lecture on naval tactics and history at the newly established Naval War College, Newport, Rhode Island. His lectures evolved into the two works for which he is most noted, *The Influence of Sea Power Upon History, 1660–1793* (1890) and *The Influence of Sea Power Upon the French Revolution and Empire, 1793–1812* (2 volumes, 1892). In addition, he published a number of articles and essays on sea power. His writings earned him worldwide fame.

Mahan concluded that England had become a great power by controlling the seas and the commerce they bore. He laid out a number of the elements of sea power, based upon England's experience, that the United States needed to achieve in order to gain greatness. He wanted the United States to abandon its isolationist (continentalist) policy and to pursue an aggressive competition for world trade, which required a strong merchant marine, colonies, and a large navy. The merchant marine would carry foreign trade and help keep navalism in the public's mind, while colonies would provide raw materials, markets, and naval bases. Mahan felt that the annexation of Hawaii would provide a stepping stone to Asia and, should the United States acquire a canal in Central America, Hawaii would be the Pacific bastion to help protect the waterway. Mahan believed that colonies would extend Western civilization. He was convinced that the navy should gain command of the sea by defeating the enemy's fleet in a decisive battle and that only battleships could fight such engagements.[37]

At the same time that Mahan began to publish his books, Benjamin F. Tracy began his tenure as the Secretary of the Navy (1889–93). Tracy has been credited as one of the leaders in the building of the new navy by some historians, while others believe that he was highly influenced by Mahan. Indeed, many of their thoughts are closely related. Tracy believed that the sea was the prime ingredient of empire and that the United States should rule the sea. To do so, America needed overseas bases and a large navy. Instead of single-ship raiding and coastal defense, he advocated command of the sea based upon battleships capable of destroying an enemy's fleet in midocean. Between 1890 and 1896, the United States departed from her traditional naval policy and, although at times balking, Congress authorized the building of nine battleships. Tracy also brought about a "squadron of evolution" in 1889, which was the precursor of a concentrated battle fleet. The squadron practiced steaming and tactical formations in large groups. By 1897, the squadron was merged into the North Atlantic Squadron and developed into a fighting fleet.[38]

On June 21, 1900, the Boxer Uprising led to the siege of the legations in Peking. As part of an international relief force, American marines, sailors and soldiers were cobbled together and struck out for the capital city. In charge of American ground forces was Maj. Gen. of Vols. Adna Chafee. In a quick and decisive victory the siege was lifted on August 16, 1900. The ending of the uprising led to the Boxer Protocols, which caused more Chinese concessions to the West.

When U.S. ground forces were withdrawn from Peking, Chafee left behind a legation guard of one army reinforced regiment. By Spring of 1901, this had been reduced to a single rifle company. In 1905, the army force was replaced by marines, and thereafter Leathernecks furnished the legation guard.[39]

The navy in the Pacific underwent major changes in 1907. The Asiatic Fleet and Pacific Squadrons were consolidated into the Pacific Fleet, with headquarters in San Francisco. The new fleet consisted of three squadrons and two torpedo flotillas, with two squadrons and one flotilla in the Orient. The navy withdrew all battleships from the former Asiatic Squadron and replaced them with four armored cruisers. A vessel was maintained at Shanghai, and three gunboats cruised the Yangtze River. In 1910, the navy once again reorganized its forces in the Pacific by reestablishing the Asiatic Fleet.[40]

The overthrow of the Manchus in 1911 brought about more United States military forces into China. Diplomats began to worry that the revolution might herald attacks on foreigners. The United States felt that it needed troops to guard the railway from Peking to Tientsin, the traditional escape route from the capital to the sea. This time the request specified a regiment of army soldiers, not marines.

The request for a regiment was pared down to 500 men because the conditions along the railroad had become "less acute," and the Chinese government promised to keep the line open. On January 12, 1912, one battalion of the Fifteenth Infantry from the Philippines was ordered to Tientsin. By March, the American minister was requesting an additional 200 soldiers to be stationed at Peking. The army was relieved by marines from the USS *Abrarenda* and from Taku on March 11. The legation guard was now at battalion size. By the end of March, there were "six companies of the [army] China contingent ... at Tientsin, and two ... [were] scattered along the railroad in detachments, varying in size from 20 to 115 men."

Conditions stabilized somewhat in China, but army troop strength increased between 1913 and 1920. World War I caused the withdrawal of most of the European forces in 1914. In September 1914, the remaining battalion of the Fifteenth Infantry was transferred from Manila to Tientsin.[41]

The 1920s were again filled with unrest in China, which once more brought about large changes in U.S. forces in the Middle Kingdom. The first change concerned the gunboats plying the Yangtze River. Navy gunboats had sailed the river since 1854, but it was not until March 21, 1921, that the patrol force was organized as a part of the Asiatic Fleet and Capt. D. M. Wood appointed its first commander. (Howell has some rather caustic remarks about Captain Wood in his diaries.) Captain Wood was replaced by Rear Adm. W.H.G. Bullard on October 12, 1921. In September of the same year, the army requested, and was granted, permission to remove one battalion of the Fifteenth Infantry from Tientsin to Manila. While the army was reducing troop strength, the navy in 1923 requested Congress to authorize funds for the construction of six new gunboats to replace the aging Yangtze River Patrol vessels.[42]

This marks the period up to the time Glenn F. Howell served aboard the gunboat *Palos*. The remainder of the years until the beginning of World War II is marked by fluctuating levels of troop arrivals and departures according to levels of unrest and perceived danger. By 1930, American military forces were at: Peking (marines); Tientsin (army); Shanghai (marines); Yangtze and Pearl River (navy); and the ships of the Asiatic Fleet would touch at various coastal ports. The Asiatic Fleet would spend the summers cruising and visiting various ports and then return to their base in the Philippines. Usually, the various classes of ships would go to certain Chinese ports. Destroyers, for example, would generally go to Chingwangto.

As Japan expanded onto the Asian mainland, concern began to be expressed within the State Department about the chance for an incident between American and Japanese troops. To head off any incident, the

Fifteenth Infantry was withdrawn from Tientsin in 1937 and marines began a slow movement away from China. When the United States entered World War II, many marines were still in China and spent the entire conflict in captivity.

Notes

1. A Chinese *li* equals ⅓ mile, or ½ kilometer.
2. Simon Winchester, *The River at the Center of the World: A Journey Up the Yangtze, and Back in Chinese Time* (New York: Henry Holt and Company, 1996), 4.
3. Ibid., 13.
4. Kemp Tolley, *Yangtze Patrol: The U.S. Navy in China* (Annapolis, Md.: Naval Institute Press, 1971; second printing, 1984), 14, all page references are to the second printing.
5. Photocopy of Howell's career from *Shipmate*, undated, sent to Dennis L. Noble by the U.S. Naval Academy Association; *Who's Who for Idaho, 1950–1951* (Portland, Or.: Capital Publishing Company, 1950), 110.
6. Photocopy from the *Idaho Daily Statesman*, February 8, 1973, sent to Dennis L. Noble by the U.S. Naval Academy Alumni Association.
7. There have been a few officers, and one enlisted man, who have written nonfiction accounts of their years in China while serving in the U.S. military. No one, however, has left contemporary diaries to the extent of Howell. Further, some of the diarist accounts were written many years after their service and it is unclear as to whether they worked from diaries or papers. See, for example, Charles G. Finney, *The Old China Hands* (Garden City, NY: Doubleday, 1961; reprint, Westport, Ct.: Greenwood Press, 1973); David M. Shoup, *The Marines in China, 1922–1927: The China Expedition which turned out to be the China Exhibition: A Contemporaneous Journal by David M. Shoup, USMC* (Hamden, Ct.: Archon Books, 1987); Tolley, *Yangtze Patrol*; William A. Williams, *The Old Corps: A Portrait of the U.S. Marine Corps Between the Wars* (Annapolis, Md.: Naval Institute Press, 1982). The one notable fiction book about the U.S. Navy in China on the Yangtze River, and from the viewpoint of an enlisted man, is by a retired navy Chief Petty Officer: Richard McKenna, *The Pebbles* (New York: Harper's, 1962).
8. Immanuel C.Y. Hsu, *The Rise of Modern China*, 3rd ed. (New York: Oxford University Press, 1983), 190.
9. Dudley Knox, *A History of the United State Navy* (New York: Putnam, 1948), 161–165; Earl Swisher, *China's Management of the American Barbarians: A Study of Sino-American Relations, 1841–1861, With Documents* (New York: Octogon Books, 1972), 56–58; Carroll Stores Alden, *Lawrence Kearny: Sailor Diplomat* (Princeton: Princeton University Press, 1936).
10. Frank A. Kierman, Jr., "Ironies of Chinese-American Military Conflict," in *The American Military and the Far East: Proceedings of the Ninth Military History Symposium, United States Air Force Academy, 1–3 October 1980*, ed. Joe C. Dixon (Washington: Government Printing Office, 1980), 183–184.
11. Nathaniel Peffer, *The Far East: A Modern History* (Ann Arbor: University of Michigan Press, 1958), 63.
12. Ibid., 60–70.
13. David Hurd, *The Arrow War: An Anglo-American Confusion* (New York: Macmillian, 1968); Peffer, *Far East*, 71–73.
14. Hsu, *Modern China*, 387–390.
15. Ssu-Yu Teng, *The Taiping Rebellion and the Western Powers: A Comprehensive Survey* (London: Oxford University Press, 1971).

16. Ibid., 390–391.

17. Hsu *Modern China*, 387–390.

18. Ibid., 392–393.

19. Charles G. Finney, *The Old China Hands* (Garden City, NY: Doubleday, 1961; reprint Westport, Ct.: Greenwood Press, 1977), 17, all page references are to the reprint edition.

20. Robert Greenhalgh Albion, "Distant Stations," U.S. Naval Institute *Proceedings*, 80 (March 1954): 265–273; Charles C. Chadbourn III, "Sailors and Diplomats: U.S. Naval Operations in China, 1865–1877" (Ph.D. diss., University of Washington, 1976); Charles T. Henson, Jr., *Commissioners and Commodores: The East India Squadron and American Diplomacy in China* (University of Ala.: University of Alabama Press, 1982); Edwin P. Hoyt, *The Lonely Ships: The Life and Death of the U.S. Asiatic Fleet* (New York: David McKay, 1976); James M. Merrill, "The Asiatic Squadron: 1835–1907," *American Neptune*, 29 (April 1969): 106–117; E. Mowbray Tate, "American Merchant and Naval Contacts with China, 1784–1850," *American Neptune*, 30 (July 1971): 171–191.

21. Peter Karsten, *The Naval Aristocracy: The Golden Age of Annapolis and the Emergence of Modern Navalism* (New York: Free Press, 1972), 140–150; Albion, "Distant Stations," 268; Henson, *Commissioners and Commodores*, 15; Merrill, "Asiatic Squadron," 108–109; Kemp Tolley, *Yangtze Patrol*, 16, 18; Robert E. Johnson, *Thence Around Cape Horn: The Story of the United States Naval Forces on Pacific Station* (Annapolis, Md.: Naval Institute Press, 1963); Robert E. Johnson, *Far China Station: The U.S. Navy in Asian Waters, 1800–1898* (Annapolis, Md.: Naval Institute Press, 1979).

22. Hanson, *Commissioners and Commodores*, v.

23. Merrill, "Asiatic Squadron," 110.

24. Quoted in, ibid., 110.

25. Edgar Standton Maclay, *Reminiscences of the Old Navy: From the Journals and Private Papers f Captain Edward Trenchard and Rear Admiral Stephen Decatur Trenchard* (New York: Putnam, 1898), 83. See also, E.R. Curtis, "Blood is Thicker Than Water," *American Neptune*, 27 (July 1967): 157–176.

26. Harry Allansen Ellsworth, *One Hundred Eighty Landings of United States Marines, 1800–1834* (Washington: History and Museum Division, Headquarters, U.S. Marine Corps, 1935; reprint 1974), 21–23, page citations are to the reprint edition; Milton Offutt, *The Protection of Citizens Abroad by the Armed Forces of the United States* (Baltimore: Johns Hopkins University Press, 1928), 23–31, 38–39, 41, 77–79.

27. Quoted in, Charles T. Hanson, Jr., "The U.S. Navy in the Taiping Rebellion," *American Neptune*, 38 (January 1978): 31.

28. Ibid., 30.

29. Ibid., 40.

30. Albion, "Distant Stations," 269–270.

31. Knox, *United States Navy*, 318.

32. Ibid., 317; Bureau of the Census, *Historical Statistics of the United States: Colonial Times to 1970*, Part 2 (Washington: Government Printing Office, 1975), 1142.

33. The United States did have property for a coaling station at Yokohama, Japan, but had "overlooked the fact" until the Pacific Mail Company requested to sublease the land in 1899. The property had been on perpetual lease since 1864. Steward W. Livermore, "American Naval Base Policy in the Far East, 1850–1914, *Pacific Historical Review*, 13 (June 1944): 114–115, 120–121; Chadboun, "Sailors and Diplomats," 200–201; Knox, *United States Navy*, 131–158; Kenneth J. Hagan, *American Gunboat Diplomacy and the Old Navy, 1877–1899* (Westport, Ct.: Greenwood Press, 1973).

34. Samuel Flagg Bemis, *A Diplomatic History of the United States*, 5th ed. (New York: Holt, Reinhart, and Winston, 1965), 474, 482, 1004.

35. William A. Williams, *The Roots of the Modern American Empire: A Study of Growth and Shaping of Social Consciousness in a Marketplace Society* (New York: Random House, 1969), 30, 319–348, 351–381, 440–445, 449–450.

36. Walter LaFeber, *The New Empire: An Interpretation of American Expansion, 1860–1897* (Ithaca: Cornell University Press, 1963), 60. See also, Thomas J. McCormick, *China Market: America's Quest for Informal Empire, 1893–1901* (Chicago: Quadrangle Books, 1967).

37. Robert Seager II, *Alfred Thayer Mahan* (Annapolis, Md.: Naval Institute Press, 1977).

38. Benjamin Franklin Cooling, *Benjamin Franklin Tracy: Father of the Modern American Fighting Navy* (Hamden, Ct.: Archon Books, 1979); George T. Davis, *A Navy Second to None: The Development of Modern Naval Policy* (Westport, Ct.: Greenwood Press, 1971); Walter R. Herrick, Jr., *The American Naval Revolution* (Baton Rouge: Louisiana State University Press, 1966); Harold Sprout and Margret Sprout, *The Rise of American Naval Power, 1776–1918* (Princeton: Princeton University Press, 1939).

39. Allen R. Millett, *Semper Fidelis: The History of the United States Marine Corps* (New York: Macmillian, 1980), 21, 216; Louis Morton, "Army and Marines on the China Station: A Study in Military and Political Rivalry," *Pacific Historical Review*, 29 (February 1960): 53. See also, William Reynolds Braisted, *The United States Navy in the Pacific, 1897–1909* (Austin: University of Texas Press, 1958); William Reynolds Braisted, *The United States Navy in the Pacific, 1909–1922* (Austin: University of Texas Press, 1971).

40. The various changes in the naval forces are covered in: Braisted, *Navy in the Pacific, 1897–1909*; Braisted, *Navy in the Pacific, 1909–1922*; Johnson, *Thence Around Cape Horn*; Johnson, *Far China Station*; Hoyt, *Lonely Ships*.

41. Charles W. Thomas, "The United States Army Troops in China, 1912–1937," (History Term Paper, Stanford University, June 1937), *passim.*, U.S. Army Military History Institute, Carlisle, PA (USAMHI); U.S. Department of State, *Papers Relating to the Foreign Relations of the United States, 1901 and 1912* (Washington: Government Printing Office, 1920), *passim.*

42. Thomas, "Army in China," *passim*; Tolley, *Yangtze Patrol*, 16, 97.

PART 1:
WANHSIEN [WANXIAN]–SHANGHAI,
JUNE 6, 1920–NOVEMBER 8, 1920

1. Making Official Calls

Glenn F. Howell begins the entries in his diary with the formalities of accepting command of the *Palos*, which is carried out in conditions other than normal fleet practices. Military China hands would say China seemed to bring out unusual practices. Howell, as has every new commanding officer before and after him, ponders his new duties: he is now in complete charge of a ship.

On his first full day of command Howell performs an official call on a British gunboat. A great deal of the gunboat captain's time is spent in paying mandatory calls upon officials, both on ships and ashore. Kemp Tolley has described official calls on the river. The visiting officer wore a knee-length frock coat, "embellished with grapefruit-sized gold-fringed 'swabs' [epaulets] which extended the wearer's beam several inches," and the pants had "'railroad tracks,' wide gold strips." A "gold-encrusted belt" held a four-foot sword. "Topping off this magnificent display was a cocked hat, projected fore and aft some eight inches, decorated with cockade and a gilt trim." It was traditional that a commodore rated having one button of his fly undone and that anyone who had rounded Cape Horn did not have to do up the top button of his jacket. "Clawing up the vertical ladder and through the scuttle hatch of a British destroyer wardroom while so attired called for finesse of a high order, especially after three or four glasses of hospitality."[1]

An incident in official calling is described by Howell in a 1938

Yangtze River gunboatmen. Officers wore white shoes, enlisted men wore black. Kemp Tolley, then a lieutenant, is the officer to the left, aboard the *Tutuila*. Lieutenant C.E. "Two-Gun" Coffin to the right. (Photograph courtesy of U.S. Naval Institute.)

article in the U.S. Naval Institute *Proceedings*. A captain from a foreign cruiser, finding the normal route to the *Palos* cut off by coaling sampans, decided to come aboard in an unorthodox manner—over the stern of the gunboat—with an unusual consequence: he landed in a tub full of water and potatoes. Howell arrived on scene and assisted the visiting captain in removing "his crushed cocked hat from his indignant head. Gawking at him in a stunned and ill-bred way were the Chinese messcooks whose morning job of peeling spuds had been interrupted in so astonishing a fashion...."

The quartermaster of the *Palos* quickly informed his captain: "'I just come around the corner of the deckhouse, Captain. He was climbing over the life lines. And his sword caught and throwed him. He went smash into the spud tub. Thought I'd better report to you, sir. Lucky he didn't fall overboard.'"

Howell "picked off a spud which seemed to be an integral part of the left epaulet," and led the disheveled captain to the wardroom. After a few strained minutes, the captain departed the gunboat over the stern.

Howell would, eighteen years after the incident, wryly comment: "The Skipper shook his head and returned to the wardroom, ruefully pondering the fact that this call had not served to promote that amity and rapprochement which is probably the purport of official calls."[2]

2. The Three Gorges Dam

In 1994, The People's Republic of China began the biggest hydro-electric dam in the world—606 feet high and 7,640 feet wide—that will back the *Chang Jiang* up into a scenic area known as the Three Gorges that provides some of the most exciting passages in Howell's diaries. The Three Gorges dam will impound a reservoir of "31 million acre-feet of water in a snakelike lake stretching 370 miles upstream to Chongqing. The reservoir will not only diminish a scenic treasure but also submerge sites of historical, archeological, paleontological, and biological interest."[3] Thus, Howell's entries concerning the area of the Three Gorges are important, for very few Westerners observed the area in the 1920s.

The Chinese, who are credited with the first in many technologies, such as gunpowder, the compass, and others, did not begin work on dams until around 200 B.C. They trail some distance behind the Egyptians, who had stemmed part of the Nile near Memphis by at least 2900 B.C. About 2500 years ago, there emerged two schools of thought on hydraulics in the Middle Kingdom: the Taoists view and the Confucian viewpoint. It may seem strange to Westerners that religion and philosophy enters into how to manage the rivers in China, but it is a sign of the importance the Chinese give to the control of them.

Taoists believed in the building of low levees beside rivers and letting the rivers run their own courses to the sea. Confucianists, on the other hand, believed massive dikes to control the river's flow along man-made courses, thus the extra land freed up could be used for agricultural pursuits. The Confucians also believed that their approach would prevent moderate floods, but would probably break during serious flooding, causing occasional catastrophes. This, according to the Confucians, was an acceptable trade-off for the years of productivity and prosperity.

The leaders of the Republican Era, beginning in 1911, had large plans for reform. The government built a nationwide school system, a network of new railways, worked in agriculture and other areas. One of the areas concerned dams.

Sun Yat-sen, in a paper written in 1919 entitled "A Plan to Develop Industry," devoted a section to rivers and canals, and suggested building many dams. The most massive of all would be the dam to tame the mighty Yangtze River. This huge structure, according to Sun, should be built somewhere along the Three Gorges. Many factors favored the location. One important consideration is that the Gorge area lies almost in the center of China, thus any development of hydroelectric power would lessen the country's dependence on fossil fuels.

From the time Dr. Sun proposed the dam, it took seventy-five years before the project actually began. The largest part of the long delay came from finding the proper location for the structure. The decision eventually became mired in political chaos. The leaders of The People's Republic of China finally announced the location of the dam: at a turn in the river, near a village called Sandouping.

The announcement of a Yangtze River dam began with great fanfare amongst the international community. This would be an expensive undertaking and many countries eyed the project with visions of huge profits. The World Bank looked into the venture, Merrill Lynch and others formed liaison groups, while Japan and Sweden talked about lending money.

Then The People's Republic of China announced the reservoir depth, or "normal pool area," would be 573 feet, making the dam's structure 610 feet high and 6864 feet from side to side, more than five times as wide as the Hoover Dam.

The huge dam wall would take up 26 million tons of concrete and 250,000 tons of steel and it would create a 600-square-mile lake stretching behind the dam for at least 372 miles. It is only natural that some writers began touting it as a "new Great Wall."[4]

The flooding would mean that at least 11,250,000 people would have to be moved. Thirteen cities, such as Wanxian (150,000 people) and Fuling (80,000) would be lost; 140 normal-sized towns and 1,352 villages would also go under. Some 8,000 recognized archaeological sites would be lost, as would many pagodas and temples. The Gorges would simply become a large lake. The traditional steep banks of Chungking would be gone, and the Yangtze's waters would now lap at the city's lower slum streets.

Shipping and power interests immediately hailed the bold plan. Ten-thousand ton cargo ships and passenger vessels now would be able to travel from the ocean to as far as Chungking, 1,300 miles from the sea. Central China now would have the ability to ship its products to the world and receive products from outside. The power generated would be more than 18 gigawatts, 181,200 megawatts, more than any other in the world.[5]

By 1997, however, there grew a steady chorus of protest against the proposed dam, both from the international community and from within China. One of the reasons for unrest in the international community: by the 90s there came the feeling that large dams were ill-conceived projects and caused large environmental impacts on their surroundings. Daniel Beard, an American hydrologist, noted that large dams are always more expensive than planned.[6] Report after report about the dam seemed to always find misgivings about the project.

While China could do little about the reports emanating outside of its borders, those that questioned within the country received special attention. Dai Qing, a Beijing journalist-engineer-environmentalist, gathered a series of academic papers of people within China who had concerns about the project. She managed to get the papers published *within* China in 1989, just a few months before the student uprising in Tiananmen Square in June. She spent ten months in prison and was threatened with execution.

In the end, the Chinese began to undertake the project, no matter the opposition. The writer Simon Winchester best sums up what eventually happened.

> ...there are those who remember that the real Great Wall of China was held together by a mortar made of the crushed skeletons of those thousands who died making it. That the Great Wall was built by slaves; there was no choice: it had to be built, or the Empire would loose face.
>
> This new great wall had to be built too. Thousands might die in its aftermath. Animals and plants and peoples would be affected in a myriad of strange and appalling ways. An immense section of China would be affected, and for the worse, by what was going up here. And yet there was no choice here too. Two thousand two hundred years separated the building of the two walls—two millennia during which the essential nature of China, by this single standard, seemed not to have changed at all.[7]

3. S. Cornell Plant and the Three Gorges

Some of the more exciting passages in Howell's diary describes his adventures in trying to navigate through the Yangtze River's Three Gorges. For any sailor, or armchair sailor, his descriptions of the seamanship required in taking a steam gunboat through the area will prove fascinating.

The historian Lyman P. Van Slyke notes the narrow passages made by the gorges area causes the Yangtze with all its melt and rain to naturally increase in force. "In full spate ... changes of water level in the gorges have sometimes reached twenty feet in twenty-four hours, seventy to eighty feet overall. The power and velocity of the water in the gorges comes less from any absolute drop in elevation than from enormous fluid pressure forcing the water through this constricted passage."[8] Seventeen years after his command, Howell would write that the *Palos* crew had played baseball on a sandy beach near their anchorage at Wanhsein. "At four the next morning we moved in and dropped the hook [anchor] on home plate. At four in that afternoon we moved and took up our old position. Twelve hours later we moved 50 feet farther out in the river."[9]

From upstream to downstream the Three Gorges are: Ch'u-t'ang, Wu (or Witches), and Hsi-ling. In Howell's time, the boatmen of the Yangtze passed on the differences among each of the gorges: Ch'u-tang held the sheerest cliffs and swiftest current; Witches Gorge the most spectacular peaks and worse whirlpools, and Hsi-ling held the most dangerous rapids and shoals.

The first of the gorges, again from upstream to downstream, Ch'u-tang is the shortest, at five miles in length. The river at one point, in what is known as the K'uei Gate, is constricted to a mere 350 feet in width, the narrowest point of the *Chang Jiang* since leaving the Himalayan Mountains. Currents can reach fifteen knots, but generally range between six or seven knots. In Howell's time on the river a large rock, the Yen-yu, dominated navigation in this gorge. Boatmen had a doggerel concerning navigation through the gorge that centered on how the river struck the rock:

> When Yen-yu's an elephant, upstream you shan't
> When Yen-yu's a horse, don't downstream course.[10]

The rock has since been blasted away by engineers of The People's Republic of China.

On the north side of this gorge, or the left bank, cut into the cliff's face is a recessed towpath for trackers. (More on trackers later.) On the south side is Windbox (or Bellows) Gorge. The gorge is named for the crevices high above the water into which cypress coffins were once placed vertically, which from below created an appearance resembling the segments of a bellows.

The river widens after leaving Chutang and then just below Wushan is Witches [Wuhsia] Gorge, twenty-five miles in length. The steep walls of this gorge, more than the others, tend to block the sun, causing it to be "the most somber and foreboding of the Three Gorges."

When visibility allows, Goddess Peak [Shen-nu feng] may be seen. One Chinese myth relates the goddess and her eleven sisters, only slightly more beautiful and able than she, came to earth to help the *Da Yu*, the flood-tamer, drain the Chinese earth to make it habitable for ordinary mortals. The eleven sisters became the eleven peaks of Witches Gorge, and she herself remains petrified, but in human form as a sentinel on the twelfth peak to help rivermen safely through this dangerous passage.

The third and longest gorge, at almost thirty miles, Hsi-ling held fear for most boatmen because of its shoals and rapids, formed by landslides into the river.

The first rapid into the gorge, New Rapids—named for a landslide in the seventeenth century—at winter low water had a total fall of nearly twenty feet, plus a current that ran at 13 to 14 knots. Three rapids, Head Rapid, First Rapid, and Second Rapid, came next and stretched for a mile and a half. Many junks had to unload and portage their cargos and sometimes up to a hundred extra trackers had to be hired from nearby villages to help the regular trackers used by the junks. This and salvaging flotsam from wrecks provided extra income to the villagers. To maintain steerage in these rapids, junks had to exceed the speed of the current. They had to do this, plus navigate through very narrow openings. "In New Rapids as elsewhere, accounts tell of junks virtually exploding in collision with rocks, and teak beams, planking, and cargo flying in all directions." Although still dangerous, much of the channel in this gorge has been dredged.

Knowing the water levels of the *Chang Jiang* can obviously help boatmen and along the river at critical areas are seen markings or inscriptions indicating levels above mean water level. Low water marks are also present. Near the village of Fuling, between Chungking and The Gorges, are carved into rock representations of carp, the most recent from 1685. "The eyes of the fish were used as reference points for recording low-water marks."[11]

Since Howell's voyages through The Gorges in the *Palos* much has been accomplished to make the passage safer. The work on the river already noted above by The People's Republic of China is an example. Another is the work of a little-known Englishman.

Samuel Cornell Plant, usually simply called Cornell Plant, was born in a North Sea-side village and became fascinated with river travel and navigation. Plant went overseas and soon commanded ships that traveled on the Tigris and Euphrates Rivers. Home on leave, he happened to be dining in the Oriental Club in London and overheard the far more famous Archibald Little extol his frustrated attempts to steam up the Three Gorges of the Yangtze River. When Little noticed Plant's strong interest, he offered him the captaincy of the first major steam boat assault on the Gorges' rapids. Plant was thirty-three at the time.[12]

The conventional wisdom of the Chinese court held that only junks, with great effort, could pass through The Gorges. Normally, the junks would be pulled by trackers and stay close to shore. Steam vessels, because of their greater draft and propellers, would have to operate out in the dangerous deeper center of the river. Another reason given for the supposed failure of steam vessels was that the cliffs of the Gorges were the home of monkeys that would become angry at the noise of a steam engine and hurl stones at the ship, disabling the ship and killing the crew.[13]

In 1900, Cornell Plant captained the *Pioneer*, Little's steam vessel and the first to arrive at Chungking without the use of trackers. Unfortunately for Little, the Boxer Uprising caused the British to commandeer the *Pioneer* for use as an evacuation ship and eventually the British government bought it and named it the *Kinsha*. (The *Kinsha* is mentioned in Howell's diary.)

Plant then went into the shipping business, but all the while studying the river. He designed a steamer, the *Shutung*, had it built in England and sent to China. With it, Plant originated a shipping service through The Gorges. He built a houseboat so he could live on and better study the river.

Cornell Plant left the shipping business and entered a very unusual colonial bureaucracy, the Chinese Imperial Maritime Customs Service. He held the title of Senior River Inspector, Upper Yangtze.[14]

The staff of the Chinese Imperial Maritime Customs Service turned out to be men of scholarship and their reports published year after year paint an amazingly accurate picture of China as seen through Western eyes during the first three decades of the twentieth century. George Worcester, who served for thirty years as a Yangtze River inspector, and until his death in 1969, recognized as the world's expert on Chinese junks, wrote after the service had vanished that the world of scholarship on China owned much to the writings of people of this service.[15]

Cornell Plant's contribution to this body of literature is a small volume entitled *A Handbook for the Guidance of Shipmasters on the Ichang-Chungking Section of the Yangtze River*, first published in 1920 and republished in 1932. For anyone interested in China and her great river, this is a treasure trove. Plant executed detailed maps and gave the name of every rock, whirlpool, or shoal in the area of the Three Gorges that would be of interest to ship masters. The work still forms the basis of all the *Pilot* guides to the river.

The guides, of course, were in English and of immeasurable help to those who read the language. Plant also devised a system of signal stations that helped everyone on the river. The small white buildings are located on cliffs, each with a flagpole with halyards. A lookout will raise and lower large illuminated arrows to advise approaching ships if the way ahead is clear or if the channel is being used by a vessel coming the other way. Howell's diaries are replete with comments of trying to dodge fast-moving junks coming down the river.

Cornell Plant retired shortly after World War I. A grateful Imperial Maritime Customs and the Chinese government gave Plant and his wife a bungalow at the village of Xintan overlooking the New Rapids in the Gorge. "Urged to retire to Hankow or to Shanghai ... [Plant] shook his head, smiled, and explained that this wild region had for twenty years been the only home known by his wife and himself. He said with some hesitancy that he felt too keen a sense of responsibility toward his 'boys' of the fleet to abandon them after his years of responsibility and patient instruction."[16]

In 1929, Howell would write of Cornell Plant: "As his hair whitened his smile became more kindly and his personality mellow. We all turned to him with our troubles, and he was ever ready with advice and instruction. His extraordinary knowledge of the Yangtze, of the Chinese, and of the ships which comprised our Upper River fleet made his opinions very nearly infallible. His hard-headed common sense coupled with his tolerant kindliness endeared him to us. He was the godfather of our whole curiously diverse river-borne population."[17]

Howell also noted as captains of ships attempted the Hsintan rapids "[w]e invariably felt as if he [Plant] were a kindly, interested spirit who was willing us a safe passage and a successful journey. We felt that under this friendly and paternal supervision we should disappoint the old man badly if we failed, and I am sure that his being presence up there above us [on the cliff] spurred the quartermasters and firemen to greater efforts and the pilots to extraordinary caution."[18]

In 1921, Plant and his wife, described "as kindly a soul as her husband," decided to return to England for a visit. They sailed down the Yangtze to Shanghai, "with a fine send-off by their friends all along the river." In the great city, the couple caught an oceangoing ship for Hong Kong. Cornell Plant contracted pneumonia on board and died at sea. Grief stricken, his wife died a month later. They were both buried in Hong Kong's Happy Valley cemetery.[19]

Eight years after Plant's death, Howell would write: "It was our unfailing custom to salute the old man in passing [the rapids]—three blasts of the whistle. The response was always immediate—the flutter of his handkerchief as he leaned from a window."[20] Howell's article in the United States Naval Institute *Proceedings* shows the almost reverence of those who sailed the *Chang Jiang* gave to the Englishman: "...today, in the midst of the tense struggle of a straining ship up the roaring Hsintan, the hand of the master sometimes reaches involuntarily for the whistle cord and to his mind comes the vision of the kindly, white-haired, elderly man who was always ready with his benevolent advice and paternal interest—Captain Plant, the pilot of the Upper Yangtze."[21]

Over seventy years after Cornell Plant's death, a Yangtze River steamer captain told the writer Simon Winchester, "Your Englishman—

we call him Pu Lan Tian, you know—he did great things. These signal stations, for example. They are a reminder of how man has done his best to make this terrible river safe, or as safe as it can be."[22]

After Cornell Plant's death, a subscription was started for a monument to be erected in Plant's memory in Xintan. The response was so great that an oversubscription resulted. The result is the only known memorial to a Westerner on the banks of the Yangtze River. The monument, an obelisk thirty feet high made of pink granite on a brown sandstone base, can be seen downstream for many miles. On it were carved inscriptions both in Chinese characters and in English.[23]

In the 1990s, Simon Winchester visited Xintan to see the memorial. As he approached the monument, he noticed that every word in English and all 130 Chinese characters had been chiseled out of the stone. The words "Plant Memorial" were just legible.

The memorial to S. Cornell Plant that overlooks the Hsintan rapid before the wording was destroyed by Red Guards in 1968. (From: *A Handbook for the Guidance of Shipmasters in the Ichang-Chungking Section of the Yangtze River,* 1931.)

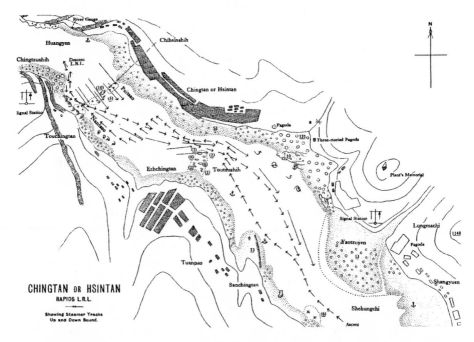

CHINGTAN or HSINTAN
RAPIDS L.R.L.
Showing Steamer Tracks
Up and Down Bound.

S. Cornell Plant's drawing of Hsintan rapids. Note the location of Plant's memorial and the location of one of the signal stations devised by Plant. (From: *A Handbook for the Guidance of Shipmasters on the Ichang-Chungking Section of the Yangtze River,* **1931.)**

A young woman approached Winchester and told him Red Guards had come in 1968 and tried to blow it up, saying it was evil to put up a memorial to a barbarian. The monument was so well built they could not destroy it, so they chiseled out the words.

Winchester's informant said how sorry she was that this had happened. She said, "My husband is a shipmaster, and so was his father. All of our families have lived in Xintan for many years. They worship Pu Lan Tan. He was a great man. We were proud that he lived here. But he has gone, and now his memorial has been wrecked as well." After the waters of the Three Gorges dam begin to back up, both Xian and the memorial to S. Cornell Plant will be lost.[24]

4. George Raleigh Gray Worcester

Prominent in Howell's diary, especially when transiting The Gorges, are comments on Chinese watercraft, and centering on junks. Most Westerners, and this included even sailors such as Howell, rarely, if ever, discussed Chinese watercraft, leaving most readers knowing very little about the maritime world of the Chinese. Yet, Sir Frederick Maze, in 1940 the Inspector General of the Chinese Customs Service, pointed out that the Chinese have shown more originality than any other people in the art of shipbuilding, and are especially good in designing vessels to suit special requirements and different conditions.[25]

The "ingenuity" mentioned by Sir Maze led to a wide variety of watercraft on the Yangtze, its tributaries, and sea-going craft. Fortunately for those in the West who wish to know about the maritime affairs of China, a scholar attempted to detail the junks and sampans of the *Chang Jiang*. Once again, as with Cornell Plant, an Englishman working for the Chinese Customs Service became enamored with The River. This man found the junks and sampans which plied the Yangtze fascinating and made it his life's work to collect not only all the information he could upon these unique Chinese craft and vessels, but he also gathered information about the people who worked them.

George Raleigh Gray Worcester (1890–1969) entered the Royal Navy during the age of sail and rounded Cape Horn as a midshipman. He came to the Yangtze River in 1919 and joined the Marine Department of the Chinese Maritime Customs Service as a River Inspector. Sir Frederick Maze recognized the deep interest of Worcester and released him from his duties so that he might spend all his time researching Chinese nautical history. This enabled him to travel to many places most foreigners never visited. He spent eight years studying and sketching the people and craft of maritime China. Both Worcester and his wife spent World War II in a Japanese prison camp. He retired from the Customs Service and authored five definitive works on the seagoing and riverine junks of China. Just prior to his death, the U.S. Naval Institute Press collected and edited these works and put them into one magnificent volume, replete with photographs and drawings from Worcester's time. *The Junks and Sampans of the Yangtze* details the craft of the various regions of the *Chang Jiang*, along with scale drawings. There is very little about Chinese riverine affairs that is not covered in Worcester's work, including such minutiae as the gods of the Chinese sailors, what the sailors wore, their superstitions, how they slept, and, in short, anything one would want to know about the Chinese who worked on the river. Unlike some Westerners, Worcester had, for his time, some fairly flattering things to say about these sailors. He noted, for example, "China, did she but know it, possesses in these industrious and fearless junkmen a treasure of immeasurable value to the country."[26]

It is beyond the scope of these introductory remarks to Howell's diary to detail all the types of junks and sampans the naval officer would encounter during his sojourn on The River. To illustrate some of the material available in Worcester's magus opus, only portions of the description of the *Ma-Yang-Tzu* type of junk that plied the Upper Yangtze between Ichang and Wanhsien will be discussed.

According to Worcester, the *Ma-Yang-Tzu* was a large junk that had "pride of place." The junk could be built to any size desired by the owner and could range in length from 36 to 110 feet. Worcester chose to illustrate one of the larger vessels.[27]

The vessel was 102 feet long, had a 19 foot beam, and drew 8½ feet of water, and was made with the cypress of Wanhsien, with fourteen bulkheads giving the appearance of great strength. (The water tight bulkhead, incidently, is a Chinese invention.) Worcester felt the heaviness caused a lack of grace, but this lack was compensated by a sturdy symmetry.

The junk's hull had a comparatively narrow deck, turret-built, with additional strength provided long and heavy wales running the whole length of the vessel. A square bow ended in a heavy projecting crossbeam, with the junk containing seven of these large beams throughout its length. A low coaming extended from the bow to the house.

The bow planking ran athwartships to a point well below the waterline, where it met the bottom planks, which lay longitudinally. In place of frames, 28 half-frames, occurred at intervals, laterally across the bottom only, between the traverse bulkheads, which were built up to the shape of the hull. The flat-surfaced high stern widened as it rose in a gentle curve from the water. The planking of the stern facing, which ascended vertically from the bottom, was laid horizontally on the top portion. A small square port with a sliding door looked out over the stern.

Worcester goes on to continue the description of the junk in the detail given above. The cargo capacity of such a junk was 100 tons down river and eighty tons up river.

One interesting service in The Gorges that is little-known, and one not mentioned by Howell, is the fleet of approximately fifty *Hung-Ch'uan*, or lifeboats, known as red boats, for their color. Worcester noted, the boats were not interesting for their design but rather for their purpose, which was for saving lives.

In 1854, a wealthy merchant named Li Yung-kuei, who lived near the Hsint'an rapids, decided to collect subscriptions from the traders whose junks had to face the danger of the rapids. With the money he raised, he built three lifesaving craft. So they could be readily identifiable, he had them painted red, from which comes *hung-ch'uan*, although the first craft used as lifeboats were known as *kan-ssu-tang*, the "'dare to die' service."[28]

Li later fell on bad times and the number of boats diminished without the financial help. Worcester, however, writes that the boats were so well constructed that one of the original boats (number 1) was seen at the rapids as late as 1901.

In 1875, 4,000 taels were given to augment the number of lifeboats. Thirteen were built and distributed so no rapids were without the services of the boats. In recognition of their work, a high official from Hunan who was rescued by the boats petitioned the Emperor that the number of boats be increased and that they should become a Government institution under the Chentai of Ichang. The petition was successful, and a special department was set aside in Ichang Yamen and known as the *Chiu-sheng Chu*, or Lifesaving Office.

The boats, in 1899, rescued 1,473 lives from 49 wrecked junks, and 11,235 from 37 junks in 1900. In 1900, the boats helped a German steamer, the S.S. *Suihsing*, that wrecked in a rapid. This brought further subscriptions from the foreign community.

By 1901, there were 44 red boats. The crew consisted of a helmsman and four boatmen, and the cost of the yearly upkeep was $200 for each boat.

The service was maintained by public subscription. The river was divided into districts, each patrolled by one of the five small guard boats. These craft acted as a river police force and supervised the work of the lifeboats.

Regulations were drawn up. Plots of ground were purchased for bodies found and for places for the crew and those rescued to live.

Usually, every upbound junk tracking through the rapids had a red boat nearby. When a wreck occurred, a gun was fired to bring the boats to the location. After the wreck, information concerning the junk was obtained. The lifeboat crew received 11,200 cash for each life saved and 400 cash for every body retrieved.

Worcester chose to illustrate a red boat 30 feet in length, with a beam of 7 feet, and very easy to handle. On its side are the seven Chinese characters for "The Lungmenhao Lower Section Life-boat," with each character within a white circle. The boat flies a flag on the port quarter with an upright line of characters in black on a red ground meaning "The Society for Rescuing Drowning People, Lower Section, Lungmenhao, South Bank, Chungking." A removable mat served as a shelter for the crew. Later, a larger type of red boat was introduced.

Prior to his death in 1969, Worcester wrote, "It is a matter for regret that this noble service has seemingly disappeared, except for an odd survival here and there."

Unlike sea-going junks, the vessels of the Yangtze River were owner run. The masters, or *laodah*, usually carried their wives and children with them. The *laodah* worked their junks until they died. The women aboard the junks, noted Worcester, may not have been able to read, but they could help at the yulohs and oars, with babies strapped to their backs, and handle the ropes and take a turn at the tiller. The wife-sailors, like sailors everywhere, were quick to voice their opinions in a loud voice.[29]

The junkman's calling passed from father to son. If one was lucky, a junk could be sailed by many generations of *laodah*. This produced, according Worcester, "a race of hardy, resourceful sailors. They are rough and tough, with plenty of pluck and endurance, and will work from daylight to dusk without shirking or grumbling. No craft in the world is more skillfully handled than the so-called 'lumbering junks;' and nowhere else do sailors work so desperately hard on such poor fare, or face so many risks for so little pay. Their amazing staying power, combined with the ability to stand hardships, has trained them in the best of schools."[30]

Their bedding was a simple quilt, about 3 feet by 6 feet. This was put over a strip of rush matting, which in the daytime was rolled up and stowed away. The junkman's raincoat was made from the coir palm. They subsisted mainly on "inferior rice" served with cabbage or some other inexpensive vegetable cooked in oil. On festivals and occasionally at other times, they received a bit of pork or fish.

Like sailors the world over, they were superstitious. It was thought to be unlucky to pass under a bridge when a woman was crossing it. It was considered bad luck to turn a food bowl upside down because it represented what could happen to a junk. The superstitions varied from area to area.

Worcester noted that sailors of the West are apt to idealize their ship. The junkman, however, is proud of his vessel too, but from "first to last she is pre-eminently a conveyance to afford him shelter of a sort and the means whereby he can buy food to sustain life in his tough and leathery body."[31]

5. Trackers

While most Westerners knew nothing of the life of the junkmen and their ships, the few foreigners who did travel to the Yangtze River all commented on one aspect of life on The River: the trackers. Trackers were China's human beasts of burden who helped pull junks over rapids and other obstructions. Junks usually carried a basic complement of trackers if they were headed up through the Three Gorges, with up to seventy or eighty on a large cargo vessel. In the Gorges, however, many more would have to be hired, sometimes up to at least 250. At times, many junks would be laid up along the shore awaiting their turn with the trackers.

Howell's diary gives a good description of how the trackers rigged their line to the junk. Each tracker would be put into a sling and this was tied on to the bamboo towing hawser. At the end of the tracker's sling was a button made of bone or wood, with the button secured by a wall knot. The trackers make a half hitch on the bamboo hawser and the button acts as a stopper when the tracker pulls upon the sling, but will easily slip loose when pressure is taken off.

Once the trackers are harnessed to the junk, they are controlled by the beating of a drum from the junk. A short sharp beat meant stop; slow, by a slow even rhythm; and full speed by a rapid, constant drumming. "The throbbing sound of the drum is a marked characteristic of the Upper Yangtze."[32]

Most junks would put the trackers ashore by sampan, or, if this was not possible, bank in. A sampan was used by many vessels to keep the bamboo hawser out of the water as much as possible. The trackers, in most cases, had regular paths. In some places the path was cut into the side of a cliff and was only high enough for bent over straining men.

Many of the Westerners who wrote about the trackers decried their life. Howell's diary lists some of dangers and hardships faced by the men. Worcester, of course, knew the fate of these men. He wished there could be some provision to provide for these hard working men, but there was none.

One had to discern between the long distance trackers, those that lived aboard a junk, and those hired at large rapids. The Victorian globe-trotting Isabella Bird wrote: "Those who crowd in hundreds to the great rapids of the season for the chance of getting a few *cash* for a haul are a rougher lot still…. At the lesser rapids the *lao-pan* goes ashore, dangling strings of *cash*, and as there is usually a village close by, he secures help, after some loud-tongued bargaining and wrangling, engaging even women and boys to tug at his ropes, and occasionally a woman with a baby on her back takes a turn at the dragging!"[33]

6. *Pumps and the* Palos

Glenn F. Howell's description of his first trip through The Gorges is memorable. It is in parts, fascinating, exciting, and humorous. Anyone reading the account of Corporal Watson and the chief watertender will think they have stumbled onto a plot for a "McHale's Navy" television episode. Humor aside, most of the trouble for Howell centers on four feed pumps that serviced the two boilers of the *Palos*. The journey from Chungking to Ichang remained so indelible, and, of course with the help of the diary, that seventeen years after leaving the gunboat Howell could write about the voyage. By this time Howell had four articles published in the prestigious U.S. Naval Institute *Proceedings* and could be considered a frequent contributor.[34] In his article, Howell explains that no one could understand the problems of the pumps: the gunboat was only six years old, so engineering officers said "the trouble would undoubtedly disappear if they were properly overhauled," which the *Palos* accomplished. Readers will see how wrong these officers were in their diagnosis.[35]

Years after his service aboard the gunboat, Howell recorded he entered into a conversation with someone who claimed to have been present at the Mare Island, California, Naval Shipyards where the *Palos* was built. Howell, "perhaps somewhat bitterly," entered into an elaboration of his problems with the six-year-old pumps.

His informant smiled at him and revealed that the pumps "'weren't six years old in 1920.... They were twenty-six years old then.... They ran out of money for those ships, so they just went over to a couple of old torpedo boats they were dismantling and took some of the auxiliaries out of them for the gunboats.'" Howell wrote that "since that conversation we have always felt somewhat better about the whole business and with the passage of the years have even arrived at a kindly feeling toward the gallant old pumps."[36]

7. Capt. Joseph Miclo

In his 1938 article on the voyage from Chungking to Ichang, Howell rightfully gives credit to the work of Capt. Joseph Miclo, skipper of the tug *Meitan*, who readers will meet in the diary. Captain Miclo "learned his trade as a captain of vessels of the Insular Coast Guard of the Philippines...."[37] Miclo worked for Standard Oil, but was later dismissed by the company. While aboard the *I'Chang* in 1931, eleven years after his adventure with Howell and the *Palos*, Miclo disappeared from his cabin while the ship was underway. The chronicler of the American merchant ships on the Yangtze River, David H. Grover, notes that Miclo may "have incurred the hatred of crewmen, whom he brutalized," or he may have been "the victim of the opium cartel...."[38]

Miclo's story does not end with his death and is the type of account that Howell would have included in his log if he had been on the river when the story began. Columbus D. Smith, a friend of Miclo, related to Grover that the Chinese believe if a body is not buried a soul will wander about the world looking for a body to inhabit so that it can eventually find peace. It is difficult "for a soul to enter an ordinary healthy body, but sometimes this can be done." This is used to explain the happenings from 1932 through 1934 on the anniversary of Miclo's disappearance. On this day a Chinese crewman aboard the *I'Chang* would speak loudly in Miclo's voice and then leap overboard. "Presumably, only the demise of the company in 1935 caused the reincarnations to cease."[39]

8. The Palos *and Opium*

Howell's 1938 article about the journey through The Gorges also mentions that a Captain McArthur, the master of British merchantman running between Hankow and Ichang, had been aboard the *Meitan* "for a quick sightseeing run up through the gorges." Captain McArthur "evolved" a cocktail for a party aboard the *Meitan* after the *Palos* had secured safely to the tug's side. Howell noted it "was a masterpiece ... [and] the last one he ever mixed."[40]

At midnight Captain McArthur sailed for Hankow in his own ship. Earlier in the evening "he had sent word to the Customs that there was a passenger on board who would bear scrutiny.... A huge quantity of opium was seized and taken ashore with its owner, a thin Chinese with one long fingernail on each hand."

Later, "some 18 miles below Ichang," McArthur turned over the deck watch to a mate and strolled aft for a smoke. "He was never seen again."[41]

Howell's diary shows the *Palos* did not escape the tentacles of the "opium cartel." The brief entries about the opium episode in the diaries need more detail. Howell realized the incident of the opium smuggling would make a good story and eighteen years later he related it, once again using his diary as his notes and once again in the U.S. Naval Institute *Proceedings*. Within the article is an important statement of the China of the 1920s that readers of today should grasp. "It is difficult to make plain to readers who have never visited the Orient the attitude of the average foreigner there regarding opium. From our griffin days in Shanghai tale upon tale had been told us concerning the power and relentlessness of the combine.[42] It was universally stated that betrayal of the opium people invariably was succeeded by disappearance and death of the offender, regardless of his position or nationality.... There were spies employed by the customs, and the [opium] combine had its spies within the customs service. It was a game run upon the most delicate of rules, and the rewards were very great." [43]

The incident began when Howell, reading in his rented bungalow in Chungking, received a Chinese visitor. "He was obviously not a coolie, and he knew the English language sufficiently well to express himself.... 'Captain, you no search ship on way to Ichang, I give you $10,000.'" At that, Howell "...flung his book at the Oriental's head, and observed him disappear around the corner of the bungalow...."

Howell informed his crew that someone had tried to bribe him and the officers would make an extra diligent search of the *Palos* for the illegal substance. Further, if any opium was found in a man's area he would receive a general court-martial. That night the ship's officers went ashore for a party leaving Chief Boatswain's Mate Smith in charge. (Smith is a fictitious name.)

The search of the gunboat found only a limited amount of opium belonging to a Chinese, which is brought out in the diary. The Chinese was put ashore and the opium thrown into the river.

When the *Palos* arrived in Shanghai, Howell received a message to report to the Commander of the Asiatic Fleet and that until further notice the *Palos* was in quarantine. Howell learned from the Admiral of the Asiatic Fleet that "customs knew as a fact that the gunboat was laden with a huge quantity of opium..." and that the captain had refused all efforts on the part of the customs to search his ship. Howell countered this comment by stating he had, in fact, diligently searched the gunboat for the illegal subsistence and he welcomed a board of officers to search the *Palos*. The admiral took Howell's word and the gunboat captain returned to his ship feeling the matter settled.

While repairs to the work on the pumps progressed, Howell noticed Chief Smith remained aboard the gunboat. The captain "was puzzled by so rigid an attention to duty. He spoke to Smith about taking some liberty while the opportunity presented itself...." The chief responded he did not feel well and Howell noted the chief's "white and haggard face and appreciable loss of weight seemed to confirm this." The doctor, however, could find nothing wrong with Smith.

Two days later, Smith went ashore, only to return within an hour. Howell noted the chief never seemed to sleep, for he could be seen about the deck when the skipper returned from late night parties.

At five o'clock in the morning of Smith's return from his very brief liberty, the chief knocked on the Executive Officer's door. Smith stammered out "they were trying to poison him ... and burst into

tears.... [The Executive Officer] decided this must be Demon Rum operating, sent the man to his quarters with the suggestion that he sleep it
off."

When the *Palos* departed suddenly for Changsha, "Smith was on
deck, but we observed that he stayed as much as possible in the lee of the
deckhouse until we were clear of the dock and out in the stream. The man
looked like a ghost. He had lost 20 pounds in 3 weeks, and his actions
were blundering and uncertain."

The *Palos* had no more than steadied up on her course up the
Yangtze, when Smith came to the bridge. "He saluted the Skipper and
said: 'I am ready to relieve you, Captain. You can go below, sir.'"

Howell immediately sent for the doctor, who led the babbling chief
to sick bay. Within an hour, shrieking could be heard coming out of sick
bay. The doctor put a strait jacket on the now screaming chief boatswain's
mate. The medical officer made notes of his patient's screechings and
reported to Howell and the chief's secret emerged. The story could be
one told in the contemporary U.S. Navy.

In Chungking, someone from the "opium combine" approached
Chief Smith and offered him "a sum which would have made him wealthy
for life, and he succumbed to this temptation." As related, a member of
the cartel made the mistake of attempting to bribe Howell, which led to
the search of the gunboat. The night before the search, two young sailors
on the quartermaster deck watch aboard the *Palos* suddenly noticed the
gunboat surrounded by sampans. Smith told the sailors these were opium
people and "that if they valued their lives they must keep silent about
this." While some of the opium people watched for the return of the ship's
officers, the others worked quickly in stowing and hiding the opium, valued at one million dollars.

The young U.S. Navy watchstanders were terrified and afraid of their
knowledge. They confided their fears to two or three of the older salts in
the crew the next morning. The old hands knew the myth of the opium
cartel and the younger men were, in Howell's words, "in a will-making"
mood. The salts went to Smith and "begged him to have the opium
removed." Smith refused. It must be understood that in the navy of the
1920s, the chief boatswain's mate would be the senior enlisted man in the
crew and enlisted men were constantly reminded they did not break the
"chain of command." That is, the procedure of going step-by-step to the
next level of seniority to speak to a commanding officer. In the case of
the enlisted men on the *Palos*, the young watchstanders would have to go
to their senior petty officer, then to Chief Smith, then to the Executive
Officer, and finally to Howell. In theory, the senior people were only to

approve or disapprove a junior person's request to see the commanding officer, but the person could still see his commanding officer even with disapprovals. In practice, however, a disapproval at any level would effectively stop the person from going up to the next level of command.

Howell warned the crew about what would happen to them if caught with an illegal substance. This caused even more agitation amongst the crew. The men again approached Smith, who replied "that it was too late, he could do nothing." The chief told the enlisted crew, "if they informed or interfered the opium people would unquestionably kill them at the first opportunity." Now the crew had a choice of a court martial or death. The crew responded in a manner as old as seafaring.

At midnight, six men, "their faces blackened with coal dust, naked to their waist," wearing dungaree trousers, grabbed Smith in his bunk, tied and gagged him. Then the men "quickly worked and tin after tin of opium slipped noiselessly over the side, sinking into the deep swift current. When the job was done the ship was free of opium, save for the unknown private venture of the Chinese member of the crew." No one knew the identity of the members of the "Chungking Tea Party." (Smith is fortunate the crew did not put him over the side, a fate of many who have placed their shipmates in such a dilemma.)

Smith was transferred, "violently insane," to a destroyer for further transfer to a hospital in Manila. Three years later Howell received a letter from Smith's father stating the chief had been discharged from the navy and in general "was in his normal mind, but that the sight of an Oriental would send him into insane spasms of terror." The father wanted to know if Howell knew what caused this breakdown in his son. Furthermore, the son "knew he had a large sum of money somewhere but could not remember where it was deposited."

Howell wrote to the father explaining the situation and suggested he try a certain San Francisco bank. The bank did in fact have Smith's account of "thousands of dollars." Smith's doctor, now knowing the cause of the trouble, started to work upon the ex-chief and told the father that the cure, however, "would be expensive. The old man remarked in a postscript that it looked as if there wouldn't be much of the ill-gotten gains left by the time" Smith finally was cured.

9. The Steam Navy

The coal burning steam navy had engineering terms now long out of usage that will appear in Howell's entries, especially when working in the rapids of the Yangtze. Firemen had to shovel coal into fireboxes to heat the boilers to make steam. The better grade of coal burned with more intensity, providing a better fire and left little ash. The poorer grade did just the opposite. A fire that burned hot, with little ash, was known as a "clean" fire and a bad fire was "dirty." No matter how clean the fire, however, eventually the ashes of the burned coal had to be removed from the firebox and this was known as cleaning a fire.

There was more to maintaining a proper fire than just shoveling coal into the firebox. For example, a fireman had to be aware of high and low spots in the fire and the proper way to distribute the coal in the firebox.[44]

10. Ship Guards

Readers will note Howell's comments about putting sailors aboard U.S. ships on the Yangtze River. This became a common occurrence. If an American ship reported that they had taken fire, either sailors or marines would be placed aboard the vessel. Howell's cryptic comment in his diary about the *Robert Dollar* being "piratical" may refer to an American ship flying a Chinese flag to draw fire in order to have the American military stationed aboard it for future trips. At times marines were stationed aboard a gunboat to give the ship the added assistance of the soldiers of the sea.

In 1934, Lieut. James F. Moriarty, of the U.S. Marine Corps, kept a log about his experiences aboard a merchant ship on the *Chang Jiang*. His duty probably reflected this type of assignment at any time and by both sailors and leathernecks. There are some entries about firing upon the ship, but most of the log is centered on how an American military man viewed service on the Yangtze River aboard a merchantman. On April 24, for example, the marine noted they were tied up at Hankow in a fog, but "so is the captain." The next day the ship got underway with the "Captain's sweetie" waving farewell. For dinner the next day, Moriarty feasted upon "rubber chicken," but at least the skipper had "come out of his fog."

Five days later, the ship was moored and everyone was "twiddling thumbs." By the end of the escort duty, the officer recommended there be no more than two men of the armed guard to a room, especially on hot days, and that there should be "ointment for bug infection or spider bites, [and] sunburn," plus medicine to combat dysentery.[45]

11. Missionaries

In this section of the diary, Howell begins to describe his feelings toward the passing scene, missionaries, and other nationalities. These will be discussed in more detail in later introductions to the sections of the diary.

Notes

1. Tolley, *Yangtze Patrol*, 188.
2. Glenn Howell, "Opium Obligato," U.S. Naval Institute *Proceedings*, 4 (December 1938): 1731–1732.
3. Erling Hoh, "The Long River's Journey Ends," *Natural History*, 105, No. 7 (July 1996): 28.
4. The Chinese in 1981 had considered a dam with a pool level of no less than 600 feet. American engineers informed the Chinese they would withdraw their support for such a large structure. The Chinese withdrew the project. Winchester, *River at the Center of the World*, 225.
5. Ibid., 226.
6. Quoted in ibid., 228.
7. Ibid., 252.
8. Lyman P. Van Slyke, *Yangtze: Nature, History, and the River* (New York: Addison-Wesley Publishing Company, 1988), 19.
9. Glenn Howell, "Chungking to Ichang," U.S. Naval Institute *Proceedings*, 65 (September 1938): 1315–1314.
10. Van Slyke, *Yangtze*, 32.
11. Ibid., 38.
12. Howell gives Plant's age as "about forty," when he came to the Yangtze. Glenn Howell, "Captain Plant," United States Naval Institute *Proceedings*, 55 (March 1929): 207. Archibald John Little (1838–1908) was an old China hand and merchant. He remained in China from 1859, departing for the final time in 1907. Very early he became determined to bring steam navigation to the upper Yangtze River. One description of Little states he conformed to the stereotype of the early Englishman on the make in China: "portly, muttonchop mustaches, pith helmet, and all." He resided for a time at Chungking and eventually had steam craft built to make their way upriver to that port. "But Little's ascent was an accomplishment of greater symbolic than practical significance." The vessel was too small to transport either passengers or cargo and, in fact, needed the assistance of trackers to make it through the difficult rapids. He financed the building of the *Pioneer*, which S. Cornell Plant captained. Van Slyke, *Yangtze*, 169–173.
13. Winchester, *River at the Center of the World*, 256.
14. Ibid.
15. G. R. G. Worcester, *The Junks and Sampans of the Yangtze* (Annapolis, Md.: Naval Institute Press, 1971), 26–27.
16. Howell, "Captain Plant," 208.
17. Ibid., 207.
18. Ibid., 208
19. Ibid.
20. Ibid.
21. Ibid.
22. Winchester, *River at the Center of the World*, 262–263.
23. Howell, "Captain Plant," 208; Winchester, *River at the Center of the World*, 253.

24. Winchester, *River at the Center of the World*, 265–266.
25. Worcester, *The Junks and Sampans of the Yangtze*, v.
26. Ibid., 11.
27. All material on the *Ma-Yang-Tzu*, unless otherwise noted, is in ibid., 498–500.
28. All material on the *hung-ch'uan*, unless otherwise noted, is in ibid., 528–530.
29. Ibid., 111.
30. Ibid.
31. Ibid., 117.
32. Ibid., 52.
33. Isabella Bird, *The Yangtze Valley and Beyond: An Account of Journeys in China, Chiefly in the Province of Sze Chuan and Among the Man-tze of the Somo Territory* (London: John Murray, 1899; reprinted, Boston: Beacon Press, 1987), 145. Page reference to reprint edition.
34. Howell would eventually have eight pieces in the journal. They reflect two periods of productivity. His first article appeared in 1927, followed by one in 1928 and 1929. A nine year hiatus followed and then publication of four articles in 1938 and one in 1939. It will be noted that most of the articles came after he had been medically retired from the navy. See Appendix 3 for citations.
35. Howell, "Chungking to Ichang," 1312.
36. Ibid., 1316
37. David H. Grover, *American Merchant Ships on the Yangtze, 1920–1921* (Westport, Ct.: Prager, 1992), 11–12.
38. Ibid., 14.
39. Ibid., 11–15. Miclo's death is also mentioned in, Howell, "Chungking to Ichang," 1316.
40. Howell, "Chungking to Ichang," 1316.
41. Ibid. Howell did not have a first name for Captain McArthur, nor did Grover in his work. See, Grover, *American Merchant Ships*, 13–14.
42. A "griffin" was someone new to China.
43. Unless otherwise noted, all material on the opium incident aboard the *Palos* is contained in Glenn F. Howell, "Opium Obligato," U.S. Naval Institute *Proceedings*, 64 (December 1938): 1720–1735.
44. For a good description of maintaining fires aboard a steam vessel, see: Commander Bruce R. Ware, Jr., "Winning the Engineering White E," U.S. Naval Institute *Proceedings* (April 1919): 593–621.
45. Papers of Brig. Gen. James F. Moriarty (USMC), China Repository, Naval Operational Archives, U.S. Naval Historical Center, Washington, D.C.

The Diary

JUNE 6, 1920. At six fifteen this morning I assumed command of the United States ship *Palos*, relieving Lieutenant Commander George S. Gillespie, who is ordered to the *South Dakota* as First Lieutenant....[1]

At six o'clock we held quarters for the crew, followed immediately by General Drills ... and in the midst of the drill I suddenly heard Gillespie bawling out for poles. A huge ancient junk was drifting down upon the ship. The entire crew rushed forward armed with poles, stretchers, and whatever was at hand, and managed to make her initial bump harmless. Then she scraped along the starboard side, and all hands clung to her against the swift current until the [*Palos'*] motor sampan could be cleared. This excitement over, we proceeded with the general drills and read our orders, after which I relieved Gillespie.

I found myself facing a new and very great responsibility. [Even though I had served in the Captain's stead on other ships,] it was not the same, for most decisions could be postponed for the Captain's approval; his was the ultimate responsibility.

The *Palos* has been cruising on the Upper Yangtze for fourteen months, except for a recent run to Nanking [Nanjing] and back. During that time, she has had no repairs other than the ship's and in consequence thereof must soon have a repair period in Shanghai. Aside from her feed pumps and blowers[,] she is in excellent condition, better, I think than the *Monocacy*, whose boilers are badly in need of an overhaul. She is very neat and clean, and the appearance of the crew is excellent.[2]

I find myself in command of two officers and fifty bluejackets....

There are also on board a raft of Chinese with apparently no names—five watsus—boatmen for the ship's sampans (she carries no boats but sampans), a barber, number two for the steward, number two for the cook, extra wardroom servants, two pilots, boys for the bunkrooms, [and] a cook for the watsus.

Before I turned in[,] I went on my fo'c'sle and sat for an hour in the moonlight. It was very beautiful.

JUNE 7, 1920. WANHSIEN. At 11:00 [A.M.] I called officially upon the Captain of the H.M.S. *Widgeon* ... [which is] a bit smaller than the *Palos*. It was the first time I had ever flown my Captain's pennant and I went alongside the *Widgeon* in style in my sampan, my boatman rowing smartly, the pennant flying properly in the bow, and the colors in the stern.[3]

I found Commander Jukes-Hughes and the doctor on the *Widgeon* very agreeable fellows, and I foresee some pleasant parties with them.[4] In the evening [Lieut. Thaddeus A.] Hoppe, [Lieut. (MC) Reuben A.] Barber, and I went to the *Widgeon* for dinner, and we played bridge afterward until midnight.[5]

Wanhsien is reputed to be ten thousand years old.... [T]he streets are of course very narrow and winding, and they are composed partly of stone steps. Like all Chinese towns, Wanhsien is very dirty with all the odors of its ilk. It is, however, the most important port between

Chungking and Ichang [Yichang], and there are at least two hundred junks lying here.

Tiffin, bridge, and tennis filled the afternoon, and we returned to the ship for dinner.[6]

JUNE 9, 1920. I have fallen into a routine of arising at half past five and of sitting on the fo'c'sle in my bathrobe while the steward brings me coffee.

Wanksien across the river is picturesquely interesting in the hot early sun. From its depth arises a great sound of many voices for the Upper River Chinese are even worse than those of the lower river in that respect.

The junks begin moving early. Those bound down stream remain in the middle of the river, swept down at a rate here of about six knots. The coolies at the oars—and there are at least thirty—stamp to and fro at their labor, singing the while—if singing it may be called. Individually, the shouting would be properly considered screaming, but the swaying rhythm of a junk full of coolies carries with it a certain sense of pleasure.

Along the bank of the river opposite the city, toil the upward bound junks. The trackers appear in their labored procession long before the junk heaves in sight. Their number depends upon the size of the junk, and it may vary from ten for a small junk to fifty for a large one. A long rope, secured to the deck of the junk, runs through a block at the top of the mast over to the beach. From the end of this rope are suspended slings in which trackers are harnessed. When all is ready, away they go, chanting to ease the strain and to insure the rhythm necessary for progress.

The life of a tracker is estimated as from two to five years. At least two hundred thousand are employed on the Upper River. Their wages on the up river trip from Ichang to Chungking are three dollars and food. The down river trip is of course rapid, though very dangerous. The up river trip cannot be made in less than two months. So their maximum wage is twelve dollars all year.

The casualties [among the trackers] are enormous. On an average, not one quarter of a bunch of trackers leaving Ichang for Chungking arrive at Chungking to claim their wages. Frequently, the junk ... pulls the tracker off high cliffs. They are drowned ... in ... crossing streams. They fall ill and are left on the shore to die or join another group of trackers. Sometimes the junk itself is wrecked. Clothes they dispense with entirely during eight months of the year.... Yet the amazing thing about the Yangtze trackers is this. In spite of the unending toil, the few years of life, ... they are an extraordinary happy group of human beings. Carefree, never thinking of the morrow, today's chow and tonight's sleep register the limits of their desire.

At 8:20 the Captain of the *Toba* called officially on me. He is quite a decent Jap, speaks English well, and is really not objectionable at all. He stayed for about an hour. He is going to Chungking for the summer.[7]

At 10:15 I returned the call ... I stayed for about twenty minutes.... He was very much interested in the Mississippi River and he fetched out an atlas to enable me to describe the river thoroughly....

The American Steamer *Robert Dollar II* came in this evening and upon the request of their Captain I sent on board [S2C(T) J. E.] Lewis,

S.S. *Robert Dollar* **steams along the Yangtze River near Chungking, with the** *Palos* **seen dimly in the background. The** *Robert Dollar* **did not escape The Gorges: she struck rocks in the The Gorges and sank in 1924. (Photograph courtesy of U.S. Naval Institute.)**

The sailors of the Yangtze River Patrol saw a slice of China most U.S. military men were unable to observe. The U.S. gunboat *Mindanao* steams along the river near Chungking. (Photograph courtesy of U.S. Naval Institute.)

a machine gun, and some ammunition. She has been fired upon so frequently by the robbers that she has requested this protection. However, unless she is fired upon this trip I shall not put a guard on board again, for the ship, although lawfully under the American flag is somewhat piratically inclined, and I am inclined to be from Missouri so far as she is concerned.

JUNE 10, 1920. Last night I sent a chit over to the *Toba* and challenged the Japs to a game of baseball.[8] So they sailed at 5:30 this morning, after the Japs had declined to play. It is evidently a good way to make them move....

In the afternoon, we had a baseball game between the deck force and the black gang, while the doctor fielded for the deck force.[9] I umped.... The deck force won—7 to 3, but vengeance is vowed and we shall have another game at the first opportunity.

Wanksien is in an uproar today. The robbers snuck in and stole a whole school—seventy fourteen year old boys, tons of leading citizens. They ran them off into the hills and will hold them for ransom.

JUNE 11, 1920. At six [this evening], [Juke-Hughes] and I went ashore for a walk in the village opposite Wanhsien. Everything is old here—the stone walks, and steps, the mud huts, the fields, the hills. We came to a temple cave in the side of a hill with a waterfall curtaining it. There were perhaps a dozen images of varying discriptude, a few villagers loafing about, [and] some soldiers idling by....

A telegram ... informed me to expect the arrival of the *Monocacy* with the Patrol Commander on board ... and that he would transfer his pennant to the *Palos* and proceed with her to Chungking.

JUNE 12, 1920. The Barber and I did a little tennis this afternoon, but it was so hot that the Barber's bulk suffered. To reach ... the tennis court, ... one leaves the sampans at the foot of a large white temple and proceeds up steep rocks into an ancient cemetery. Through this area treads a devious route—always uphill—until the court is reached. It is leveled off in the very center of the cemetery with graves all about it, and much cumshaw must have been required to have established it....[10]

JUNE 13, 1920. A horrible night...! [T]he river ... fell with rapidity. I slept from ten to eleven—no more. I was resolved not to move until dawn unless I had to; so I had to sit up and watch....

At a quarter to four I shifted berth—not a bit too soon, for when we hauled up ... our anchor we had just six inches to spare under our stern ... I shall take no more chances like this.

At six fifteen this evening ... I shifted berth about twenty yards further out from the bank.... Of course, immediately—[after] I shifted the river began to rise again. I do not like Wanhsien.

JUNE 14, 1920. At 10:30 the *Monocacy* hove in sight ... flying the Patrol Commander's pennant. As soon as she anchored, I went over and called.

At 1:05 Captain Kearney called officially on the *Palos*.... At 3:05 the Patrol Commander transferred to the *Palos*, and we broke his pennant.[11] From the *Monocacy*, in addition to Captain Kearney's servant and his body guard of two blue jackets and two marines, there reported on board a squad of eight marines and a corporal. These men will remain on board the *Palos* until we go down river next fall.

Lieutenant B.O. Wells came on board with Captain Kearney as the latter's aide.[12]

JUNE 15, 1920. At 4:55[A.M.] the *Palos* hove up and stood up river. It was rather a peculiar sensation to realize I was solely responsible for the safety of the ship and lives of my people.

At 6:15 [A.M.] we entered the Ho Tan, the worst rapid on the river at this water level.... [T]he whole volume of the Yangtze at this point is compressed into a rapid of great current. It breaks along a distinct V and within ten feet falls six. So it is necessary for the ship not only to overcome the current but also to accomplish the feat of climbing up hill.

We crawled up in the lee of rocks on the left side of the river, suddenly veered out and dashed at the rapid, and as suddenly found ourselves in the midst of its roar with a bow wave ten feet high mounting over the fo'c'sle. The foc's'le buried itself under water for a time and then slowly struggled up. The instant we climbed the hill the pilot eased the ship over to the right, for our port side was only four feet from the rocks.

Then we eased across the river on the top of the rapid, losing a bit of what we had gained. There, almost touching those rocks, we resumed our struggle against the current. But it was a losing fight. We began visibly to go astern. The pilot eased back toward the left bank, but I then found that the steam had dropped to eighty pounds. So we gave up temporarily, stopped the engines in order to give the black gang a chance to get up a full head of steam, and drifted over the rapid and down the river.

Presently we tried it again, and this time won through. I do not know of anything more thrilling than to battle through an Upper Yangtze rapid. The great roar of the water, the charging of the wall at full speed, the burying of the ship's nose, the dangerous nearness to jagged rocks, the inch by inch gain upstream—all combine to make skipper and pilot give sighs of relief when comparatively easy water is reached.

At 10:52 we anchored about twenty feet from a mud bank to clean fires. Many poor natives came to sit and stare at us. However, their apathy was soon galvanized into activity for the Commissariat of the ship indicated a desire for fowls. One and all the population disappeared over the hill only to be back again shortly bearing chickens.

The infamous Hsintan rapids in the Three Gorges area. This photograph was taken by Glenn F. Howell to illustrate an article he wrote on S. Cornell Plant. Howell pointed out the memorial to Plant sat atop the dark hill in the middle background. (Photograph courtesy of U.S. Naval Institute.)

The procedure of the barter was as follows. A coin was flung to the beach. There was a mad scramble, and out of the melee appeared a lad bearing off the coin. Promptly he threw off his scanty garb and plunged into the river, carefully holding up his left hand clear of the water so that the chicken in it would be delivered properly in a not bedraggled condition. The chickens did not seem to mind this precarious sort of journeying. I presume that the fatalism of their owners has infected them also.

At 1:15 we got underway again. The river is obviously narrower with high rolling hills on each side but without the gorges which make the river below Wanhsien so grandly beautiful. The whole appearance of this country impresses one with its great age. The covering of the hills has in many places been washed away by the rains of centuries, and many hills are but bare rocks. There are hundreds of little waterfalls. Often a dozen will be seen within a mile.

Wherever there is a patch of earth it is under cultivation. I was very much surprised to see Indian corn under extensive cultivation. Everything is apparently grown here: maize, tobacco, rice, tea, potatoes, and vegetables of all sorts.

At 7:09 we anchored three miles below Kao-Chia Chen [Kao Jiachen], tying up to stakes as usual to insure our anchor not dragging.[13]

JUNE 16, 1920—UPPER YANGTZE. At the unholy hour of 4:10 [A.M.] we got underway and stood up river. There is a certain satisfaction in starting out in the early dawn. One gains so much distance before eight o'clock, when your normal world is just beginning to move.

At 11:34 we anchored perhaps a mile above Tuchow [Tuzhou], a city of considerable size. I was a bit worried during the forenoon on account of the lowness of our coal, but we got in with two tons to spare. However, I made a resolve today to cut out this business of moving with six inches [of water] under the bottom and landing in port with two tons left. In the future we are going to run on a little margin.

At 2:30, having coaled and cleaned fires, we got underway. At 6:15 we moored to the bank one mile above Chang Chou [Zhangchau], a little city surrounded by a wall. At dark there came a boat load of soldiers who evidently were arriving for their squeeze.[14] But when they learned that we were not a passenger vessel and that we had ammunition on board they left without argument.

JUNE 17, 1920—ABOVE CHANG CHOU. At 4:23 [A.M.] got underway for the last leg to Chungking. We had all sorts of trouble with the feed pumps. They were continually stopping, and at one time we thought that we would have to haul fires in #1 boiler.[15] However, we worried through, and at 2:40 moored to our summer moorings at Chungking....

[T]he American consul, P.R. Josselyn, called.[16] He is a very nice chap, and I am sure that he and I will get along well together. Walter Halliday, whom I knew so well in Shanghai in 1916, and the other Standard Oil people called before dinner.

The *Robert Dollar II* arrived this evening, and since she had not been fired upon or otherwise molested[,] I took Lewis and the machine gun off her.

JUNE 19, 1920—CHUNGKING. At 9:40 Captain Kearney, Wells, and I left the ship to call on the Taoyin and the Commissioner of Foreign Affairs.[17] We crossed the river in the borrowed launch ... and landed at the foot of a stair that [at] a distance reminds one of biblical times. Only a few feet from where we landed there lay a man dead from the cholera and another was dying on the steps. Everyone gave them a wide berth, not through any particular fear of contamination, but on account of the unwritten law that he who gives assistance to a dying man must pay for his burial.

The Consul met us near the landing, and we proceeded in state to our destination. Two coolies ran before [our procession] shouting for gangway. Then came Captain Kearney, the Consul, myself, Wells, and the interpreter. Two sailors wearing straw hats (a foible of the Patrol Commander of which I disapprove) walked on either side of Captain Kearney's chair, and two marines guarded me. In all, counting runners, guards, and chair coolies, the retinue consisted of twenty-six people.

The Taoyin received us with much state in an apartment in sad disrepair. The table cloth was dirty, as were the wine glasses, and we drank the toasts with a reluctance sharpened by the cholera dread.

The Commissioner of Foreign Affairs wore European clothes and lived in better surroundings. He spoke more French than he did English, and he knew only a dozen works of French. So the interpreter was busy.

At one o'clock we had a tiffin for ten.... It rather was a squeeze to get everyone into our little messroom, but we managed ... and had really a very nice party.

JUNE 20, 1920—CHUNGKING. At 4:00 we all turned out to say goodbye to the Patrol Commander. They left for the *Widgeon* ... for Wanhsien....

After tiffin we went by chair up on the country to Bollard's for tennis. I returned to the ship during dusk.

JUNE 21, 1920—CHUNGKING. About one o'clock this morning robbers attacked the village across the Little River from Chungking. About thirty shots were fired, and then the Jap put his searchlight on the scene and we heard no more shooting.

The Taoyin has quite an interesting history. Along in 1910 he threw a bomb at Yuan Shi Kai [Yuan Shikai], but it exploded prematurely and wounded the thrower in the hand. He was thrown in prison to await execution, but before he could be executed the revolution of 1911 occurred, and the new party released him. His name he then discarded and took a new name which means literally "Man born again." He is the magistrate of the city and looks quite young for so responsible a position. The Commissioner of Foreign Affairs is the only official from Peking in the province. He is tolerated only because his salary is paid by the white customs people, who do not recognize the independence of Szechwan.

JUNE 22, 1920—CHUNGKING. Hoppe, the Barber, and I have rented the top floor of an empty Chinese house that is within a stone's throw of the ship.... I am going to be very contented here. This existence is peaceful, there is no rushing around and hurrying, time there is and to spare, and we are forgotten by the outside world. I have not seen a daily paper since the seventeenth of May, nor have I received one bit of news prior to that date other than local. The prohibitionists may have been put to routing New Jersey mets, the American Republic may have disappeared in an earthquake, old Woody Wilson may have snapped out of his hop—one cannot tell.[18]

I am really eager to know of but one thing and that is—who was nominated by the Republicans on the seventh of June and consequently will be the next president? I can only conjecture somewhat wildly. I have no objection to any of the leading Republicans.... Any of them would make an immeasurably better president than poor, foolish, old, grandeur-obsessed Wilson has. I am a little doubtful about Hiram.[19] He is very much on the Roosevelt style without Roosevelt's fine judgment in crisis. If Roosevelt were alive, he would be elected by an overwhelming majority.[20]

Just about today, the Democrats are making their decision at San Francisco and I am equally at sea regarding their ultimate candidate.... Of this trash, the best would be McAdoo or Palmer.[21] Hoover has a very strong following throughout the country, but his affiliations with either party are considered too slight to give him a chance.[22]

I inherited my sedan chair from Gillespie. It is an ordinary wicker chair mounted on two long poles. Two coolies support it from the front and two in the rear. I have only two of Gillespie's coolies. The others died of the cholera about three weeks ago.

The chair coolies have but two gaits. One is a short, swinging trot, the other a slow, careful step employed in climbing hills. It is the only method short of walking that is feasible in the country for getting about, for the up and down trails with their succession of steps preclude any wheeled conveyance being employed. There are ponies, but they are not as dependable as coolies.

During the summer here, practically all the foreigners live in bungalows on the first or second ranges.[23] These high hills, almost mountains, can be reached by chair within an hour or two from the river, and their breezy coolness makes them delightful after the filth of the city and the heat of the river. The trip up any of the paths is beautiful, and it is also thrilling, for the trails round precipices and across unwieldy bridges. However, accidents rarely happen.

JULY 3, 1920—CHUNGKING. We all went up to the Standard Oil bungalow tonight for dinner, but at half past ten I heard shots fired in the distance and so came hastily back to the ship, only to find everything quiet. Had a good sleep in consequence thereof.

JULY 6, 1920—CHUNGKING. Rumor has it that Admiral Gleaves is contemplating a visit to Chungking in the near future.[24] I am getting fed up to the neck with people coming up here to muddle into a mess that is already sufficient.

AUGUST 3, 1920—CHUNGKING. Did forty pages on the Lazarettes today.[25]

Jukes-Hughes called and thanked us for half masting colors with him on account of the death from heatstroke of his Chief Petty Officer. I attended his funeral that afternoon with three of my gobs.... We went up the Little River about four miles to the foreign cemetery.... Then a brief service was held.... The whole thing was very sad. The man ... [had] but a few more months to serve before retiring. The plain black box, the chattering coolies, the sickening heat of the afternoon—all made the affair depressing.

The British Navy sends the bodies of neither officers nor men home. We do, and I am glad of it. In the cemetery were several graves of British sailors and officers. A few German sailors are buried here....

AUGUST 26, 1920—HOKIANG [HEKIANG]. The *Shuhun* got underway today at dawn and proceeded up river. She is a passenger vessel owned by the government and a Chinese company. This trip is to Luchow [Luchow], one hundred and forty miles above Chungking[,] for no less a purpose than to get the Civil Governor of Sechwan's [Sichuan] wife—one of them at least—and to fetch her to Chungking ... I have a large cabin.[26]

The Governor has sent his soldiers on ahead, and as a consequence we have seen no robbers.

The river above Chungking runs through a much more open country than between Chungking and Ichang.... The terrain gives one the idea of the great age of the land itself. At point after point, the rains of thousands of years have washed the hills bare of all soil, leaving the naked rock with an occasional tree. The country is much less densely populated than below Chungking, although all tillable land is under intense cultivation.

We moored for the night at Kokiang [Gekang?], because it is friendly to the Governor and there is little likelihood of being attacked by robbers.

AUGUST 27, 1920—LUCHOW [LUCHOU]. We arrived at Luchow at ten A.M. It is a town where a small river flows into the Yangtze from the Chengtu [Chengdu] plain. It's population is about 100,000 Chinese and 13 adult foreigners. It's importance lies in the fact that it is the gateway from Yunnan into Szechwan. It is under the Yunnanese with a Yunnanese general as governor.

Szechwan has been in an uproar since 1911. It's revolution with the rest of the country was accomplished very quietly, but in 1913 the province declared itself independent of the Peking Government. Since then it has been one long drawn out, balled up mess. About three years ago those provinces south of the Yangtze seceded from the Peking Government. Consequently, when the Peking Government attacked Szechwan in force, the Szechwanese called in the Yunnanese and the Hweichowese [Huizhou] troops to assist them to repel boarders. But when the Northern troops were successfully driven out, the Yunnanese and the Hweichowese demanded pay for their aid. The Szchwanese have never paid them. So they have remained ever since, occupying most of the important cities except Chengtu, which is now held by the Szchwanese. The Hweichow people hold Chungking and all towns below it except Wanhsien, which is independent of everybody.

The Yunnanese hold Luchow and the surrounding country. This particular general is friendly to the Civil Governor. Hence, the safety of the visit....

[C]alled on Joliffe, a Canadian missionary, who had lived there twelve years, completely surrounded by a large and growing family. He seemed happy and contented, but what an existence![27]

[Howell returns to the *Palos* August 28, 1920]

SEPTEMBER 1, 1920—CHUNGKING. Arriving back at the ship, I found a large mail waiting, and to my joy our movement orders directing us to proceed to Shanghai for leave, liberty, and repairs. I plan to leave on September 9th with the *Meitan* as convoy, for our pumps are going to worry me constantly until we reach Shanghai.[28]

SEPTEMBER 6, 1920—CHUNGKING. I was offered today ten thousand dollars if I would not search the *Palos* for opium on her down river trip.[29]

SEPTEMBER 9, 1920—CHUNGKING. What is commonly known as a large day.... Sailed from Chungking at 4:50 A.M. followed by the *Meitan* towing an oil barge on her starboard side. We had a little trouble with the feed pumps from the start, but we stood down river without serious trouble until 6:30, when Hoppe reported that the pumps showed imminent signs of failing.

I therefore made signal to the *Meitan*, who came within hailing distance, and told Captain Miclo that I wanted to be taken in tow as soon as he could manage it. He promised to take me in tow at a point ten miles further down where there was room for both of us to turn. The *Meitan* then passed us and stood on down river.

At 7:00 all feed pumps failed. Efforts to start them again were of no avail. I gave orders to haul fires as soon as the water disappeared from the glass. Accordingly, at 7:04 fires were hauled in both boilers.

In the meantime, I made signals of distress to the *Meitan*. Captain Miclo acknowledged the signals, but could do nothing but stand on, as it was impossible to turn at that point. We cut off all auxiliaries except the steering engine in order to husband the remaining steam, and the engines continued to turn over dead slow. We went steadily on down the river, still under control, with rocks staring at us from either side of the narrow channel. At 7:14 the engines stopped. At 7:18 the steering engine failed, and I shifted to hand steering. At the same moment—I put the rudder hard over right in order to get headed up stream before all way was lost. We managed to complete the turn, and then drifted rapidly down the river, the ship still under very slight control through the rudders. A swirl set us nearer the rocks, but we passed the nearest ones with a few feet to spare.

A great silence settled over the ship. The sampans were tended, and lifebelts quietly distributed. No one said anything. Not far below us was a heap of rocks through which we could not hope to win.

But in the meantime, Miclo was turning the *Meitan* and the barge, and taking a fearful chance, for where he turned he had a clearance of less than two feet over the rocks. He stood up to us, and at 7:22 we gave him our first line. It was his intention to tow us well clear of the rocks and then secure us alongside. But swirls forced us up alongside him. So very quickly we secured to him port side, the *Meitan* using the engines to keep all three vessels clear of danger during the evolution. At 7:25 we completed the securing. As soon as we reached a clear space, the *Meitan* turned the tow and headed down river.

All hands then drew several long breaths.

Examination of the boilers showed no damage, and aside from the feed pumps the ship is entirely all right. The passage to Wanhsien was accomplished without further incident, although the combined beam of the three vessels was 66 feet, and the passage of three ships lashed together has never before been attempted in the Upper River.

This is the second time the *Meitan* has saved the *Palos*. In 1917, the *Palos* struck a rock in the gorges, arriving at Ichang with her decks awash. She went alongside the *Meitan*, who pumped her out, and towed her all the way to Shanghai.

We anchored in triple tandem at Wanhsien at 6:30 P.M. The *Widgeon* was there, and a number of merchant ships—the *Dollar*, the *Shuhun*, and the *Mechuen*. From the *Mechuen* took on board a marine corporal and a private, thus removing the last remaining guard we have had on merchant vessels here....

Had a long conference after dinner. Jukes-Hughes strongly advised me not to go on, but to remain at Wanhsien until the *Meitan* should return to Wanhsien alone to tow me down. This I refused to consider. Finally Miclo and I decided to proceed on down river in the same manner the next morning. We determined to withhold decision on attempting the worse gorges until it could be seen how the tow maneuvered in the first rapids....

SEPTEMBER 10, 1920—WANHSIEN. We lighted fires under #2 boiler at midnight. Steam formed at 2:40, started up three feed pumps, and experienced no more than ordinary trouble. Turned out at 4:30 A.M. and got underway at 6:08 alongside *Meitan* as before. At 7:00, went ahead slow speed on one engine for a double purpose: to assist speed of the *Meitan* through rapids and bad swirls, and to learn if it were practicable to steam slow on one engine and under one boiler below Ichang.

I found out. At 9:00 all feed pumps slowed. At 9:15, all failed, and we hauled fires. I shall make no further attempts to use the engines until new feed pumps are installed. At 10:35, the *Meitan* anchored us off Hwe-ichowfu [Hweichoufu], three miles above the entrance to Bellows Gorge, and proceeded on down river with her barge. Had we been able to keep steam up, I rather believe that we should have attempted to go on through to Ichang. But with a dead weight on either side of him, and with that great beam in the narrow gorges, to proceed was merely to challenge our luck. So we waved goodbye to the *Meitan* with a marooned feeling, Miclo promising to return for us by Tuesday, the fourteenth.

I then telegraphed Captain Kearney all about it, telegraphed the Standard Oil people in Ichang requesting the *Meitan* to return for us, took a good look at our moorings, and then went sound asleep.

Hweichowfu is a town of 60,000 people, 110 miles from Ichang, 90 miles below Wanhsien, and 290 miles below Chungking. It is garrisoned by 10,000 Szechwan soldiers, but is peaceful at the present.

SEPTEMBER 11, 1920—HWEICHOWFU. Naturally a very quiet day. I sent the Doc ashore to make an intelligence report on the city. In the afternoon, I took about twenty of my gobs for a hike along the beach. We visited a pagoda and then wandered on to a point where we could see the entrance to the Bellows Gorge. It is extraordinarily impressive—a great gash in the mountain range with a sheer cliff on the port side two and a half thousand feet high. The river narrows to a mere thread between those mighty walls.

Received a telegram from Ichang that the *Meitan* will return Monday for us.

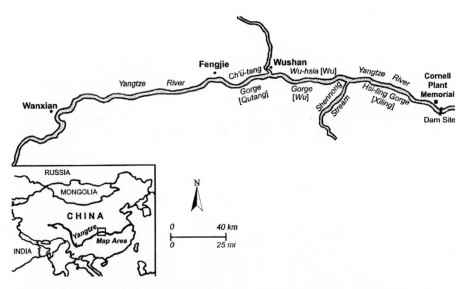

The Three Gorges of the Yangtze River. (Map by Susan Browning.)

SEPTEMBER 12, 1920—HWEICHOWFU. Another quiet day, spent largely by all hands in sleep. Received a telegram from Miclo to have steam up if possible when we go through the gorges, as they are bad. We shall, but not for the main engines.

Found a bottle of sauterne in my cabin today, placed there by the faithful Joe. [Howell's Chinese cabin steward.] We braved the dictum of Sir Josephus.[30]

SEPTEMBER 13, 1920—HWEICHOWFU. I carried out my threat about the opium today, and the mate and the Doctor spent five hours searching the ship for it. The result was about 30 catties of it, worth probably in Shanghai $3,000.[31] We found it in the after bunk house, and it belonged to Peanuts, the men's cook. I contented myself with bawling the weeping Peanuts out and confiscating the opium.

In the midst of the opium raid, I heard a great shouting from forward. I rushed out on the fo'c'sle to see a great junk drifting helplessly down upon us. We grabbed poles and boat hooks and tried to stop her, but her stern drifted neatly down upon our bow. There was a long splintering crash, and out sharp bow made stove wood out of the junk's broad stern. I was rather worried for a moment, but our lines held with the anchor. Hundreds of cash spilled out of the gaping stern, within which was revealed an old Chinese grandmother, who screamed and howled as she tried to stop the outflow of coin.

Had the junk drifted broadside down upon us with more way upon her, there might have been a different tale to record. However—

Had a quiet afternoon, and as evening approached, all hands kept an eager lookout for the Meitan. When the signal was at last made a great shout went up over the ship. The Meitan tied up alongside our port side for the night. She had on board six or seven Ichanger, and there was consequently much gossip to exchange....

SEPTEMBER 14, 1920. HWEICHOWFU. Got underway at dawn in tow alongside Meitan, and stood down river. Had steam up, but did not use main engines, as it proved unnecessary. Had an uneventful shoot down the gorges, and after I found that we were negotiating the swirls and rapids with ease, I had time to devote a little attention to the marvelous scenery. The trip through the Upper Yangtze gorges is one of the wonderful journeys of the world. Vast cliffs overhang the rushing, boiling river; ancient shale and worn out rock fringes into the edges of the river; an occasional mud house [?] sits a precarious existence

Top: "The trip through the Upper Yangtze gorge is one of the wonderful journeys of the world." The Gorges will be largely lost after the completion of the Three Gorges Dam. *Bottom:* "[O]ne rounds each bend only to have his eyes greeted by grander and even more magnificent sights." Photographs taken in 1921. (Photographs courtesy of U.S. Naval Institute.)

under an overhanging mountain; one rounds each bend only to have his eyes greeted by grander and even more magnificent sights.

But I sighed with relief when we passed the last danger spot, the gorge where the new *Loongmow* was wrecked on her second trip. Then we steamed out into quiet waters, the low, green banks giving me the first glimpse of flat country for many weeks. We were back in he world once more.

The *Meitan* anchored us off the Standard Oil Hong [warehouse], and an hour later I went over to H.M.S. *Kinsha* and paid my respects to Rear Admiral [George H.] Borrett, the Commander of the British Yangtze Squadron. He is a very charming gentleman.

The Doc and I went ashore for tennis with the *Kinsha* officers, followed by a little session at the Customs Club. I returned to the *Palos* just in time to welcome on board for dinner Flag Secretary Hamner of the *Kinsha*, who is a friend of mine from Vladivostok days, when he and Admiral Borrett were on H.M.S. *Cairo*....

The *Kinsha* is a funny, old thing, a side wheeler. She was formerly the S.S. *Pioneer*, and she was the first steam vessel to negotiate the Yangtze gorges. The British Navy bought her in 1900 for use as their Yangtze flagship.

SEPTEMBER 15, 1920—ICHANG. ...the plot now is the *Elcano* is coming from Hankow to tow the *Palos* to Hankow.[32] There, experts are going to attempt temporary repairs in order to give us a chance to make Shanghai under our own steam. I don't think anything short of new pumps will do the slightest bit of good. However, I am willing to be shown.

Walked ten miles this afternoon out to the large pagoda below here. It is fine to have a flat space long enough to take a walk.

SEPTEMBER 17, 1920—ICHANG. ...[C]alled officially on the British Consul.... The Consul is an interesting antiquarian.... [H]e is a collector of fossils, Buddhas, and old books, and is known up and down the river as Fossil Smith. I found him an interesting old bird.

The Frenchmen I have met in the Orient do not seem to be as contented as is the average Britisher or American. The Britisher calmly settles down for life, importing most of his own customs and assimilating those necessary to his comfort.

The American arrives here chock a block with energy, and goes hard after the game. There is no doubt in my mind. China is his oyster, and he will be just about beginning to enjoy it some ten years from now. The British firms who have been controlling Yangtze traffic all these years must either snap out of it and adopt modern business methods or be left hopelessly behind. They are still subscribing themselves "I have the honour to be, sir"—a pretty enough form, but one hardly conforming to the present day snappy ways.

It appears that the *Elcano* is waiting for us at Sunday Island; her draft is too great to take a chance on coming up to this place. The *Monocacy* left Hankow, however, on the 14th, the plot now being that ... [she] will tow us to Sunday Island, and the *Elcano* on to Hankow. I expect the *Monocacy* in tomorrow night, at the earliest. At Hankow is the Engineer Officer of the *Wilmington*, who will endeavor to fix us up sufficiently to let us make Shanghai under our own steam.

SEPTEMBER 20, 1920—ICHANG. I was awakened at six this morning by one of my kid quartermasters, who informed me that the ship was in his young opinion dragging. It was mine, too. In fact, it had already dragged a ship's length.

So I turned out and sent a warning to the Pacific Mailer *Mechuen* astern of us to stand by to duck if we went cruising down upon him. He retaliated with the offer of a loan of his anchor, which offer I promptly accepted. This 350 lb. anchor I chucked out on our port bow running a wire from it to our fo'c'sle bitts. So we were all snug again.

I wish to heaven that the *Monocacy* would shake a leg and get here and give us a sort [?] of anchor to windward. The river is rising rapidly.

[Coded notes on the opium smuggling.]

SEPTEMBER 20, 1920—ICHANG. Returned to the ship at 6:00 to let the mate go ashore, for the river is rising and the current so strong that I have ruled that one or the other of us must be aboard at all times. Around 7:30, the ship started off on an independent cruise down the river, dragging both anchors about thirty yards before she fetched up in better holding grounds. I'm fed up with this constant worry about our berth, I let go our big 750 lb. anchor, although I doubt very much if we ever get the darned thing up again. However, I bent [tied] an extra wire on it—which should help.

SEPTEMBER 21, 1920—ICHANG. Came back to the ship at 1:30 [A.M.] to find her dragging merrily down the river in a pouring rain with my kid quartermaster snug and comfortable in his poncho and oilskin pants serenely unconscious of anything wrong. He and I had quite an interview. I veered [let] out some more chain, and that stopped her. I am anxious to get down river, but I prefer to go bow first.

SEPTEMBER 23, 1920—ICHANG. [The *Monocacy* arrives.] _____, the *Monocacy*'s skipper[,] ... had a dreadful trip up from Shanghai. He joined the *Monocacy* two days before she sailed and made the trip to Hankow without an Executive Officer. Out of Shanghai he ran into a typhoon and lost his foretopmast and jazzed up his radio. He burns three times as much coal as we do.... He was nine days coming from Hankow to Ichang, and twenty-three out of Shanghai.

SEPTEMBER 25, 1920—AT SEA, YANGTZE KIANG [WEST-ERNIZATION OF CHINESE NAME FOR YANGTZE RIVER]. Got under-way at dawn alongside *Monocacy*.... For a few hours the *Monocacy* kept up a fair speed, but by noon she had slowed to about minus zero. All hands heartily cursed her, and about two o'clock she picked up again. However, during the intermission the current swept both ships down the river at the rate of five miles an hour; so it wasn't so annoying as it might have been, although it was a case of the blind leading the blind. It was with relief that I sighted the *Elcano* near Sunday Island.

Captain McCauley came over in his motor boat, and we decided to tie up together at daybreak tomorrow. Then he went over to the *Monocacy*, and gave _____ permission to shove off.

Then the drama began. _____ had been trying to persuade me all afternoon to take a drunken chief watertender of his, and I had con-sistently refused. But both Hoppe and I had a hunch that they would try to slip him over on us anyhow. So Hoppe inspected the ship, and, sure enough, there was this bird sitting in the after bunkroom with bag and baggage. So we fired him back to the *Monocacy*, and I gave Corpo-ral Watson of my marines instructions to keep him off the ship.

McCauley brought his dog and Sam Haight's dog on board with him. Sam's dog, of course, was formerly on the *Monocacy* when Sam was. So the *Monocacy*'s gobs promptly pinched the dog and hid him in a storeroom.

Just as the *Monocacy* was about to shove off, McCauley discovered the loss of his dog. The *Monocacy* was ordered to hold fast until the dog was found. Scouts were sent out. Every face on the *Monocacy* registered inno-cence [sic] and ignorance of the whereabouts of the dog. Matters impassed.[33]

In the meanwhile an awful row arose aft. It appeared that McCauley had agreed to take the drunken watertender. So the *Monocacy* tried to get him plus his baggage over to the *Palos* in order to put him into McCauley's motor boat. But Corporal Watson maintained a firm stand.

"You let him on board!" cried the *Monocacy*.

"No!" replied Corporal Watson nervously but firmly.

"Here, go ahead anyhow," urged the *Monocacy* to the befogged chief watertender.

Corporal Watson drew his gun.

"Stand back!" he cried valiantly. "He shall not pass!"

All hands fell back a little before the brave youth.

"The Captain of the *Elcano* orders his transfer," shouted the *Monocacy*.

"My Captain said not to let him on board," couraged Corporal Watson.

"The Captain of the *Elcano* is Senior Officer Present," volunteered the *Monocacy*.

Corporal Watson's reply was a flourish of his revolver.

By this time Sam had arrived to rescue his devoted dog from the toils of the infamous ship.

Then all at once the situation cleared.

SEPTEMBER 25, 1920—AT SEA YANGTZE KIANG. We got underway around six o'clock and both ships turned easily and headed down river.... [W]e ran on until eleven o'clock, when the *Elcano* anchored.

SEPTEMBER 26, 1920—AT SEA YANGTZE KIANG. At daybreak we pulled up to the *Elcano* and secured to her port side.... [G]ot underway around six o'clock ... and headed down river.... [W]e ran until eleven o'clock [P.M.], when the *Elcano* anchored.

SEPTEMBER 27, 1920—HANKOW. [W]e cruised easily along to Hankow ... [and] arrived about half past one in the afternoon, and anchored near the American Consulate....

The port is one of the best laid out in China, with a handsome and dignified Bund, wide streets, and stately buildings. The harbor was full of shipping, and there was a whole fleet of war vessels.... It seems that this assemblage is a protest by Great Britain, France, and Japan against a proposal of the Chinese to take over the Russian Concession. After the World War ended, the Chinese took over the German Concession, and of course the Allies could not protest.

Now that Russia has no government, the Chinese propose to take over the Russian Concession as well. This will result in isolating the British from the French. The French are isolated from the Japs already; and if the Chinese carry out their intention it will result that the European city will be divided into three cities with a Chinese section separating each two. Hence the row.

McCauley's bride came on board the *Elcano*, and I went over and met her. She is very attractive.

Cozine, the Engineer Officer of the *Wilmington*, came on board to assume charge of repairing the pumps. He reported their disease to be as we had diagnosed it, i.e., old age. Tomorrow we shall have three of them taken out and renew the steam and water ends. When that is completed we shall attempt to make Shanghai under our own steam. The date of departure is as yet uncertain.

Received from the *Elcano* a General Courtmartial Prisoner for transportation to Shanghai. This man, a ship's cook named _____, came from liberty here in Hankow one morning about three weeks ago. He was intoxicated. A Chinese cobbler was on board the *Elcano* awaiting him with a bill. _____ told him to beat it, but the Chinaman persisted. Another gob watching the scene said laughingly: "Why don't you throw that Chink overboard?"

"I believe I will," replied _____.

"I'll bet you two dollars you don't," taunted the gob.

Whereupon _____ heaved the cobbler overboard, and he was never seen no more. We are taking him to Shanghai to be tried for manslaughter. Corporal Watson is in general charge of the prisoner. I feel assured that there is no chance of an escape, not with Corporal Watson around.

Sam Haight and I went ashore at four o'clock to the Race Club and played four sets of tennis. I have a cold and played badly, but I enjoyed it just the same. The Hankow Race Club is the most beautiful club in China, and it is one of the best in the world. In the afternoons, all Hankow repairs there for tennis, football, tea, and dancing.[34]

After tennis and a bath, Sam and I with Doc Carll and Cozine had a mint julep on the terrace. Admiral Borrett came over from his table and congratulated me on the safe arrival of the *Palos*.

Back to the ship we went at seven thirty. Doc Kelley and Sam came over and dined with us.

I am certainly off that *Monocacy* gang for life. My mail, which I had so carefully planned to have here upon our arrival, is enroute to Ichang. Why? Because [?] idiotic *Monocacy* told them to send it there, although my telegraphic instructions were to the contrary. I hope that I won't be sent down river to straighten out that mess on the *Monocacy*.

OCTOBER 2, 1920—HANKOW. The pumps came back this morning. So, with coal sufficient to take us to Nanking and provisions sufficient for all the way to Shanghai, I prepared to get underway the moment the pumps were installed. By two o'clock it was evident that the pumps would not work without further fixing. So I sent Cozine ashore to make the arrangements, and at 4:15 the Yangtze Engineering Company's tug came alongside.... Off again, towed by the fourth ship since Chungking.

A frightful battle has been underway the last three nights between the American bluejackets and British bluejackets. The *Palos* had no casualties, but several men on the *Elcano* bear visible evidences of the war. It appears eight men of the *Hawkins* are laid up in sick bay and Admiral Duff told the *Hawkins* crew that they must either stop fighting the American gobs or he would kick them off the river. However, I think our men started the affair. That is one more reason why I am glad that we are moored quietly here, although my little gobs need no nurse-maiding to be able to look out for themselves.

OCTOBER 3, 1920—KANKOW [GANKOU]. If anyone ever mentions the word[s] "feed pump" to me after we reach Shanghai, he is due for the count right then and there. I am certainly fed up to the neck with our damn things.

OCTOBER 4, 1920. I got hold of a tug this morning and moved first thing.... Once clear of our berth it became speedily apparent that the tug had about one leg less power than that required to tow us. So we got well out in the stream and started drifting down river. Of course, by this time I am accustomed to drifting helplessly around. I don't suppose that I shall know how to act when we get under our own power again, if that ever happens. However, it seems with the *Palos* that she has two josses—one good, one evil. The bad joss gave us a tug with too little power. The good joss then turned around and caused the wind to blow harder, with the result that we virtually sailed up to Seven Mile Creek.

At ten o'clock, I put my foot down on the pump question. I told Cozine to hire two feed pumps capable of taking us to Shanghai. That means a definite two or three days longer stay here, but it is a definite decision, and I am sick of fooling with pumps I am convinced never will run. The new pumps will come on board tomorrow.

OCTOBER 7, 1920—BELOW WUSUCH [WUSU]. Finally got the second feed pump running, and at 7:19 A.M. got underway for down river. It was fine after all those helpless days ... to stand out of Seven

Mile Creek and Boldly [go] down river under our own power. The day
was pleasant and for the first time since I joined the *Palos* I enjoyed
cruising in her.

I made the above entry ... early in the afternoon. I should have
waited until night.

At 4:05 P.M. both pumps failed, and the *Palos* was once again helplessly drifting down the Yangtze. I headed her for the beach with the
remaining steam, then headed up stream, and drifted along vainly trying to get bottom with the lead. Finally got a sounding—11 fathoms and
immediately let go both anchors, although the ship was drifting down
river at the rate of five or six knots an hour. Veered and veered, but
finally snubbed her down. I fully expected to loose both anchors in the
maneuver, but there was nothing else I could do, and luck was with us.

Half an hour later, ... heard loud cries from outside. Out we rushed.
Drifting helplessly down upon us was a large, two masted junk. A collision was inevitable, for her people were jumping about screaming and
crying and making no effort to use oar, rudder, sails, or grappler. It looked
like a badness, for I was pretty sure that our chains would part with her
impact. However, I shouted to clear away the boat on our starboard-davits
for if we withstood the initial smash, the junk would be sure to go scraping along the starboard side. I also stationed men at the chains to veer.
Others stood ready with poles, fenders, and whatever was at hand.

Just as she was upon us, the men at the chains began to veer. I
shall never forget that old junk ... [towering] over us as she struck. There
was a crash, the rattle of the chain, as we veered and snubbed in the
double necessity of not parting the chains[,] not letting the ship take
charge and start dragging down the river. Finally the junk tore itself
loose from our bow, bumped and scraped its way along the starboard
side, and [was] finally clear.... [F]inally [the junk was] clear astern, a great
gash in [her] side.

We checked the chains and secured them, examined our bow and
forward compartments and found no damage to us, and them beat it
to the bridge and watched the end of the junk. Screaming howling the
Chinese abandoned her in their small boat. Nine minutes after she
struck us the junk capsized and sank, the cries of her crew coming to
us as they pulled over to shore.

We had just 10 fathoms of chain left in the starboard locker.

This trip from Chungking down is the most damnable trip I
ever made in my life. I am fed up to the neck with hair-raising experiences.

OCTOBER 8, 1920—KIUKIANG [JIUJIANG]. There was noth-
ing else to do this morning but to go on, ... although I was convinced
that we were due for further troubles. We were.

At 6:30 [A.M.] everything failed. However, I am now an expert in
the art of handling a helpless, drifting ship. I eased her into the beach
and let go both anchors in what appeared to be a nice spot. It was.

First we swung around in a back current that headed us downstream. I kept our stern from whacking the beach only by going ahead
on the engines with the last of the steam. Then we swung back again,
and I dropped our kedge anchor over the stern and held the ship there.
Then Cozine informed me that number one boiler was burnt out, and
that it would take the boilermaker seven days to reroll the tubes in it.
However, I had expected this to happen ever since we started this whole
business of pumps failing and of fuel having to be hauled. So I didn't
say much. However, what I did say was to the point.

There being utterly no sense in sitting there and looking at the
marshy bank, I determined to make a last, final effort to reach Kukiang,
twenty-odd miles away. So presently we up-anchored and limped slowly
downstream under the remaining boiler, and to my great surprise we
arrived at Kiukiang shortly before noon and anchored comfortably outboard of our friend, the *Elcano*. Captain McCauley came aboard, and
we ... agreed that the *Palos* should make one last try tomorrow morning and the *Elcano* should go along as convoy.

OCTOBER 9, 1920—ABOVE ICHANG. Got underway at six,
accompanied by the *Elcano*. A new misfortune! Broke a part of the
anchor engine, and must not in the future use the port anchor if it can
be avoided. This part has been cracked for some time; so its breaking
was nobody's fault.

We made as much as five knots for the first hour. That plus the
five knots of current gave us ten knots an hour over the ground. However, bit by bit we petered out, and finally I signaled to the *Elcano* that
I had to anchor and clean fires.... Then he came in ahead of me and
anchored, and then floated his towline down to us.... Then both ships
up-anchored, and we stood down river once more, this time towing
astern of the *Elcano* rather than alongside her.

During the day, we helped ourselves along a little with the engines,
but we had constant pump trouble. So I finally quit monkeying with
the engines, and towed thankfully along astern of the *Elcano*.

[*Elcano* receives orders to tow *Palos* to Shanghai.]

OCTOBER 11, 1920—BELOW CHINKIANG [JINKIANG]. This is surely an enormous river. It is in flood again now, and without a pilot a skipper not thoroughly familiar with the river would be sure to get completely lost. The charts are some good, but they cannot be trusted for overnight the river may cut itself a channel miles away from its former course. According to the chart, the place where we first tied up to the *Elcano* below Ichang was four miles inland from the river. Creeks, bayous, and lakes branch off from the main river, and there are frequently two or three channels which may be used. There are beacons and lightboats here and there, but they are unreliable and serve only to confuse one the more. So the thing to do is trust in the lead, the pilot, and your luck, and not trust any of them too much.

After the marvelous scenery of Szechwan, the Lower River offers little to attract the eye. The banks are very low, and most of the villages are built several miles back from the river proper. There is an occasional hill or bluff, and those with the pagodas are the landmarks which prove to one that he is not hopelessly lost.

OCTOBER 13, 1920—SHANGHAI. ...[A] horrible night.... [T]he tide turned and we did a great bit of rolling when we fell into the trough of the sea.... On the third roll, there was a tremendous crash from above, followed by shouts from the people on watch. I rushed out on the fo'c'sle to be greeted with the information that the mainmast had gone by the boards....

At 3:00 [P.M.] secured to the Old Dock Company's warf, only seven blocks below the Astor [Hotel].

OCTOBER 19, 1920—SHANGHAI. Spent a large proportion of the day in search of American gold with which to pay the crew.... Returned to the ship and paid my gobs. They made about a thousand dollars more by this method; hence my efforts to get it. The government rate for Mex is $1 Gold= $1.32= Mex.41. Consequently, if I pay my gobs in Mex at the government rate, that is all they get. However, if I can obtain gold, ... the gobs can take the gold and buy Mex from the money changer ... at the rate of $1 gold = $1.50 Mex. They therefore gain .18 Mex on each gold dollar. Some high finance![35]

OCTOBER 20, 1920—SHANGHAI. Convened my first court on the *Palos* today ... [and] tried by summary courtmartial the ship's cook for sneaking off the ship a night or so ago when he did not have liberty.

NOVEMBER 8, 1920—SHANGHAI. ...Issued orders to get underway at daybreak.... Shanghai will always be like New York in that one is always eager to get there and after a two or three weeks' fling is always ready to leave.

Notes

1. George S. Gillespie was born October 11, 1889, in Missouri and appointed to the naval academy on June 8, 1909, from Michigan. The *South Dakota*, later the *Huron*, was an armored cruiser built by Union Iron Works, San Francisco, in 1907. She was 15, 138 tons, could make 22 knots and 505 feet × 70 feet × 27 feet. She had a compliment of 822. Four 8"/45, fifteen 6"/50. Six-inch belt, 6½" turrets, 4" deck, 9" conning tower. The *Huron* was sold in 1930. Tolley, *Yangtze Patrol*, 315.

2. The *Monocacy* in service during Howell's period of time on the Yangtze was the second gunboat of the same name on the river. The second *Monocacy* was constructed and then disassembled at Mare Island, California, then reassembled at Shanghai in 1914 by Kiangnan Dockyard. She was 204 tons and made 13 knots. 165½ feet × 24½ feet × 2½ foot. The gunboat had a complement of 47 and carried two 6-pdr, six .30 cal. MG. She was sunk by demolition charges on February 10, 1939, at sea off Shanghai. Tolley, *Yangtze Patrol*, 313.

3. HMS *Widgeon* was built in 1904. 180 tons and 13 knots. 165 feet × 24½ feet × 2½ feet. Two 6-pdr guns, 4 MG. Carried a crew of 35. Tolley, *Yangtze Patrol*, 316.

4. Comdr. Edward Glyn de Styrap Jukes-Hughes, date of rank June 30, 1916. *Navy List for July 1920* (London: His Majesty's Stationary Office, 1920), 345, 899.

5. Lieut. Thaddeus A. Hoppe, born January 2, 1896. Appointed to naval academy from Illinois, class of 1918. Number 43 in a class of 199. Resigned as a lieutenant on October 9, 1923, *Register of Alumni Graduates and Former Naval Cadets and Midshipmen* (Annapolis, Md.: U.S. Naval Academy Alumni Association, 1982), 216; Lieut. (MC) Reuben A. Barker, born July 23, 1899, and appointed to the U.S. Navy on July 19, 1917, *Register of Officers*, 146–147. Hoppe would be replaced by Charles Julian Wheeler, born Mobile, Alabama, July 27, 1895. Appointed to naval academy July 1912. He first came to Asia in 1919 aboard the *South Dakota* and was assigned to the *Palos* in 1920. Photocopy of undated material sent to Dennis L. Noble by the U.S. Naval Academy Alumni Association.

6. Following the British, the American military China hands referred to lunch as "tiffin." Tolley, *Yangtze Patrol*, 125.

7. The officer was Lieut. Comdr. Otakita Inase. The name was obtained from a calling card pinned in Howell's diary.

8. Hindu word *chitti*. Letter, note, bill, voucher, or receipt ... The word has wide use in the Far East and is used throughout the British Army and Navy. The U.S. Navy on the Asiatic Station adopted it many years ago from the "pidgin" (business) English. Leland P. Lovette, *Naval Customs, Traditions, and Usage* (Annapolis, Md.: Naval Institute Press, 1934), 199.

9. The "black gang" is a naval term for the engineering force on a ship. The term comes from the steam navy when the engineering force had to contend with coal dust in the engineering spaces. John V. Noel, Jr., and Edward L. Beach, eds., *Naval Terms Dictionary*, 5th ed. (Annapolis, Md.: Naval Institute Press, 1988), 35.

10. "Cumshaw" used in China connotated bribes. Most U.S. military men believed that the Chinese always needed to obtain some cumshaw to transact business.

11. Thomas A. Kearney was born February 15, 1875. Appointed to the naval academy

from Missouri and graduated class of 1896. He was number 19 in a class of 38. Kearney was the first Commander, Yangtze River Patrol. Retired as a captain on June 31, 1931, and died on October 7, 1941. *Register of Alumni*, 166.

12. Lieut. Benjamin Osborne Wells born October 26, 1896, in Wisconsin. Appointed to the naval academy on May 8, 1913, from Wisconsin. *Register of Officers*, 56–57.

13. This was known as "spar mooring."

14. Another term used by military China hands to denote bribery.

15. Haul fires means to put out the fire.

16. Paul R. Josselyn was born in Iowa and appointed to the Department of State on April 15, 1918. He was transferred on July 8, 1921, to an unknown new post. Letter with enclosed photocopied personnel information from Office of Historian, Bureau of Public Affairs, Department of State, to Dennis L. Noble, April 27, 1993.

17. *Taoyin* was the westernized title of the Chinese official in charge of a city.

18. Howell is referring to President Woodrow Wilson and the "hop" is a reference to Wilson's disability caused by a stroke.

19. Hiram Warren Johnson (1866–1945) was elected governor of California on a Republican reform ticket in 1910 and was reelected in 1914. He was Theodore Roosevelt's running mate on the Bull Moose ticket in 1912, but returned as a Republican in 1916. Johnson was eventually elected to the U.S. Senate, where he served for twenty-eight years and was a strong isolationist. He refused to accept the vice-presidential nomination in 1920 on the Republican ticket with Warren G. Harding, thus missing the chance to become president upon Harding's death. John Garraty, ed., *Encyclopedia of American Biography* (New York: Harper & Row, 1974), 587–588. Warren G. Harding was eventually the Republican nomination and became president in 1921.

20. Howell is referring to President Theodore Roosevelt.

21. Alexander Mitchell Palmer (1872–1936) a Democratic reformer and Congressman, served as the chairman of the Democratic National Committee executive committee and was elected chairman of the Democratic caucus in the House of Representatives and acted as Woodrow Wilson's liaison man with Democratic progressives. In March 1919, Wilson appointed him attorney general. This reformer, however, is most noted for his reactions to the so-called Red Scare of 1919–1920. Responding to a widespread conviction of a conspiracy, Palmer directed raids against thousands of suspected aliens. On January 2, 1920, some 7,000 aliens were arrested, "mostly without proper warrants." He failed to win the 1920 Democratic nomination and left public life, but remained active in Democratic politics.

William Gibbs McAdoo (1863–1941) became a leading figure in Woodrow Wilson's 1912 presidential campaign and later married Wilson's daughter. He was secretary of the treasury under Wilson. He as mentioned as a runner in the 1920 campaign and actively sought the nomination in 1924, but did not receive it. Garrity, *Encyclopedia of American Biography*, 700, 833–834.

The 1920 Democratic party nomination for president was Gov. James M. Cox, of Ohio. His running mate was Franklin D. Roosevelt.

22. Herbert Clarke Hoover (1874–1964) became president in 1929 on the Republican ticket.

23. China hands called anyone living in China, except the Chinese, "foreigner."

24. Albert Gleaves, born January 1, 1858, Nashville, Tennessee. Graduated from naval academy, class of 1877. Promoted to captain in 1909. Appointed Commander in Chief of the Asiatic Fleet as an admiral in 1919. Retired on January 1, 1922, and died Haverford, Pennsylvania, January 6, 1937. Undated biographical material from U.S. Naval Academy Alumni Association.

25. An unpublished play that Howell was writing.

26. This may be Chow Tao-kang. *China Year Book*, 308.

27. May be the Rev. Dr. R.O. Jolliffe of the Canadian Methodist Episcopal Mission, affiliated with the National Committee for Christian Religious Education and the United Church of Canada. Jolliffe appears to have served twice in China, arriving for the second

time in 1904. Kathleen Lodwick, *The Chinese Recorder Index: A Guide to Christian Missions in Asia, 1867–1941*, vol. 1 (Wilmington, Del.: Scholarly Resources, Inc., 1986), 245.

28. The 135-foot *Meitan* was a river tug of the Standard Oil Company and the first of the company's boats on the upper Yangtze. Grover, *American Ships on Yangtze*, 11.

29. This marks the beginning of opium incident discussed in the introduction to this portion of the diary.

30. Josephus Daniels (1862–1948) newspaperman and politician from North Carolina. A Progressive who started as publicity director for Woodrow Wilson's presidential campaign. Wilson appointed him secretary of the navy in 1913. Daniels was noted for his reforms in the navy, some of them highly unpopular, such as prohibiting officers from drinking aboard ship. He left office in 1921. In 1932, he campaigned for Franklin D. Roosevelt and became ambassador to Mexico after Roosevelt's election. In 1941, Daniels again returned to the private sector. Garraty, *Encyclopedia of American Biography*, 252–253. For an interesting article on Daniels influence on enlisted men, see: Richard McKenna, "The Wreck of Uncle Josephus," in Eva Grice McKenna and Shirley Graves Cochrane, eds., *New Eyes for Old: Nonfiction Writings by Richard McKenna* (Winston-Salem, NC: John F. Blair, 1972): 40–59

31. 1 catty equals 1½ pounds, or 604.53 grams. Hsu, *Rise of Modern China*, xxxiii.

32. *Elcano* built in Spain and commissioned as *El Cano*. Captured at Manila, May 1, 1898, and commissioned in U.S. Navy in 1902. 620 tons. 165 feet in length. Four 4" and four 3 pdrs. Sunk as a target October 4, 1928. Tolley, *Yangtze Patrol*, 312.

33. A dog played an unusual part in the history of the *Palos* prior to Howell's taking command of the gunboat. Gillespie had an English bull terrier named "Sooner" that slept in Gillespie's cabin. Normally, the dog was very quiet, but one night when the *Palos* was at anchor the dog's growling awoke Gillespie, who ordered an extra sharp deck watch. The watch reported that a boatload of soldiers were drifting down upon the ship, but the watch had caused them to turn away. Kemp Tolley has noted that it had been a long time since an American ship had been "taken by boarding, and it is just possible that an English bulldog … kept the record clean." Tolley, *Yangtze Patrol*, 86.

34. When Howell mentions that "all Hankow repairs" to the Hankow Race Club, he means all of the Westerners in the city. Chinese were seldom, if ever, allowed into white clubs as guests.

35. The money situation in China may seem strange to readers. In fact, it could be complex to China hands. When most of the silver was drained out of China at the end of the nineteenth century, replenishment came from silver dollars minted in Mexico. These silver dollars were not reminted, but circulated "as was" and prices in China were quoted as "dollars mex." Some inventive Chinese found ways to split the dollars lengthwise, scoop out the silver, and then refill and seal the coin with lead, producing what was known as a "three-piece mex." Most shop owners would bounce a silver coin, known as "dinging," against a hard object to hear the proper ring before accepting a silver coin.

By the 1930s, the silver Mexican dollar had largely disappeared. The official basic unit of Chinese currency, the Yuan, inherited the name "mex." When a price of twenty dollars mex is mentioned in the 1930s, what is usually meant is twenty Yuan.

Other coins were called "small money" and consisted of copper and silver. The value of the copper coins would fluctuate from day to day, depending on the price of scrap copper. Silver coins were somewhat more complicated. "Ten smaller dimes or five twenty cent pieces did not equal a paper or silver dollar … [T]he smaller coins in total equaled the value of the silver content of a dollar."

Paper money, called "big money," was made up of a galaxy of currency from various sources and never seemed to be withdrawn from circulation due to wear. Big money was usually in denominations of less than one dollar and China hands used them for tips and rickshaw fare. Kemp Tolley, "Three Pieces and Other Dollars Mex," *Shipmate*, 28, No. 10 (December 1965: 8–10.)

PART 2:
SHANGHAI–SHANGHAI,
NOVEMBER 9, 1920–MAY 22, 1921

1. Views of China and the Chinese

The foreigners living in China, in the main, never became a part of the country. Most lived in their own settlements, called concessions, that in many cases resembled their homelands. Areas of Tsingtao [Quingdao], for example, resembled Germany. Very few people bothered to learn Chinese; there was no need to in the concessions. All of this, of course, also applied to the U.S. military in the Middle Kingdom. One service publication, for example, in describing a foreign concession noted but for the "absence of a red front five and ten cent store, the new arrival might easily forget, that for the moment, that the United States is some 7,000 miles away."[1]

Sailors on the Yangtze Patrol, because of their abilities to visit more cities during their time on the river, had a better chance to see a "slice" of China than the rest of the American armed forces. The gunboat sailors for the most part, however, also tended to gravitate toward the areas where other Westerners resided. Again, this is not altogether unusual, for very few could speak Chinese. Further, many of the bars that the sailors frequented were run by retired sailors who decided to remain in China rather than return to the United States, or were sailors from other Western nations.

One of the problems stemming from this type of arrangement is that to most military men the Chinese were never seen as human, with some very bad results, such as the throwing of the Chinese man into the river described in the first section of the diary. During his third tour of duty in China, Howell would write that it was no wonder the poor of China hated Westerners, "who make it possible for thousands of them to exist [in poverty.] We, with our comfortable food, our warm clothes, our leisure, our golfing, our riding while they pull, our overseeing while they work. The Negro slave in the South before the war had an infinitely better time of it."[2]

There is an interesting dichotomy in the views of the military on China. As noted earlier, the China Station achieved an almost mythical reputation among those serving in the armed forces. Many military men chose to remain in the country instead of returning to the United States when they retired or took their discharges. It is interesting to note, however, that this feeling came very slowly during the decade of 20s. When examining the newspapers and magazines published by the military in China, one is struck about the amount of racist and derogatory comments about the country. Corp. Vance Lyndale, in 1921, wrote if anyone found a soldier who enjoyed serving in the Middle Kingdom it would be evident "there was something queer about him."[3] By 1925, however, the same army newspaper that published Lyndale's comments, noted in an editorial that the longer one remained in a country, the more one was inclined to see the good points of the country's customs. By the 1930s, the regimental newspaper was encouraging its readers to make an effort to travel and see China.

Most Western military service people also held the Chinese in low regard as military personnel. "We didn't have much respect for ... Chinese soldiers," recalled marine officer George H. Cloud. Military men, in fact, ignored the fighting going on about them because the Chinese seemed to have been fighting forever.[4] This disdain is illustrated in this section of Howell's diary when he writes, "I see no reason why exercise and pleasure should be suspended while we wait for Chinese mutinous soldiers to pull something...."

Military men, like other Westerners living in China, developed a love-hate relationship with the country they were living within. The soldiers, sailors, and marines in general had easy duty days and the cost of living made their meager pay stretch much further than in their own country. On the other hand, they could not understand or read the Chinese language and, in most cases, they certainly did not understand the culture they lived within. In the end, most military men simply ignored the Chinese and saw them as a faceless backdrop against their lives in a strange country.

Howell's diary is an excellent example of the love-hate relationship of the military men in China. Unlike many in the American armed forces who did not venture far from their station or ship, Howell went on an overland "expedition" with two enlisted men, and this is detailed in this section. As a part of their normal duties, officers of all the armed forces gathered intelligence reports of the areas they visited in China. This especially applied to the officers of the Yangtze Patrol. Thus, Howell's foray into the countryside had a military role. His entries for the journey shows he relished the role, even adopting an assumed name. There is also no doubt Howell undertook the expedition because he really wanted to see the countryside.

It is during the foray into the country that the diary entries at times become almost lyrical. Howell's accounts of most of the people he meets are sympathetic and very descriptive. It is obvious from this journey that the naval officer means it when much later in this section he writes, "I like China."

The Historian Harold R. Isaccs has written that our "sympathies about the Chinese have ranged between sympathy and rejection, parental benevolence and parental exasperation, affection and hostility, love and a fear close to hate."[5] Within the diary entries of Howell's tenure aboard the *Palos* and his third tour in China are all the aspects Isaccs mentioned. On his journey into the country, Howell is trying to see as many carvings of images as he can. On the return portion of the expedition, he even has the junk he is aboard stopped so he can go ashore to examine two images. He becomes angry about the Chinese using the statues as stepping stones. In short, the Chinese were too ignorant to understand the riches around them. Scattered throughout the diary are entries where one moment Howell can make insightful and sympathetic observations of China and the Chinese and then, later, just the opposite. On his third tour of duty in the Middle Kingdom, when Howell penned the lines about the poor of China quoted above, a month later the naval officer wrote that the Chinese "are a lazy people.... The moment a Chinaman gains sufficient money to support him[self] he ceases to labor with his hands." Christianity was not "for these exasperating people." The Chinese, according to Howell, were not capable of appreciating any of the world's great religions. "A joss or two, dimly recognized and dimly and spasmodically worshiped is apparently about the limits of their intelligence." The naval officer also saw nothing wrong in beating a rickshaw puller who shoved a white woman in a fare dispute. In short, the observations of Glenn F. Howell reveal exactly what Isaacs so aptly described.[6]

If the China Station seemed to be the ideal duty location for the American military, why then this love-hate relationship? There are two main factors. The most important is that very few Americans could speak the language. Further, many did not make the effort to do so. In 1919, the army began to assign officers to Beijing for formal language training. There were also sporadic attempts by some military commanders to have their troops understand the language. Brig. Gen. William D. O'Connor, in the 1920s, initiated a program where all officers of the 15th Infantry at Tientsin studied an hour a day, five days a week for one year and then were examined in their abilities. If found qualified, the officers were considered interpreters and received a patch worn on the right sleeve of the uniform blouse with the Chinese character *zhong*, which combined with the character *guo*, represents China.

In time, a similar program for enlisted men began. This enlightened program unfortunately stopped when Col. Reynolds J. Burt took command of the 15th. Burt felt Chinese was a "fool language," but conceded that it would be useful for dealing with tradesmen."[7]

While the army began language training, both formally and informally, during the same period of time, the 1920s, of the 317 line officers who were assigned to the Asiatic Fleet, not one had a Chinese language qualification. There were naval officers who were listed as fluent in Spanish, French, and Italian, but none in Chinese. There is some evidence, however, that some officers and enlisted men learned the language informally.[8]

Without the ability to speak or read the language it is difficult to learn anything about a people or their country. There is some evidence that those who did learn the language were the ones who enjoyed China the most. Marine officer Samuel B. Griffith II is an excellent example of this generality. Griffith attended the formal training in Beijing when the navy began sending officers to school. Many years later, when asked what he found most interesting about the duty in China he replied, "The Chinese people." When an interviewer remarked to the retired marine officer that the Chinese were corrupt and cruel, Griffith responded with a very emphatic: "Oh no! I think that is terribly wrong." Upon his retirement from the marine corps, Griffith received his doctorate from Oxford, with his dissertation the translation of Sun Tzu's classic work *On the Art of War*, written between 400–320 B.C.[9]

The second major reason most American military men had such a love-hate relationship is they simply could not fathom the culture they served within. In the main, the enlisted men who served in China until well into the 1930s came from the lower economic strata and did not have the education to prepare them for such a shift in culture. Officers, even with their higher education levels, could not escape the cultural baggage they brought to the Middle Kingdom. The longer the U.S. military spent in China, some of the strangeness ameliorated. This came about because there were efforts to let people know the country through tours and language lessons. In general, however, the majority of American military men in China could not rid themselves of the mindset they brought to Asia and the inability to speak the language that caused most of the difficulties. A lack of comprehension produced a lack of contact. As one naval officer put it, "we generally followed the British system of not associating with the 'natives,' unfortunately."[10]

Most of the people who visited or were stationed in China during the 1920s commented upon the "cheapness of life" in the Middle Kingdom. Robert O. Bare commented that when he arrived in Tientsin, the street poles were festooned with the severed heads of Chinese. One of the duties of the deck seamen on the Yangtze Patrol when in port "was to free floating bodies which had become trapped by the gangway." It is interesting to note, however, that many military men and their families would go to great lengths to witness a beheading, with *The Sentinel* reporting one group walking 21 *li* to see an execution. In this section is Howell's determination to find the head of General Li. In other words, Westerners bore as much responsibility for the cheapness of life as did the Chinese.[11]

2. Officer–Enlisted Relationships

If Western military officers with their superior education had difficulty understanding China and the Chinese, interestingly this same education and training also made it difficult for them to understand the men they led. Howell discusses forming portions of the *Palos'* crew into two football teams. All of the U.S. military tried to have enlisted men participate in sports. The interest in sports was so great that during unrest around Tientsin in 1927, *The Sentinel*, the newspaper of the 15th Infantry, devoted more space to athletics than the fighting around the city. The reason given for this strong interest: it built team spirit and could foster leadership. Left unsaid, it kept the men from sampling some of the delights of the surrounding cities.

Off-duty sports is one example of how some sailors on the Yangtze Patrol spent their time away from their ships. Much of what has been published about sailors is far from flattering. Most are pictured as carousing, with little care except for the next drink and the next woman, with the occasional brawl thrown into the mix. Richard McKenna, years after his retirement from the navy, wrote about a shipmate, Coxswain Duke Lee, "who wore chin whiskers, went barefoot, scarcely even talked, kept an ancient and equally silent parrot in number four hold and smoked opium in the cordage locker." Lee, while on liberty in Shanghai, would heat Chinese pennies red hot and then throw them out the window to beggars. In a bar in Shanghai's Blood Alley, he "vomited the contents of his stomach over a table, then used a pair of chopsticks to pick up the solid pieces and swallow them again."[12]

One of the problems for sailors on the Yangtze Patrol was the lack of off-duty activities. The greatest obstacle the men had to overcome was their status. Sailors were, and in many cases still have this stigma put upon them, considered by Western society in China as uneducated and boorish. In the early years in China, enlisted sailors could only pass their off-duty hours in the red light districts. Officers, on the other hand, were considered gentlemen and could mingle with almost all levels of Western society. Howell gives a short biography of a sailor called "Ski." It is one of the few of the enlisted force for this period of time.

For the gunboat sailors, there was so little in the way of wholesome activities for the men to do on their off-duty time, it is no wonder many drank. Richard McKenna has noted the lack of libraries on the ships he served in prior to World War II. Howell, and other commanding officers, recognized this fact. To offer something other than drinking, Howell often organized walking tours, as described throughout the diary. On his second tour of duty on the Yangtze, Howell would write in his log about sailors' clubs at Ichang, Changsha, and Chungking. The naval officer felt they were "very vital necessities if anything resembling spirit is to be maintained in the crews [on the Yangtze.]"[13] In most cases, however, the sailors aboard the gunboats had little choice in what they did on their off-duty time. They could do some sight seeing in the cities they visited, but, in the end, it really came down to visiting in a bar frequented by their shipmates, or staying aboard the gunboat.

Howell's entries about enlisted men represents the tensions between the officer corps and the enlisted force. At times, the naval officer shows a sincere effort to better their stay aboard the *Palos*. Then, like with China and the Chinese, he shows the difficulties his education and training causes in completely understanding the men. In 1925, for example, he confided to the diary that one of the "greatest responsibilities of a naval officer is that of punishment of men." Howell would also write that sailors are "a particularly irresponsible group" in their conduct ashore. Further, the only difference between a young sailor and a grammar schoolboy "is that the latter wears knickerbockers."[14] In this comment, Howell only reflected what Capt. Eugene H. C. Leutz twenty-two years earlier had written about enlisted men. The captain observed that because the navy did not "get the best elements of the male population," it followed that those who entered the service were men of "poorer ... roving and adventurous dispositions. These men have never known restraint, so that the discipline and routine work of the Navy is irksome to them."[15] Howell mentions in the diary how he feels brig time on bread and water does help to cause the men to stay within regulations. Later still, after seeing a military prison at Bilibid, in the Philippine Islands, he observed how confinement sapped a man's self-respect. He would then write that slapping a sailor in the brig on bread and water was ludicrous, because it so resembled "shutting little Willie in the closet without any supper."[16] While Howell does show a real effort on his part to help the enlisted men who served on the *Palos*, his education and training made it very difficult, if not impossible, to completely understand these sailors.

3. Howell's Views on Other Foreigners in China

Howell in this section of the diary again gives his views of other nations and missionaries. The concluding section of the diary gives even more on missionaries and this subject will be addressed in the introduction of to that portion.

Howell had unflattering remarks to say about most of the foreigners in China. He did not trust the English because, as he saw it, they knew the United States now was in the ascendancy and did not care to give up their former position in the world. Howell's most strident comments are those directed at the Japanese. In this, he reflected the comments of many Europeans and Americans in Asia who felt war with Japan was inevitable.

4. Two Views of Howell

Two interesting characteristics of Howell emerge. The naval officer is quick to scribble a caustic remark about a superior, such as the offhanded remarks about Admiral Strauss. As soon as he meets Strauss, however, his entries read almost like a sycophant's writings.

Howell's desire to be published in some form comes through strongly in this section. The naval officer even takes himself off to a nearby Taoist monastery for a short period of time to write a play. The caliber of his writing can be judged by his diary. The diary, as noted elsewhere, did provide a memory jogging tool and a source for much of Howell's eight published articles in the U.S. Naval Institute *Proceedings*. His articles are very readable. Howell's articles have been used by the few scholars and writers who have written on the American military in China and the Yangtze River. It is ironic, however, that Glenn F. Howell's only recorded published book deals with American naval heroes and not China. It came onto the market a year before he left the navy.

Notes

1. *The Sentinel* (Tientsin, China), 24 September 1926, 1,041.

2. "Log of Glenn F. Howell," Vol. XL (1925), 11,132, Naval Operational Archives (NOA), Naval Historical Center (NHC), Washington, D.C.

3. *The Sentinel*, 22 April 1921, 1.

4. William J. Scheyer, "Diary," 4, Papers of William J. Scheyer, P.C. 115, Personal Papers Collection (PPC), U.S. Marine Corps Historical Center (MCHC), Washington, D.C.; MGEN George H. Cloud, interview by Benis M. Frank, (1970), 42, Marine Corps Oral History Program (MCOH), MCHC.

5. Harold R. Isaacs, *Scratches on our Mind: American Images of China and India* (New York: John Day, 1958), 64.

6. Howell Diaries, XLI (1926), 11,248; XL (1925), 11,140–11141; XXXIX (1925), 10,857.

7. Dennis L. Noble, *The Eagle and the Dragon: The United States in China, 1901–1937* (Westport, Ct.: Greenwood Press, 1990), 143–145; Quoted in, Roy K. Flint, "The United States Army on the Pacific Frontier, 1899–1939," in *The United States Military in the Far East: Proceedings of the Ninth Military History Symposium, United States Air Force Academy, 1–3 October 1980*, ed. Joe C. Dixon (Washington: Government Printing Office, 1980), 149.

8. *Register of Commissioned and Warrant Officers of the United States Navy, 1923* (Washington: Government Printing Office, to 1923), *passim*.

9. BGEN Samuel B. Griffith II interview by Benis M. Frank (1970), 41–43, MCOH, MCHC. The dates I have used for Sun Tzu are from, Samuel B. Griffith, *Sun Tzu: The Art of War* (New York: Oxford University Press, 1963), 11.

10. Quoted in Noble, *Eagle and the Dragon*, 165.

11. LGEN Robert O. Bare, interview by Benis M. Frank (1968), 16, MCOH, MCHC; Papers of Henry J. Poy, China Repository (CR), Naval Operation Archives (NOA), NHC; *The Sentinel*, 18 April 1924, 6.

12. Richard McKenna, "Life Aboard the USS Goldstar," in *The Left-Handed Monkey Wrench: Stories and Essays by Richard McKenna*, ed. Robert Shenk (Annapolis, Md.: Naval Institute Press, 1986), 130.

13. "Log of Glenn Howell," XLI, 11,277, NOA, NHC.

14. Ibid, XL, 11,094–11,099, NOA, NHC.

15. Quoted in Frederick S. Harrod, *Manning the New Navy: The Development of a Modern Naval Enlisted Force, 1899–1940* (Westport, Ct.: Greenwood Press, 1978), 118.

16. "Log of Glenn Howell," XL, 11,094–11,099, NOA, NHC.

The Diary

NOVEMBER 9, 1920—TEN MILES BELOW CHINKIANG.
...Between 11:00 and noon we cracked out 13¼ knots. Then #1 feed pump failed. I saw red instantly.... [I]t developed that rust must have been in the new feed pumps packing and that was largely the matter. It was fixed, but fooling with it spoiled our speed for the rest of the day for the fires got very dirty.

NOVEMBER 14, 1920. FINE CRUISING! This afternoon passed three villages on rafts floating down-stream to market. It takes perhaps a year to construct these rafts. They are built on low land which is flooded at high water, and after the bodies of the rafts are constructed then houses are erected, streets are laid out, the community moves on board. The main purpose, of course, is to float the lumber to a market, but in addition to that, quantities of produce are carried. How the three or four hundred people who live on the raft get back up river I do not know, but I suppose that the majority of them simply remain where they chance to land. With their flags flying, drums booming, their rafts were a fine sight as we passed them.

    Then I saw four or five hundred ducks being herded down river

"This afternoon passed three villages on rafts floating downstream to market.... The main purpose, of course, is to float the lumber to a market.... [The] rafts were a fine sight as we passed them." (Photograph courtesy of U.S. Naval Institute.)

to market, swimming in the center of the stream and shepherded by three boatmen in as many small boats.

NOVEMBER 17, 1920—HANKOW. Everyday or so I manage to pick up a detail or so that makes the opium story a little clearer. Today I learned that all the money [Chief Smith] received from the [Opium] Combine in Chungking he turned over to various gobs on the ship as hush money. Then when we arrived at Shanghai he accepted $4000.00 more from the Combine, who were under the impression that the opium was still on the ship. He certainly played a double crossing game all around.

NOVEMBER 20, 1920—CHENGHI [CHANGHAI OR CHANGHEI]. The Commissioner of Customs ... is Bryant, he is an American, he is seventy and looks fifty-five.... He has been in China fifty years, and he had many stories to tell of the old Asiatic Fleet....

NOVEMBER 21, 1920—ELEVEN MILES BELOW CHANGSHA. At about five o'clock [P.M.] we reached a stretch of [the river with a] ... depth of six feet. I even got used to that after a bit, though when your ship is churning along with less than two feet under her bottom you cannot be expected to be exactly easy on your mind.

Today a fish twenty-four inches long jumped out of the water and landed right outside the door of my cabin, and one of my boatmen pounced upon him. We had him for dinner, and he was very good. This is a new way to catch fish.

NOVEMBER 22, 1920—CHANGSHA. ...I am mighty glad to have won through and to have arrived safely at our winter quarters....

The *Palos* moored opposite the American Consulate close to the shore of an island on which many of the foreigners have their houses. The offices and business places are opposite us on a bund, the only bund in China built by the Chinese themselves independent of foreign suggestion.

There are about 175 Americans here with missionaries in a considerable majority. We shall have to do with the minority naturally.... There is the usual balled-up mess of local affairs.... However, the situation is in no wise serious and nobody seems worried.

The American Consulate Meinhardt, (I thought we were still at war with those people)—called officially at 11:00 and I returned his call at 2:00.

He is a pleasant enough young fellow, good to his mother, does not beat his wife, and smokes not neither does he drink. However, I think that in spite of all this he and I will get along together all right. If we don't it will be his fault.[1]

The Doc left for Hankow ... to bring his wife up here.

NOVEMBER 29, 1920—CHANGSHA. At 2:30 P.M. the mate and I and twenty-three of our gobs got into football suits and bent it for the football field on the island, a good mile away from the ship. Here we held our first football practice, handling the ball, formations, kicking, and punting. It was great to lace up in the old harness and go out and cast care and dignity to the winds. Nobody, not even the captain of a super-dreadnought like the *Palos*, can be very dignified when he winds up in a mud puddle with a couple of padded gobs on top of him.

DECEMBER 3, 1920—CHANGSHA. We are chipping the whole ship preparatory to painting her, and the racket is deafening....

DECEMBER 3, 1920—CHANGSHA. Hell broke loose in Ichang on the 1st. It appears that the soldiers there, after having received no pay for practically a year, suddenly mutinied and looted the city, including the banks, the hanger of the Standard Oil and Robert Dollar Companies, and all the foreign godowns [warehouses]. Then they set fire to some more buildings, including the Customs Club. I never thought that this outfit would have nerve enough, but their Bolshevism is slowly spreading.

DECEMBER 5, 1920—CHANGSHA. ...Brannon and Foley, two of the younger Scononys came in, and the mate and I took them on for a rubber. We had them set horribly, I had just bid three spades, been doubled, and had redoubled, when the telephone bell rang and De Ballard was informed by an outlying missionary that one thousand soldiers had suddenly appeared at the North Gate, had entered the City with the announced intention of looting and that soldiers within the City had mutinied and joined them. De Ballard called up someone else and found that the soldiers had torn up the railroad north of the City, had put the telegraph lines out of commission, and had surrounded the mint.[2]

So I first played the hangfire spade hand, incidently making my bid and two extra tricks and winning the rubber, a $16.00 one, and the mate flew back to the ship to recall the crew from liberty and get the Landing Force ready, while De Ballard and I proceeded to the Consulate to confer with Meinhardt, whom I am going to like all right, although I didn't think at first I would. Wild rumors were pouring into the Consulate. We chased down the report that the mint had been surrounded, discovering over the telephone from a German living out that way that it bore its usual appearance. Chinese had arrived earlier in the afternoon at the Consulate desiring to know if the new Military Governor had sought refuge there. It seemed that the Governor had disappeared with the first news of the affair. We received a report that the Chinese Chamber of Commerce was meeting with a view toward bribing the malcontents to leave the City. A messenger was sent to the Chamber of Commerce only to return with the news that the members had fled.

I arranged signals with the Consulate and the Asia Bank and returned to the ship, though Mr. Mellows, the Postal Commissioner, shrieked from the upper floor of the Asia Bank for me to come back for more bridge.

We held the Landing Force ready until nine o'clock [P.M.] and then turned in, leaving instructions for a bright lookout to be kept for signals from the Consulate or the bank. Once every half hour during the night, our search light swept the bank, but nothing happened. Had an excellent sleep.

DECEMBER 5, 1920—CHANGSHA. ...[I]nformation from the Consul that matters were still in a hang fire state, the mutineers still in possession of the City, and no looting but much talk going on.

At 2:00 [P.M.] donned football togs and left the ship with the team. I see no reason why exercise and pleasure should be suspended while we wait for Chinese mutinous soldiers to pull something. We might have to wait a month. Left arms, ammunition, and equipment at hand and ready while we were on the football field, and decided that if matters were really desperate, we could land in the football suits, though I doubt if that has been done very often in the past.

[Incident ends inconclusively on December 7, 1920.]

DECEMBER 11, 1920—CHANGSHA. In the midst of [playing] bridge, there arrived on board the river police, the spokesman of whom was so excited his conversation was entirely falsetto. Through the ... steward, we learned that some of our men while out hunting had shot a Chinaman. I dispatched Wheeler and the Doc to investigate.

It developed that a stray shot had pinged the bird in the hip. Of course, no one knew who fired the shot. We shipped him out to the Yale Hospital, and I am going to make [the] four gobs who were hunting near him pay all the expenses of the affair. I am secretly glad they will not confess who fired the shot, for that means a courtmartial with resulting unpleasantness.

[The *Palos* football team plays it first game on Christmas Day, 1920.]

[A *coup de etat* which has General Chao taking command and beheading several generals, including General Li, Chao's "most active enemy."]

...[We learned] General Li's [head] ... had been nailed up over the Hunan Bank.... We left [in the afternoon] in search of General Li's head. It was not at the Hunan Bank, but some soldiers there told us it had been put up on the East Gate.... It was not there.

By that time the mate and I were quite obstinate over finding that head. We proceeded to the Yamen of General Li. The officer on duty there was very courteous. He told us that the head, after being exposed on the Bank and over the East Gate, had been returned to the body of the General, which was lying inside. He invited us to come in and take a look around. In we went.

In the center of the Yamen was a modern brick house, and into that our guide led us. The interior of the dwelling looked as if a typhoon had swept down upon it. Every lootable article had been removed.... Nothing remained but a trestle in an inner room, and on that trestle lay the body of the assassinated general. The upper part of the body was covered with a cloth, which was probably [just] as well. It was evident that a furious struggle had taken place. Blood was in evidence everywhere, and there were marks on the walls. A great sound of wailing filled the place, for Li's women had been permitted to return to mourn him. They were in another room, but their crying permeated the place, and we were glad to leave. We had[,] however, ... run down the head of General Li.

DECEMBER 28, 1920—CHANGSHA. ...[After a visit from a Yale missionary group.] It is refreshing to play around with honest-to-God, young Americans after the awful type of Britishers that exists in the East.

JANUARY 1, 1921—CHANGSHA. Came back to the ship to find Joe all agog with a story.... It seems that Ski, Keller, and Joe went to a show [sponsored by a Reverend My Qyng]. They had not been there twenty minutes before soldiers surrounded the place and demanding the box office receipts and free admission. This the gallant missionary refused, but while he was arguing in front the soldiers entered from the back and proceeded to put the place on the bum. They tore down scenery, chucked the audience about, knocked over the benches, and then cleared the place at the point of the bayonet....

Well, Ski and Keller and Joe came immediately back to the ship, having quite enough of the show. This is the first time Joe has been ashore in two months, and I think it will be the last time in Changsha for him.

[On January 3 Howell began a trip with two enlisted crewmen, an interpreter, and a young Chinese boy from the *Palos*. There were two purposes for this journey. First, from asidisms much later in the diaries and the insistence on not using real names, intelligence gathering. Second, Howell was truly interested in seeing the Chinese countryside.]

JANUARY 3, 1921 [ABOARD THE MEITAL]. ...[W]e stopped at Siangtan [Xiangdan] ... [and] visited the YMCA first. Crouched in a

"We crossed the river ... and landed at the foot of a stair that [at] a distance remind one of biblical times." The River Gate at Chungking. (Photograph courtesy of U.S. Naval Institute.)

corner over a miserable inadequate little stove was the American missionary in charge of the place. He was about forty, needed a haircut horribly, was obviously a failure in this world, and was equally obviously completely satisfied with himself. He was ... inquisitive about who we were.... I told him I was James McDonald, reporter for my New York paper ... George remarked that he supposed the reason that his disguise was no good was that he looked so military. One must know George to appreciate this.... [W]e [will] leave Hengshan for Hengschow [Hengchou] by chair tomorrow morning....

JANUARY 4, 1921. [We went aboard a launch, which was] about fifty feet long with a beam of ten feet and a draft of twenty inches. On it were packed probably a hundred Chinese, wrapped in pukows and wadded garments, crowded, miserable with the cold, yet uncomplaining. One never complains about inconveniences to which he had been accustomed all his life.

At 10:30 [A.M.] secured alongside a dock.... Soldiers were massed on the dock, and I found ... that they were to search the passengers and their baggage for ammunition and opium. I had no intention to permit my party or my baggage to be searched. So I directed all hands to remain on board until the other passengers had landed.

We watched the search. The soldiers appeared honest enough, though they were full of the sense of their importance and a desire to impress the bystanders. Neither ammunition or opium was found. When all the other passengers were off, I told Yong Ki [the interpreter] to get the equipment ashore to the Standard Oil Agency and strode haughtily to the beach through the soldiers, who fell back and made no effort to stop me. Yong Ki explained that the baggage was mine, and it was passed without argument.

Polly [a Chinese boy aboard the *Palos*] was halted by the soldiers and asked who we were and what our business was. Whereupon the little rascal struck his tongue out at them and sauced in English—"Oh, you shut up!" and the[n] scuttled up the steps to the safety of our presence. He got away with it.

JANUARY 6, 1921. [We set off on foot today.] The caravan was quite appalling in its length and size. First came the chair of Mr. James McDonald [Howell], ... borne by four coolies, of whom was Number One, through who Yong Ki did all business with the coolies, and who is their manager. Second came the chair of Mr. Red Evans, borne by three coolies, one of who was intelligent. Next came Mr. George Smiley, also carried by three coolies. Yong Ki came next in a two man chair. Fifth came Polly borne by two grinning coolies, who knew they had a cinch with his less than one hundred pounds. Next came a coolie bearing the oil stove and two of my bags. There followed my bedding and cots and lanterns and cases of condensed milk, soda water, canned fruit, three live chickens unresigned to their ultimate sacrifice, and this and that, and so forth, and as viz. There were twenty-nine coolies in all.

It appeared that one man's chair coolies were assigned in the order of one's importance, that one's weight had nothing to do with the matter. Yong Ki had agreed with Number One to pay him sixty cents Mex per day for each coolie and six cents per day for each one's cumshaw. (I see now where those New York waiters get that stuff.) That meant ... less than ten dollars American money per day for the whole outfit. Number One paid each coolie fifty cents per day wages and five cents cumshaw, paid for their chow and lodging, and still made money on the eleven cents per day per man he reserved unto himself.

Number One was not large. He was active and was distinguished by a complete set of teeth of which you remembered but one. But he proved active, willing, and efficient, and he expressed a desire—nay, a determination—to follow us to the ends of the earth....

The road was of stone and a good three feet wide. The snow and sleet had made it slippery, but the coolies were careful and did not fall.

[At the first inn we] were much amused at the cash register of the mistress of the inn. It was merely a hollowed out bamboo joint four feet long and four inches in diameter, locked securely in an upright position to a stanchion. Anyone could drop money in, but none could remove a coin except Madame, who carried the key and wore a very severe expression when she had occasion to unlock the bank. And Madame was very much on the lookout for business. There was a rival inn across the street. And Madame of necessity must hail each potential customer when he was a hundred yards away. There was an uproar when a traveler halted undecided between the two inns. It was evident that Madame and Monsieur, her rival across the ten feet wide street, hated one another with sincerity.

...[M]y morning in the chair had made me very cold. So Red and I walked all afternoon. The stone trail was easy to follow, and by avoiding slippery places we found it simple to pick out our way. The country was slightly rolling, covered in the main by scores of frozen rice paddies through which the trail wound.

At four-thirty Red and I stopped in a village, doubtful whether the caravan, which was miles behind us, could get past it before night. In the village street was an ancient stone pestle with a primitive tread on it. Two men were stamping on the tread with their feet, while an old woman fed in the rice to be threshed.

I was amused at the village boys. They had a little toy with feathers on it. They kicked it with the sides of their feet, and the idea of the game was to see how long it could be kept in the air. It interested me because it is the only instrument of play I have seen the Chinese boys indulge in.

At five the caravan came up, and Yong Ki decided upon the village as our stopping place for the night. We selected the best inn, but at that we had to sleep uncomfortably close to the pigsty.... It was a damp, dismal hole with a dirt floor, a papered window full of holes, and an allaround, suitable place for a murder. But Yong Ki fetched in the oilstove, the brazier, lantern, our cots, a table—. The place began to heat up, we gathered around the glowing charcoal, cheered up enormously, had an excellent supper in honor of George's birthday and turned in early.

JANUARY 7, 1921. After an excellent breakfast, ... waited on the street for the caravan to get underway. I was interested in a family at chow across the way. They all sat crouched about the fire on which breakfast was cooking—the wrinkled old grandmother who kept an alert eye upon the cooking but was not too much occupied to miss anything that was going [on] in her little world; the shy, quaint, small mother, with her baby unwinking...[?] in her arm, its vivid red cap standing out as a blob of color; the little cheeseeye [child] hiding behind his grandmother and peeping out upon us; two hens pecking away at the ground; a pig grunting comfortably near the fire; three ducks ... [quacking] at the strangers; the man of the house dignifiedly at one side, inspecting us with expressionless eyes, smoking his long pipe with an occasional puff.

There was the usual shouting and arguing amongst the coolies, but whatever the quarreling was about it presently smoothed out, as it always does in China, and at eight we got underway.

Red, George, and I walked all morning, got far enough ahead of the caravan, and managed to select the wrong road. Small joss houses were numerous and appeared to receive some attention. The haystacks were constructed in trees, where they were protected from marauders of all sorts.

At half past ten[,] Number One found us and patiently led us back to the proper road. The trail still wound through frozen rice paddies, though the country was a bit more rolling than yesterday.

[After a brief break for lunch at an inn,] ... [w]e rode in our chairs until half past three and then walked the rest of the afternoon to keep warm. It is noticeable how few graves there are. In Szechwan each hillside is dotted with hundreds of mounds, but so far we have seen surprisingly few graves. Yong Ki says that there are many graves but they are not visible from the road, but I am not convinced that he is right. There are fewer roadside shrines, but those that exist are about equally proportioned between Buddha and Confucius.

At 4:45 anchored for the night in a new inn in a small village that was very comfortable, though it was impossible to heat up our room much. This inn, like all others, is built with mud walls, earthen floor, paper windows, and a precariously tiled roof with openings to let the smoke out.

It is but thirty li to Leiyang, but I decided to cut the place, as it is slightly out of our way, and accordingly, gave orders to Number One to take the direct trail to Chenchow [Chenchou] tomorrow. It is two hundred li there.

JANUARY 8, 1921. ...We left the main trail immediately and struck off on a muddier, slipperier stone road not well traveled.... During the forenoon I saw the first cattle I have observed on this journey, smaller and scrawnier than our well fed beasts at home.

At eleven I was amazed to come upon four stone images of animals. They were half buried in the rice paddies under an over hanging hill, and they were arranged in pairs exactly as are the approaches to the Ming tombs at Nanking and near Peking. Though I am lamentably weak on details of this nature, I have thought that all along this guarding of the approaches to a tomb with images of animals and men was strictly a custom of the old Ming emperors. But here, along a disused, old trail, half buried in rice paddies was mute evidence to the contrary.

I examined the hill, but there was nothing on it but a few modern tombs. I went back to the images and looked them over with care. They were very old, and two were sunk so deep in the paddies as to barely be visible. Their lineaments were so worn by the weather as to give but a slight indication as to what they originally represented. I wanted to hire a hundred coolies to dig out that hill, but instead of that I went tamely on with my caravan. The place was about ten miles to Leiyang....[3]

Many peasants passed en route to market at Leiyang. They carried in the inevitable baskets swung from their shoulders on the inevitable pole turnips, onions, cabbages, and red peppers.

The trail was so muddy and slippery that the coolies tired early; so we anchored for the night in town called Chow Su [Chou Su], having made good 50 li today.

The country is still one vast rice paddy with the hills serving only to supply the water from their melting snow. The whole country is wonderfully irrigated. The first tiny paddy is at the very top of a hillside valley. It discharges exactly the correct amount of water into the paddy below it, which process is repeated perhaps thirty times before the plain itself is reached. The overflow is taken care of in little brooks which parallel the paddies. Not five years nor one hundred could ever have produced this system. Yong Ki says it has been working for a thousand years, and I think he is right.[4]

Directly after we came to anchor, we heard much booming of firecrackers and discovered that a wedding was being celebrated in the neighborhood....

JANUARY 9, 1921. ...The terrain is no longer one mass of rice paddies. It is more mountainous, and there are numerous coal mines worked by the natives. Hunan abounds in coal, tin, antimony and iron, and its metallic resources have but been tapped.

About every mile along these trails is erected a resthouse of stone, usually with open sides, but always with tiled roof and with stone benches for the weary wayfarer to sit upon. This afternoon we passed two new and beautiful ones with crossed national and army flags carved over the entrance and the inscription—"Remember the law." These were erected by General Mao, a Hunanese, after the Southerners obtained possession of Hunan last summer and drove out the Northerners.

I am interested in observing how easily the coolies bear great weights long distances on their shoulders. They are little, undernourished men, but they have an endurance which is nothing less than remarkable. I doubt if their average height is over five feet four inches or their weight much over one hundred thirty pounds. Yet our coolies carry one hundred ten pounds a piece for eight hours, and a little lad passed this afternoon bearing twice his weight in lumber.

At five ... [stopped] in an inn at the village of Gaojosi. [Gaozhouxi?] Yong Ki told us that ... early marriages still exist up country, but that in Shanghai and the larger cities the Chinese are ceasing it and that the day is coming when the youth of China shall select his own helpmate.

Just before we turned in, George went out into the inn to investigate a racket. It seemed that a married couple jointly own a store next door. They sell wine amongst other things. Now the merchant who sold them this wine had come this evening to collect the money. The husband was out and the wife in his absence paid the bill. The merchant left, the husband returned, and the wife was properly beaten for paying the bill without her husband's knowledge. She came crying to the inn with her ten month's old baby in her arms. I shall write this to Mr. W. J. Bryan, for he must be running dry on new arguments in favor of prohibition.[5]

JANUARY 10, 1921. Eggs, hotcakes, and molasses for breakfast! What more could mortal desire? Yet Yong Ki and Polly as always ate some damned Chinese concoction.

The country is more mountainous, somewhat wooded, and less cultivated ...[T]he trail was much drier and easier for the coolies. We passed a large seven story pagoda, one of the four we have seen thus far....

The stone road climbed higher and higher, and at eleven [A.M.] we came out on the backbone of the range to find blue hills in every direction with those ahead lost in the grey mist. We descended into the valley along an avenue bordered by splendid fir trees, crossed a rice-paddied plain, and paused outside a village to observe a wedding procession across the paddies . . [T]he sedan chairs [of the bride and groom] were covered with red drapery. A band went ahead with much wailing and squeaking of flutes and stringed instruments, beating of drums, and banging of cymbals. Before the chair of the bride marched coolies bearing four banners, two red, two blue.

We waited until the booming of giant firecrackers announced that the bride had crossed the threshold of her future home, and then we entered the village. We wandered through it waiting for our coolies to come up, and found at the far end of it a delightful, little island as well kept as a park, with trees, a temple, and three charming bridges. I took a time-exposure of the temple—the day was grey as usual—we watched a small junk shoot the rapids, and then another wedding party hove in sight. They had evidently been traveling for some time, and part of the procession had fallen behind. The poor, little bride, locked into her closed chair, was wailing out her grief at leaving her parents.... The groom, aged eight, was arrayed in what they call raiment, and his shoes were too large for him. His chair was open, and he seemed entirely unconcerned about the whole affair. There were several coolies bearing wedding presents, which consisted largely of shoes and red lacquered furniture.

One of [our] ... coolies was sick of a fever, and the village doctor came in to treat him. The handling of the case was simple. The coolie's loose skin on his neck was pulled out and snapped back until a blood clot formed. Then the same thing was done to his chest and back. I tried to find out their reasoning regarding this, but I could get nothing more than the fact that is an old custom which had proven good for fevers.

JANUARY 11, 1921. The farther we penetrated into the interior the more curious regarding us are the natives. They block up the inn doors watching us eat.... [T]in cans, bottles, knives, forks, spoons, and tin cups are all delightful mysteries. They evidently see very few white men this far up.

The narrow stone road broadened into a respectable highway, and at eleven the caravan entered Chenchow and finally accumulated itself in the Standard Oil building.

The country is no longer composed of rice paddies. It is entirely mountainous with cattle grazing as the principal industry.

Caravan after caravan of ponies with their jingling bells walked by. Ponies and coolies coming from Ichang carried salt and sugar; those from Chenchow bore woodoil, eggs, chickens, ducks, produce, and pigs—all destined ultimately for Canton.

[The room in the inn we stayed at] proved impossible ... to heat.... It is almost inconceivable that these people, surrounded on all sides by rich coal fields, should pass their winters in miserably cold huts, huddled over tiny braziers which give forth as much gas as heat, when all that is necessary to a comfortable existence is two days work or a fireplace and the digging out of a winter's supply of coal. But one cannot change China.

Half an hour after we left, ... the trail left the slowly rising plain and entered a very beautiful, little canyon, which we promptly named McDonald Canyon. The rice paddies, all flooded, paralleled the brook down its purling course. The rocky sides were precipitous, with great faults in places, and the stone trail wove back and forth the canyon through the paddies. It was a delightful lost corner of the world, and it is almost unfortunate that but a few appreciative eyes will ever behold its beauty. We named the brook Smiley's Slough, and a ravine which led off from one side became Evan's Valley. The boy explorers were on the job.

The canyon apparently ended abruptly against a great wall of stone which blocked its lower end, and sweeping diagonally down the rock was a great black fault. It was as if an artist had begun a picture in the intention of sketching it with bold, sharp lines, had drawn a single, broad black line sloping from left to right, had idly put in two or three experimental cleancut curves, and then had altered up a palette, and filled up the picture with soft brown rocks and gray stones and green bushes and silver paddies, fringing his

"Red" Evans on Howell's "expedition" in January 1921. Note that Evans is wearing Chinese shoes. (Photograph by Glenn F. Howell, located in his diary.)

original sharp lines with delicate, trailing vines. It was [a beautiful] scene.

Shortly we left the stream and began climbing up the ridge. The road was still of stone, three feet wide, and it soon became entirely a stair bordered by ancient pine trees. I counted over a thousand steps as the coolies toiled upward and then gave up and settled back in my chair, for the higher we went up the mountain the more the wind rose.

...I found myself on the top of the world. Directly behind me was a hillock that hid but a small sector of the horizon. Ahead to the right, to the left, lay revealed, misty blue, range upon range, the nearer one curving sharply silhouettes of those behind. There was no horizon. The distant mountains resembled clouds; the clouds were distant mountains.

Left: **Polly, one of the Chinese aboard the *Palos* and on Howell's expedition. *Right:* George Smiley in his chair during the expedition. (Photographs by Glenn F. Howell, located in his diary.)**

And the gray of the sky melted unto the blue of the mountains, and the blue of the mountains into green and silver of the paddied valleys, and from the valleys up to my feet rushed the red and yellow earth laid bare by recent landslides. Pinshek [Binshek] lay visible a thousand feet below us, nestling on either side of its river ... and the coolies were impatient to go on, but I could hardly tear myself away from [the] vantage.

[We remained briefly in Pinshek and entered into Kwangtung [Guangton] Province.] I was surprised to find stone images in pairs in Hunan. I was amazed to find them in Kwangtung. [We returned to Ichang through the canyon.]

JANUARY 14, 1921. I cannot make out whether the Chinese really believe their religions a little. I think that the situation is best summed up by what Lee [Li], my old pilot, said to me last summer. We

Top: "The caravan was quite appalling in its length and size." The January 1921 expedition. (Photograph by Glenn F. Howell.) *Left:* Glenn F. Howell fitted out in foul weather gear during his expedition. (Photographs located in Glenn F. Howell's diary.)

were going up the Gorges, and I noticed that whenever we passed a river joss old Lee always chin-chinned [chanted] to it. Through Yong Ki I asked him why, since he must know better than to believe in river josses. Lee's reply explained everything. He argued that he knew better but that it did no harm to chinchin, and if by any remote chance the river joss did have any influence he had gained its protection and lost nothing.

[En route to ship.] Scores of coolies passed us bound for Ichang with their loads. I fell to wondering what they will do when the railroad comes through as it is sure to within

(*L-R*): **Polly, Pedro, and unidentified boy on return trip from expedition. (Photograph by Glenn F. Howell, located in his diary.)**

the next decade. I suppose that they will move back into the untouched interior. They must live somehow.

The pony caravans were plentiful. Along this road are the only fences I have seen in China in the country. I assume that they are to keep the ponies out of their fields. The fences are hedge and thick.

Beyond the divide there made up on our right a wonderful mountain, huge, bleak, barren, and topped with snow.

At five thirty [P.M.] came to anchor in our former ancient inn and partitioned off our apartment as before. After supper, a fiendish noise outside required investigation, and we went out to find the whole village alight with a candle before each door and chinchin joss procession in full swing. They came by: a Chinese band of flutes, squeaky stringed instruments, drums, and cymbals; an array of small boys carrying lighted tapers; and a man at the end bearing an open book. As they came abreast [of] each house, its inhabitants fired off firecrackers, the drums and cymbals were whacked, and there was a high old time generally.

Yong Ki explained that eight or ten times a year each village hires a band and has a chinchin joss night. The chinchinning works equally well for any joss you may select. Each householder subscribes his share of the expense, and if he "stinges" on the party, as Yong Ki expressed it, he simply loses out on good joss. That is what the man at the end of the procession carries the book for. In it are the names of the subscribers, and his function is to warn the musicians to be silent while passing the house of the one who has "stinged" lest he get some good joss without paying for it.

We turned in, to be disturbed at decreasing intervals by our coolies, who were gambling in another inn and came to the door to request more money from Number One, who fired them away with increasing vigor. Yong Ki said they were not playing fantan, but that they were at a version of American poker. I understand that Yong Ki is rather an authority on gambling.

JANUARY 15, 1921. Everybody was up at a quarter to seven.... After last night's chinchinning, the villagers were sleeping in....

The caravan hove up anchor at seven thirty and sailed for Chenchow. The sun was out, but it was cold, there was frost on the ground, and the rice paddies were frozen. However, there was no wind and I was comfortable in my chair in my windproof suit.

The coolies, the end of their journey in sight, made haste, and the whole caravan arrived at the Standard Oil Agency in Chengchow at eleven o'clock [A.M.].

We were ready enough to gather around the charcoal fire.

About noon I went around to the Presbyterian Mission to call on the missionaries, but found everybody out except the Chinese clerks who spoke English. They said everything was serene—no trouble brewed or brewing—and wanted me to go to the missionaries' home, a li away. By this time my enthusiasm for seeing the missionaries had entirely evaporated. So I sat down and wrote a note to them addressed "Gentlemen" and told them how sorry I was to have missed them and how I hoped to have the pleasure of meeting them some day. I signed the note "James McDonald," and I fancy the missionaries will wonder for many a day just who James McDonald is and what business could possibly have brought him to their remote Chengchow. Possibly they will scent a rival in their sacred precincts.

I absolutely cannot see missionarying in China or any place else. The Yale Mission at Changsha does a great good, but it is educational rather than religious. Its medical section is of course a godsend to this part of China. Then, too, its people are broad-minded, well-educated men and women, who are a community sufficient to keep them up to the mark and up with the times. But deliver me from these upcountry missionaries! Their creed they believe not because they have ever thought it out; but by sheer repetition. You are saved to glory if you believe with them. You are damned if you drink. You are close to it if you smoke or swear. You are irrevocably damned if you venture to hint that it is not what you believe in this world but what you do that counts, that it does not really make much difference whether your darkened heathen mind calls the dim divinity he vaguely worships God, Buddha, Brahma, Confucius, or just plain Joss, so long as he worships something, and in that worshipping is kinder to his neighbor, sincerer, more honest, a better citizen.

China at present is having off her old gods. Her temples are falling into decay, are not being replaced, her priests are decadent—they have no grip on the people. It would appear that now is the time for Christianity to step in. It is, but not through the medium of smalltown religious freaks. Open the Chinese minds with proper, sensible education, the three R's, develop their bodies at the same time with sitting up exercises and suitable games, and season with some good, wholesome religion. The Chinese is a reasonable being. He absorbs a program like the one I have outlined. But let some freak with spectacles and common sense squaretoed shoes that squeak get at him and tell him that his parents lied to him, that there ain't no joss, that there is a being on high named God who sits on a throne and deals out justice with mercy, surrounded with a mob scene of angels twanging away at harps, that this mercy is only for those who believe a certain narrow creed, that ninety-nine percent of the world must needs go straight to hell, that only the remaining one percent can hope to obtain the mercy—all this stuff is received by the Chinese with bland faces. They listen with grave attention and go away. That is why Christianity is not advancing in China.

If the people at home must spend money to convert the heathen, for Bud's sake splurge on the medical missionaries. Better a bum doctor for thousands who need him than a bum preacher, his wife, seven kids—(your salary is increased one hundred bucks a year for every new one)—all of whom are neither useful nor ornamental nor desired, and who are firmly convinced that the harp and crown are cinched and waiting—.

I returned to the Standard Oil Agency to find that Yong Ki had hired a junk to take us down river to Hengshan. It appeared that six junks had arrived this morning from Changsha laden with oil ... I went down the river and looked it over. It was new and clean, and told Yong Ki we would take it. The big junkmaster grinned his thanks.

[A dispute over the junk ensues between soldiers, the junkmaster and the Standard Oil Company.]

...[We] had got past the annoyed stage and were rather amused. I became quite absorbed in [the novel] "Main Street," but after half an hour with no results as to our departure I strolled up to the Standard Oil people, and Yong Ki bawled out in English—"Five minutes more!" and I mutely retired to the junk and "Main Street," hoping that we could get away before dark. One hour later, Yong Ki appeared quite out of patience. He explained that we must select another junk.

We did.

...We bowed farewell to the ... [city]; we eased out from the other junks; we took our last look at the crowd assembled on the beach; we shoved off. It was 3:33 [P.M.].

At 3:34 we ran aground. We ran aground ten times before dark.

JANUARY 17, 1921. ...We passed other coal mines ... there is apparently an enormous quantity of coal in this province.

At ten ... passed a temple built at the entrance to a great cave in a solid cliff which formed the bank of the river. It was eight stories high; the lower part of weathered brick; the upper section all columns and oxblood balconies, tiled roofs and carved ridges; the exterior a mere suggestion of the mysteries within. The temple can be reached only by water.

JANUARY 19, 1921. ...The junks toiling up stream sometimes [use] sails, sometimes pole, and in the bad places track. The junkmen set up the most hideous cries as they exert themselves to pole and track over a rapids. Those on the beach with the tracking line are bent double. Those on board the junk shove the poles with might and main, and all hands bawl out and groan and exhort themselves and their comrades to greater efforts. And always do they get over, even when the bystander is convinced that they will never make it. I am sure that there is no such thing in China as a dumb coolie. He could not exist, for none of them can possibly work without a flow of chattering; of chanting, of yelling....

JANUARY 19, 1921. At 1:36 came the piece de resistance of the expedition so far. I, Jimmy McDonald, fell overboard.

The boatmen were aft chowing, and the junk was drifting slowly down stream. I was sitting on the bow, writing up the log as usual. Red and George were stretched out on deck, further aft on the fo'c'sle, absorbed in their working.

I got up to go aft and fell headfirst neatly and completely overboard. I have never been so surprised. One moment I was peacefully scribbling; ... the next moment I found myself paddling frantically upward from the depths of the river. Red and George extended helping hands, I got my wet clothes off on the fo'c'sle, ducked inside, rubbed down, dressed, took a shot of whiskey, and felt fine, even though it is January.

It appeared that a portion of the decking had given away. I returned to the bow and resumed writing up the log.

JANUARY 20, 1921. Yong Ki is very ill, complaining of much pain, and has a walloping fever. He has something....

At eight [A.M.] Red shouted from the stern that he saw a stone cut on the beach.... There was nothing for it but to land, and Red and I jumped ashore and raced back to the object.... It was the granite image of a crouching animal some four feet high with wattles on its back and a head shaped like that of an anteater. And in the edge of the water lay on its side its mate. And they were being used by the junk coolies as Stepping Stones from the beach to their junks. It made me furious....

We arrived off the American Presbyterian Mission Hospital at ten thirty, and I went ashore immediately with Number One and Polly. Number One assuming the role of guide. We visited several backdoors, three kitchens, two bedrooms, and a chapel before we finally found Doctor Robertson, a Canadian and the only white doctor attached to the hospital. Obviously, due to Yong Ki, I had to drop the Jimmy McDonald and open up with who I was. I went over to his home and met Mrs. Robinson, an Ohioan. They were both very agreeable and invited me to tiffin. We went back to the hospital, where the doctor had a case on the operating table waiting for him.

He sent a Chinese doctor, his assistant, back to the junk with me, and after an examination he found that Yong Ki had pneumonia and temperature of 104. There was no doubt about the necessity of his immediate transfer to the hospital.

Red and Polly packed up his things, and Red, who now becomes Cook for the rest of this cruise, got from him how to make pancakes and dumplings. George went ashore with the doctor and me and obtained a stretcher and an attendant, returned ... and convoyed Yong Ki to the hospital in the stretcher. I saw to it that he was in a separate room and in a good bed.

When Doctor Robertson finished operating, he confirmed his assistant's diagnosis ... and promised to give him every attention.

Then ... [Doctor Robertson] took me for a walk about the city, which has a population of fifty or sixty thousand.

...[After walking about the city,] the Doctor and I went to Hell. A temple not far ... [away] contains the dreadful place. In the center of large earthen-floored room is a small pagoda with folded Buddhas peering out from each aperture. On each side of the pagoda are represented six stages of hell in booths built into the wall. Each booth contains one large devil with two smaller sidekicks and then five or six little devils below the dias raising hell with the helltourists—immersing them in blood, sawing them in two, pulling out their tongues, sticking wires in their ears, gouging out their eyes, boiling them in oil—woodsman spare that tree!

I had just come to a firm resolve to be a good boy in the future when I caught sight of a poor Chinese helltourist about to be beheaded. But the artist, with the final touch that kills so many pictures, had crowned the victim with the kind of an American hat they call a Fedora. And somehow the sight of a Fedora hat on an agonized Chinaman about to be beheaded in hell was too much for me, and I departed hastily, chocking with illbred mirth.

...I had no more time to waste at Hengchow [Hengchou]. So I ordered the junkmaster who had been summoned from the beach, to get underway for Hengshan immediately.

JANUARY 21, 1921. ...Polly woke us up [in the early morning hours] with information that we were surrounded by pilories (robbers). We leaped up, our movements somewhat accelerated by Polly's assertion that pilories were already alongside. I crawled out on the fo'c'sle with a revolver in my hand; the boys went aft.... Red sang out that the men were not pilories, but that Polly said they were "Posters" and were merely giving us information that the pilories were all about us. That made the situation different.

The "Posters" talked excitedly for a bit in guarded tones—the first time I have ever heard a subdued Chinese conversation. Then they shoved off for their village on the banks, which was alive with lights and chinchinning at the top of its lungs with an infernal racket to persuade their joss to keep the pilories away. All hands were evidently in a panic.

The junkmaster ... [decided] he would run on a bit further until he found a safe place and then would anchor for what remained of the night.

[The junk remained anchored and the alarm proved false. Howell and his expedition arrived in Hengshan and engaged a steam launch to return them to the *Palos*.]

JANUARY 22, 1921. The pleasure of putting foot again upon my own little ship, of receiving and returning the quartermaster's salute, of entering my warm cabin, of chucking off my leather suit, and diving into a huge pile of Christmas mail!

JANUARY 23, 1921—CHANGSHA. [After discussing the shooting of navy Lieut. Warren H. Langdon, engineer on the USS *Albany*, by a Japanese sentry.] Yet I don't think that the Japs are quite ready for war just now, though I do wish that we would hurry up and get it over with.

JANUARY 28, 1921—CHANGSHA. I am going up to Yoloshan [Yue Lu] often. I had no idea that so lovely a view existed around Changsha. Yet half the foreigners here have never visited it.

[Yong Ki returns to the *Palos* on January 20.]

FEBRUARY 14, 1921—CHANGSHA. [Rehearsing for an amateur play written by Howell.] There exists in Changsha three distinct Sets [of Westerners], each Set hating the other two. There are also people who hate each other privately. In fact, there is quite a bit of hating going on all the time. One might even go so far as to say that it is ad lib.... The standards of the Sets differ one from another.

My official duty requires me to play with all Sets. I do not like any of them collectively, [but care for only a few in each set.] Hence, playing with these Sets is dangerous, for the slightest favoritism shown by me is immediately resented by both the others.

FEBRUARY 17, 1921—CHANGSHA. I held mast this afternoon, derated four men—no, three, gave one gob a Summary Court Martial and slapped a couple of them into the brig on bread and water.

I wish I could handle [the] women [in the play] that way.

MARCH 5, 1921—CHANGSHA. ...It gives one a sort of wholesome feeling to wake up in the morning and realize that the flag flies over a safe, sane bunch of people who will not forever be making one ashamed of the country. I am sure that this administration will arise to its responsibilities. And the pleasure of being able to say—"Now when Josephus Daniels was Secretary of the Navy!"

MARCH 7, 1925—CHANGSHA. I decided yesterday to run away for a week and work on "Landry Sterrett" while I feel in the mood. It will do me good anyhow to get away from the ship....

The Taoist Temple, my home for a week, is built on the crest of the southern knob of Yoloshan on the edge of the sacred forest. It is old—very old—and its Buddhas or josses are covered with dust, but the view from it to the South and East is marvelous. There are two priests, one great, and fat, and old to senility—the other young and rather

shrewd. There is a room with a balcony devoted to tea, for which the pilgrims pay, and three or four coolies look out for that. Only the young priest has anything to do with religious part.

I am going to like it up here.[6]

[Howell returns on March 11.]

MARCH 16, 1921—CHANGSHA. Ski told me his history—very interesting. He is the child of Polish parents, and his father died when he was one month old. His mother turned him over to an orphanage, Catholic and eight miles from Pittsburgh, when he was two. For twelve years he was shut up in this place with about ten trips of less than three hours away from it. At three they put him into the orphanage uniform, a straight waist, straight short trousers, no cap, shoes or stockings, except for three months of the year, and turned him over to an older boy to be looked out for by him. In due course of time, Ski in turn was given a baby to care for, and then another, and another. At six he ran away and was

"Ski told me his history—very interesting." (Photograph by Glenn F. Howell, located in his diary.)

returned. At eight he ran away and was captured and returned after only two hours of freedom. He had no pockets in his clothes, no newspapers, no books, no pleasures except games invented by himself and his messmates. His ideas of the world were of the vaguest. The Sisters had a school for them, but the most advanced textbook that he saw was a Fourth Reader.

Twice a month came adopting day, and on that day all the children stood in a row and were looked over—but nobody ever adopted Ski. Each occasion was a bitter disappointment to him, for he longed desperately to get out of his prison.

At last came his opportunity. A youngster who had been in the place returned to call and got Ski out by promising to look after him. His release came in 1917, when he was fifteen. For two years he worked at odd jobs, but finally fell into success as a bellhop in a Pittsburgh hotel. Then his mother traced him. She had remarried again—a worthless fellow—and she demanded Ski support her now that he was earning enough. He told her to go to the devil—that she had let him go through all that childhood hell without extending a helping hand—and then he ran away from her and enlisted in the Navy.

He came out to the Orient with me in 1919 in the *South Dakota*.

MARCH 21, 1921—CHANGSHA. I had a most amusing mast this morning. Theisen, a fireman, lost a razor yesterday, and proceeding to the Chinese quarters to search, discovered the Wampus (aged twelve) and Colonel Cootie (aged ten) at their locker. Upon his approach, the Wampus flung something into a far corner, which Colonel Cootie retrieved for Theisen. 'Twas the missing razor. Then Theisen searched their locker and discovered his crucifix and some other articles of his. The outraged Theisen reported the affair to me last night, and I held mast for the culprits this morning.... [T]he Wampus made a most impassioned defense, but Yong Ki settled the matter by denouncing the lad as a thief, and he further stated that the Wampus to be instantly fired from the *Palos* forever. The court then proceeded to the case of Colonel Cootie. There was nothing provable against the Colonel, other than he had shared a locker with the Wampus. Colonel Cootie was quite eloquent in his defense. He stood stiffly at attention during his trial, and I learned afterward that he practiced for fifteen minutes on how to carry out himself before the "Meigue Binchwan Twanzu," which is my official title in Szechwanese. I let the Colonel off with the warning to watch his step in the future, and mast was over.

MARCH 25, 1921—CHANGSHA. I held mast first thing this morning, and slapped my young friend _____ into the brig for five days bread and water. A gloomy day, with me still feeling rotten. I am sick of Changsha, but our departure is sure to occur soon.

APRIL 7, 1921—CHANGSHA. ...Met the Captain of the *Woodlark* out walking with his dogs, and went part way with him. I rather like him, but I distrust all Britishers on general principals. Those in Changsha are under the surface distinctly anti–American, for our position in the world is now predominate, and it is growing in the Orient by leaps and bounds.

Selby, my yeoman, had a fit down in the office after tiffin today. I am not sure whether I had better stop writing so many letters or whether Selby had better go on the wagon. This Orient certainly gets the boys if they don't watch out. There is but one way to live successfully out here without danger of slipping. Boil your water, touch liquor gingerly, and exercise yourself into a perspiration once a day.

[Howell returns again to Yoloshan April 8 and the next day departs on a houseboat cruise for two days.]

APRIL 11, 1921—CHANGSHA. [A quartermaster fails to notice a boat has drifted away.] As it was, no one was put into the brig over the affair. I have come around to using the brig frequently. It is strange that with the world in its theoretically advanced condition it is actually necessary to shut men up in solitary confinement on bread and water for five days in order to straighten them out. I have never been keen about using that punishment, but I have used it five or six times since the first of the year with excellent results. It completely straightened _____ and _____ out; they have been like lambs ever since then. It merely made _____ more careful in wrongdoing. I think it scared _____ into temporary good behavior. I was amused one morning to discover that the occupants of the fo'c'sle at that moment were Hollander, _____ and myself, who fought shoulder to shoulder against the *Palos* Palons in December as the three backs of our team. But _____ was in the brig, I had put him there, and Hollander was the sentry. Yet how many times had _____ and I had flung our padded bodies against the enemy to let Hollander through! How many times the three of us—judge, prisoner, and sentry—had rolled in the mud in a confused tangle of arms and legs!

I think that bread and water will soon be abolished in the Navy as a punishment, but I hope not, for properly used it brings results.[7]

[April 14 to 17 makes a trip to Changteh.]

APRIL 19, 1921—CHANGSHA. We received our orders today to proceed [to] Shanghai day after tomorrow, but I have a hunch we won't go just yet....

APRIL 22, 1921—CHANGSHA. [A] telegram from the Patrol Commander directing me to stay here until the *Villalobos* relieves me....[8]

APRIL 23, 1921—YOLSHAN. It is Saturday. So I inspected the crew and passed out 32 victory medals and had Julian read to the crew "Rocks and Shoals," a senseless proceeding, but one required.[9]

[Howell then proceeds to Yoloshan.]

APRIL 30, 1921—CHENGLIN. We shoved off at six this morning and departed ... wildly blowing the whistle with Joe de Borgia leaning from his windows and waving as long as were in sight.

I have checked Changsha off the list as a set of peculiar incidents. The winter has not been a loss rather a distinct gain, for I have done quite a bit of writing, and I had the opportunity to study a dozen very interesting characters. The main result of the past winter is that I know Hunan, and I am the only naval officer who does. And that knowledge may come in handy some day, Quien sabe [who knows]?

We learned tonight that Selby, my yeoman, and Pope, the machinist's mate, won second prize in the Hankow champion sweeps—$4,450.00. That's not a bad haul for a pair of gobbies.... Just after I've got Selby firmly on the water wagon!

MAY 2, 1921—COCK'S HEAD ABOVE KILLIKANG [JILIKANG]. At 9:30 [A.M.] sighted the *Elcano* and stopped to obtain a new chief bo's'ns mate. He had little to tell me save the target practice is delayed.... While I was stopped the steering gear jammed, ... but we eventually fixed it and proceeded. Half an hour later the rudder jammed again and the packing in the forward blower blew out. So I anchored at ten thirty and directed that the steering gear and blower should be thoroughly overhauled.

Got underway again at four, but directly [after] we got the anchor up the steering gear jammed. This time we found the trouble—an elusive wire in the conning tower. We undamaged it and stood downriver....

MAY 4, 1921—ABOVE NANKING [NANJING]. Got underway at five as usual. At six anchored on account of fog. Immediately upon anchoring, Pat O'Grady rushed up out of the forward fireroom crying out water was coming in and that it was over the floorplates. There was an anxious ten minutes, and then we got all pumps working on it, found that we could pump faster than it was coming in, and then proceeded to investigate. I suspected personnel, and I was right. What had happened was this: The syphon out of the forward fireroom had broken as we left Changsha. Consequently the bilges had not been pumped. But since Changsha each successive fireman when he found the syphon out of commission merely stated the after syphon and failing to report the trouble, apparently concluding that either syphon functioned on both firerooms and never bothering to look to see. But unfortunately, the after syphon operates only upon the after fireroom. Consequently, the water had slowly accumulated day by day, and the listing of the ship as we turned to anchor revealed it presence.

We got underway again at seven thirty, the fog having lifted, and steamed all day until six thirty when I anchored for the night....

MAY 5, 1921—NANKING. Selby discovered a ricksha coolie on shore this afternoon wearing a regulation United States Army blouse. Selby cut off the buttons, but permitted him to retain the blouse. Where did he get it? There are certainly no American soldiers in this part of China.

MAY 6, 1921—TUNGSHAW. Today is my eleventh anniversary; that is to say, I have been in command of the *Palos* for eleven months.... Somehow I feel that tomorrow ushers in a new era. We shall have target practice, of course, and inspection; but after that, quien sabe?

There are a lot of people who want my job, and since I am going home anyhow in two or three months I don't particularity care what happens.

I want to see what Admiral Strauss assumes about my intelligence reports. If he is interested, I shall propose that Chungking, Yunnan, French Indochina, Siam, Singapore, Java trip and see what happens.

I like China. My cruise on the Yangtze River has been fascinating. But I am beginning to look forward to other countries.... I am certainly going to break out in print soon. It seems to me my life so far has been one thorough preparation for the literary and dramatic work I expect to ease into during the coming two years.

MAY 7, 1921—SHANGHAI. ...[A]rrived at Woosung in ample time to moor off the Old Dock before noon.

Shanghai and New York! Two great cities for us sailors to come
to.... We moored and I left the ship all sworded up to pay my respects
to the Patrol Commander.

I received delightful orders. The *Monocacy* limped in here two weeks
ago at a speed of nine knots and with bottom on gimbals, so to speak,
and filled with cement, due to hitting rocks at Chungking and also
bumping the beach below Ichang a couple of times. We came snorting
in at thirteen knots and all right. So the *Monocacy* stays here for two or
three months complete overhaul, while the *Palos* will have a week or
ten days to put in our new feed pumps and blowers, will take a rapid
crack at target practice if possible, and then will head for the Gorges,
where there is a lot of pirates screaming to be shot up and subdued.
The *Monocacy* will relieve us about August first, at which time we shall
return to Shanghai for a complete overhaul and I shall be detailed and
start home.

MAY 9, 1921—SHANGHAI. Captain Wood inspected the *Palos*
today, and since he took from 9:30 to 2:00 P.M. for it, it is evident that
he did a thorough job. He went over the ship with a fine toothed comb
and was quite pleased with her.[10]

My new blowers and feed pumps are here.... At last the *Palos* will
be in efficient steaming condition. When I leave her, I shall have the
proud satisfaction of having taken command of a wreck and left her in
excellent shape....

MAY 11, 1921—SHANGHAI. ...[W]e went to the *New Orleans*,
where everybody had a conference which lasted three hours and left me
horribly bored.[11] The only thing of interest I gathered was that I am to
take the *Palos* outside as soon as the repairs are finished and fire her
through all forms of target practice.[12] It is rather amusing to spend all
that time on two toy popguns when the American firms above Ichang
are yelling for protection from bandits. But Joe Strauss, having really
done two big jobs in laying the North Sea Mine barrage and removing
it, is evidently now determined to crown his lifework by making the
Gunnery of the Fleet efficient. Some fleet! And some Gunnery![13]

It was decided at the Conference to recommend to the Admiral that
the *Palos* and *Monocacy* be assigned the two senior commanding officers
on the gunboats, due to the independent nature of the duty we perform.
I was amused at this, for I am years junior to Miles of the *Elcano* and
_____ of the *Monocacy* and a bit junior to Petersen of the *Quiros*. A year

ago I should have been concerned over such a decision. Now it makes no difference, for my time on the station is rapidly reducing to zero.

MAY 13, 1921—SHANGHAI. ...I returned to find old Lee [Li], the Number One pilot through the Gorges, awaiting me with his son ... [?] and I persuaded him to stay on for another year. We took his son on as his father's Number Two.

It was vital to ... retain old Lee, for I' m sorry for the *Palos* and the *Monocacy* when Lee retires. The trouble seemed to be that _____ ripped the bottom out of the *Monocacy* by disregarding Lee's advice, and old Lee lost much face by the affair.[14]

MAY 14, 1921—SHANGHAI. ...At eleven I paid my official respects to the Admiral.... He is conscientious, hardworking, thorough. He is not given to speech making, and he has the idea that ships of the Asiatic Station can be kept as efficient as those of any other fleet. I like his looks and way of doing business, but he is not going to be popular out here either with the Fleet or with civilians, for he is going to make the one work and he will not play with the other.

Alas for _____! They are on his trail, for the *Monocacy* would not have hit bottom had he done what old Lee wanted him to do. I have little sympathy for him, for it is a case of darned foolishness and not one of hard luck.

MAY 17, 1921—WOOSUNG. We shoved off at 2:35 [P.M.], blew attention to the *Huron*, and stood down river to Woosung, where we anchored for the night....

MAY 18, 1921—WOOSUNG. We got underway at seven and joined the *Elcano*, the *Quiros*, and the *Pompey* on the range about eight miles above Woosung at a bit past eight o'clock.[15] The *Elcano* was firing; so we kept clear of her and anchored at 9:30.

MAY 19, 1921—SHANGHAI. ...[W]e took the range and fired spotting practice without any casualties. It is the first time the *Palos* ever fired a gun in target practice. Spotting practice finished, we fled to Shanghai for coal, mooring in gunboat row about eight....

It seems that there has been another row in the Gorges. Night before last, an armed junk guarded by two of *Monocacy*'s men was boarded while they slept by bandits. A sharp fight ensued during which one of the men, Connelly, who was on the *Palos* last summer, was badly wounded in the leg, but eventually they got the Lewis gun going and killed six or eight of the bandits.[16] Captain Wood said the Admiral was not pleased at _____'s leaving American gobs on Chinese-owned junks as guards. I must admit that I agree with the Admiral on that point. I was told to expedite the practice of the *Palos* in every way so that I can get up to the Gorges in the earliest possible time and try to straighten out the mess there.

MAY 20, 1921—WOOSANG. We unmoored and left about ten ... and arrived at the range.... [W]e fired short range battle practice. The forward gun did splendidly, but the after gun with the firing of the third shot jammed, and we had to cease firing. [The extractor had burned.] After the firing we returned the unfires to the *Elcano* and steamed for Woosang, where we anchored for the night....

MAY 21, 1921—SHANGHAI. We arrived on the range at eight ... and finished short range ... and then fired long range battle. A defective shell misfired in the after gun and that rather spoiled our time. However, immediately afterward we fired submarine target practice and swung on that heavy for we got twelve hits out of twenty shots—one a bullseye—and the time was excellent. Directly [after] we had finished [,] away we ran for Woosung for I had orders to dine officially with the Patrol Commander ... at the French Club in Shanghai....

A telegram received today from Chungking is to the effect that Connelly was shot just above the knee, that his leg had been amputated, and that gangrene had set in....[17]

MAY 22, 1921—SHANGHAI. _____ was suddenly detached from command of the *Monocacy* this evening and ordered to the *New Orleans* as Executive Officer. To be detached without relief one week before target practice is a pretty severe blow, but he certainly deserved it and I have little sympathy for him. Old Yens Hansin, my classmate and intimate friend of 1916, is ordered to command the craft, which makes it fine for both *Palos* and the *Monocacy* this summer, for Yens is a good man.[18] He will join her about the tenth of June and then bring her up to Chungking.

Notes

1. Carl D. Meinhardt was born in New York and appointed to the State Department from New York. On April 20, 1920, he reported to this post. He had previously served in

Canton. On March 9, 1927, he was assigned to Shanghai. The Changsha Consulate was closed on October 15, 1929. Historian, Department of State. Today, Changsha is most noted for being the location where Mao Tse-Tung [Mao Zedong] spent his adolescent schooldays and used the city as a base to spread his ideas.

2. Joe DeBallard, manager of the Asian Bank in Changsha. Calling card pinned in diary.

3. There is a chance that Howell stumbled upon an old lesser imperial tomb site. Under the modern tombs on top of the hill might have rested a tomb of an early southern dynastic ruler. Letter, Prof. Leonard H. D. Gordon, Purdue University, to Dennis L. Noble, 13 February 1995.

4. Irrigation in China began in pre-imperial times by carefully channeling river water or snow melt through the Chinese farmland.

5. William Jennings Bryan (1867–1925), Secretary of State in Woodrow Wilson's cabinet, a staunch believer in prohibition.

6. *Fodor's* travel guide mentions that Yue Lu Hill "is a beautiful wooded area with a path leading to the peak; on the way you will pass an old temple. Clustered at the base of this hill are Hunan University and Hunan Teachers' College." John Summerfield, *Fodor's China* (New York: Fodor's Travel Publications, Inc., 1992), 311.

7. It did not go out of use.

8. Named after Magellan's first lieutenant. Built by Hong Kong and Whampoa Dock Company, Hong Kong, for Spain in 1896. Captured at Cavite, Philippine Islands, by the U.S. Army and transferred to the U.S. Navy and commissioned March 1900. Composite, single-screw gunboat. 350 tons. 11 knots. 138 feet × 22 feet × 9 feet. Compliment 44. Two 6-pdrs, two 3-pdrs, two 1-pders, 2 Colt MG. Sunk as target on October 9, 1928. Tolley, *Yangtze Patrol*, 314–315.

9. It was mandatory for an officer to read to the crew the Navy Regulations, properly entitled, *Articles for the Governance of the Navy*, but called by sailors "Rocks and Shoals." Leland P. Lovette, *Naval Customs, Traditions, and Usage* (Annapolis, Md.: Naval Institute Press, 1934): 66.

10. Duncan Mahon Wood, born October 27, 1876, in Maryland and appointed to the naval academy from Alabama on September 30, 1892, *Register of Officers*, 14–15.

11. *New Orleans*, originally *Amazonas*, steel protected cruiser, sheathed with teak below the waterline, built by Elswick, England, for Brazil in 1897. Acquired by the U.S. Navy in 1898. 3,950 tons. 20.5 knots. 355 feet × 44 feet × 19 feet. Compliment 300. Six 6"/50, for 5"/50. Sold at Mare Island, California, in 1929. Tolley, *Yangtze Patrol*, 313.

12. Howell's comment about taking the *Palos* "outside" refers to taking it out of the river and into the sea.

13. Joseph Strauss, born November 16, 1861, Mount Morris, New York. Graduated from the naval academy in 1885. Rear Admiral and Chief of Bureau of Ordnance, October 21, 1913. Commanding Officer, Mine Force, Atlantic Fleet, March 1918. Responsible for laying North Sea Mine barrage. Commander in Chief Asiatic Fleet, March 1921–October 1922, thence to General Board. Retired November 16, 1925. Noted for work in ordnance. Designed first spring recoil mount used in the U.S. Navy and the first disappearing mount for deck guns of submarines. He developed the 12-inch gun which became forerunner of the big gun batteries and a pioneer in the field of smokeless powder development. Karl Schuon, *U.S. Navy Biographical Dictionary* (New York: Franklin Watts, Inc., 1964), 238–239.

14. "From the ranks of ... [the junk pilots] came the real VIPs of the river, the steamer pilots themselves. But whether one began as the apprentice of an old veteran or came up from the ranks, the trip would have been long and arduous, a constant struggle with the never-sleeping demons of the wicked river and the sometimes even wickeder fellowmen who fought for bare survival. The steamer pilot would have spent twenty years of an adult life, the total span cut to perhaps half a century by earlier hardship and later opium. When at last he could let fingernails grow long, like gently curving yellow claws, and don the long-sleeved black gown and skull cap of a steamer pilot, one could honestly say he earned his stripes." Tolley, *Yangtze Patrol*, 227.

15. *Pompey* was purchased from James and Charles Harrison, London, April 1898. 3,085 tons. 10.5 knots. 245 feet × 33½ feet × 16 feet. Compliment 114. Four 6-pdrs. Decommissioned in 1921. Tolley, *Yangtze Patrol*, 314.

16. According to Tolley, the person wounded was Seaman (SN) Everett Conely. Tolley, *Yangtze Patrol*, 99.

17. See also, ibid.

18. This may be Edward W. Hanson, born February 12, 1889, in Minnesota. Appointed to the naval academy from Minnesota. Class of 1911 and number 37 in a class of 193. Retired as a Vice Admiral on February 1, 1952. Died October 18, 1959. Photocopy of biographical material from U.S. Naval Academy Alumni Association.

PART 3:
SHANGHAI–HANKOW,
MAY 25, 1921–SEPTEMBER 23, 1921

1. Military Retirees in China

In one of his entries Glenn Howell again mentions he loves China, but does not want to be "a confirmed Easterner." This again illustrates the love-hate relationship most U.S. military men had about China. The passage also may cause some to wonder: If military people felt this way, why did some choose to retire in China?

Those serving in China helped to coin a new phrase into the military lexicon: "he has gone Asiatic." The term had two broad connotations and neither was altogether flattering. A serviceman in East Asia who had eccentric ideas and plans was said to have gone Asiatic. (While the term may have started on the China Station, it quickly spread throughout the military and, indeed, can still be heard today.) The largest use of the expression, however, dealt with those men who decided to remain in China rather than return to the United States. Former sailor George St. Lawrence recalled a shipmate, Boatswain's Mate Leo Bauman, who went by the nickname of "Chino Ah Hee." Chino Ah Hee had spent at least fourteen years in China, and "his only fear was receiving orders to the U.S." The boatswain's mate dressed in traditional Chinese clothing whenever possible and spoke excellent Chinese. "He paused long moments when speaking English as if he [had forgotten] the language."[1]

Those military men like Bauman who chose to remain in China

had, interestingly enough, at least two assumptions made about them, especially if they lived with, or married a Chinese woman. Most Westerners knew little about the Chinese and considered them inferior. Furthermore, China itself was deemed below any Western nation. Therefore, if anyone wished to live with a Chinese woman and remain in the country they must be suspect and had probably gone Asiatic. To explain away why white men would want to remain in China, many began to say only those who would lead lives of dissipation were apt to stay in China.

In some cases, the men who did remain in China fit neatly into the persona of wastrel. Even with their meager retirement pay, military men could live far better in China than in their own country. It must also be pointed out, however, that the retirees would, in the most part, live in the concession areas and thus not really be a part of China in the true sense.

While there is evidence to support the popular view of retirees in China, there is also compelling contrary evidence to support just the opposite viewpoint.

In 1926, Howell mentioned he met a man by the name of Wokinsin who was the agent for Standard Oil Company. Wokinsin had first come to Asia as a chief yeoman in 1919. A retired chief commissary man ran a bakery and gave out baked goods to gunboat sailors. Another sailor became a U.S. Marshall and Kemp Tolley recalled a former chief who ran an ice plant in Chungking. A retired soldier ran a dry cleaning establishment in Tientsin.[2]

True to part of the mythology of the retired military China hand, some did operate drinking establishments. Many of these establishments in Yangtze River ports passed to other retired military men when the proprietor died or decided to give up the business. The writer William Leaderer, who served in the navy in China during the 1930s, mentions the Poema Cafe in Chefoo run by an ex-chief by the name of Blackie. Navy men could run up a bill and Blackie would present the total each month. The running of drinking establishments catering to military men would not be considered an approved type of business by most of the Western society that lived in China.[3]

There were some military men who chose not to work in retirement and did not spend all their time in drinking establishments. Charles G. Finney, while serving in the army in the 1920s, wrote about the man he identified as Msgt. George Smith. Smith, born in 1872, had enlisted in 1893 and first came to China during combat operations in the Boxer Uprising. He served in various posts before returning to China again, retiring at Tientsin in 1923. Breaking the stereotype, Smith enjoyed reading and the young soldier and old master sergeant discussed books and authors in his apartment in Tientsin.[4]

What is absent from the mythology of the China Station is the fact that many men who, at the end of their first enlistment, took their discharges and remained in the Middle Kingdom. Former marine Corp. David Adix decided he would remain in Shanghai and enter the business world, as did Virgil Findley. Findley is one of the rare mentions of an enlisted man with a wife in China. The men who chose to leave the military and enter into business would be accepted by Westerners in China.[5]

Why did these men decide to remain far from their own country? In general, those that remained were enlisted men. Some officers did elect to stay in China, but preliminary research indicates they were few in number. For an officer to remain in one location for a long period of time while in the service would do harm to his career. Most officers who served in China had well-established careers and, unlike the enlisted men, brought their families with them. It would take a great deal of fortitude to give up their security, especially in the Depression years, to remain in China. More importantly, many officers saw themselves as either middle-class or upper-middle-class and to remain in China would be living below what they perceived as their station in life.[6]

The enlisted men of the pre–World War II era, except during the Depression era, were poorly educated and most came from poor families. Even if they retired from the military, the amount of money they received would not be sufficient to live comfortably in the United States. Where else could an enlisted man with a pension amounting to only a few hundred dollars live as well as in China? Charles G. Finney's classic work on the army China hands in the 1920s puts it very succinctly. A senior noncommissioned officer's retired pay in 1927 came to approximately four hundred Chinese dollars a month. This small amount "represented wealth, when one considers that the average coolie in Tientsin ... grossed less than eighteen dollars American a year."[7]

The enlisted men who took their discharges after their first enlistment and remained in China did so for basically the same reasons as those who retired. This is especially true for the Depression years. They perceived China as the chance to rise above, at best, the blue collar status that awaited them in the United States.

2. The U.S. Military and Missionaries

Scattered throughout Glenn Howell's diary are his constant refrains against missionaries in China, and in this section there are a number of these entries. The naval officer was not in the minority on his feelings about missionaries. Richard McKenna, in *The Sand Pebbles*, arguably the best novel about the Yangtze Patrol, details some of the conflict with the missionaries. One of the main duties of the American military in China was the protection of lives. Most of the people who came under this rubric for the navy were missionaries.

William Sims, in 1901, informed a friend that he did not care for missionaries. Marine officer William A. Worton felt the missionaries in Peking were "a sorry lot." They were anti-military and did not care to mix with military people.[8] Another marine officer, James P. Berkeley, recalled when the American legation in Peking received a call from the American Board mission to help bring in the children from a school some fifteen miles north of the city. Berkeley assembled a platoon of marines and six trucks. The officer ordered machine guns mounted on the vehicles and large American flags were attached. The small, armed convoy departed "for the hinterland." They passed through a relative no man's land between Japanese and Chinese troops. The entire journey was made in a highly charged atmosphere.

The convoy arrived at the mission, only to have the person in charge inform the military rescuers that the children had already departed. As an afterthought, the missionary said that "since you are here with all those trucks, would you mind taking this silver and these rugs back to the American Board mission in town?" Berkeley, many years later, recalled: "So we rescued the missionaries' rugs and silver, anyway!"[9]

The religious zeal and inflexible morality of some of the missionaries helped to further the animosity of the military men. Berkeley recalled that at the opening of the Peking hotel there were naked mermaids painted on a wall. The "missionaries made them put bathing suits on the mermaids!" A former Yangtze Patrol officer recalled that when visiting a temple at Yochow with his captain and a missionary, the two naval officers removed their hats. The missionary thereupon wrote to the commander of the patrol admonishing the two officers for showing respect to heathen idols. The same officer recalled a hot July afternoon near the Wuhan area. The naval officer lead his landing force on a familiarization trip to a mission. He planned his arrival at the mission at noon so his sailors could rest in the shade. Upon reaching the site, however, they encountered eight-foot walls "topped with broken glass" and a refusal to allow the men inside. Only reluctantly were the sailors given even a drink of water. The officer then moved his men down the trail about a mile so they could sit under the shade of some trees. An elderly Chinese farmer appeared and invited the men to sit on benches under his fruit trees. Once settled in, the farmer brought out tea. The naval officer reflected on the difference in the "hospitality between a wealthy American mission ... in a large compound of allegedly Christian[s] ... and an elderly Chinese farmer to whom a loss of a single crop would be a disaster."[10]

Howell's entries makes it clear there existed a hierarchy of likes and dislikes among the military concerning missionaries. Usually, Catholics were accepted because they were well-educated. Medical missionaries, as Howell's entries clearly indicate, met with approval, as were those who tried to introduce better agricultural methods to the Chinese. What brought the most censure and outburst of anger were what would now be labeled fundamentalist.

The criticism of the missionaries in pre–World War II China is not relegated to only the military, some of it has been echoed in scholarship. The historian Nathaniel Peffer, for example, observed that some missionaries "were barely literate," and they never attempted to learn China's philosophy and religions.[11]

The friction between missionaries and those in the profession of arms may be seen as a natural thing, after all, their callings were diametrically opposed to each other. The missionaries could point to many of the men in the ranks as not "good people," as they drank and womanized. On the other hand, some military men would see people who did not drink as somewhat strange. (It should be pointed out, however, there were military men who did not drink, smoke, or womanize.)

An objective view of the missionaries in China prior to 1949 shows they were in the middle of a serious and, for the times, an insoluble problem. If the missionaries were seen by the Chinese as supporting the military, it would appear to many Chinese they also favored the unequal treaties. Further, they could be despised for supporting the gunboats. On the other hand, in times of turbulence and unrest, when large groups of undisciplined Chinese soldiers roamed the countryside, could they take the chance of gaining protection from anyone but Western military forces? Did they want to put themselves at the mercy of the courts of China? This conundrum never found a satisfactory solution. Instead, the military continued to supply protection while the two groups continued to warily eye each other, both trapped by their stereotyped visions of each other.

3. A Voyage up the Min River

In this last section of Howell's service aboard the *Palos*, the naval officer describes his voyage up the Min River. Howell also wrote about the ascent of the Min in the U.S. Naval Institute *Proceedings* in 1939. In the article, he also spoke about an unusual discovery in an unnamed village. In the summer of 1920, Howell took ashore with him Polly to act as an interpreter and began to walk inland to a village to obtain "information concerning the operations of farmers and fishermen."[12]

In the village Polly and Howell met the priest of "a ramshackle temple which stood on a high point beyond the hamlet." The priest took the two on a tour of his temple. They were led into a long, narrow hall. "An atmosphere of great age hung about the apartment." Running the length of the room and in the middle a long platform stood with "rows and rows of wooden images." Howell remarked, "We regarded without much interest the crudely carved and painted images…. Then abruptly we came to a stop."

Seated at the end of row sat the image of Marco Polo. "There was no doubt about it, for he wore the hat and costume of Venice in the thirteenth century. The artist had done well with Marco, and the Venetian sat there gazing out upon his dusty compeers with a haughty look as if he were sneering at the placidity of his piefaced fellows."

Through Polly, Howell asked who the image represented. The priest told him it belonged to a white who had come this way many, many years ago.

Upon his return to the *Palos*, Howell began to read about Marco Polo's journey's in the Middle Kingdom. Upon reading that great early traveler's description of the Chengtu plain, Howell became "determined to visit that place when and if we could manage it."

A year later a combination of very high water in the upper reaches of the Yangtze River and high water in the Min made Howell believe he could make the attempt and judged the activity as "dangerous but possibly practicable."

The patrol commander approved the attempt as it would "show the flag" and possibly have a "good influence" on Americans in the region should trouble happen in the future. Again, the value of Howell's diaries, and his reminiscences, is illustrated when he mentions that in 1921 there was a "considerable number of Americans in this region above Chungking. Some were scattered in towns along the river. There was a small colony at Kiating. There was a large group at Chengtu, the capital of the province, and there were others on beyond toward Thibet. Nearly all of these people were missionaries."

Howell's narrative in his diary is clearly the material he used to help write the article eighteen years after successfully completing his plan to ascend the Min.

Notes

1. George St. Lawrence, China Service Questionnaire to Dennis L. Noble, 6 June 1984, now in the China Repository (CR), NOA, NHC.

2. "Log of Howell," XLI, 11,311; China Service Questionnaires to Dennis L. Noble, all 1984, from William R. Hardcastle, Lawrence VanBrookhaven, Garry L. Murphy, Glen R. Smith, Kemp Tolley, all now located in CR, NOA, NHC.

3. William Leaderer, *All the Ships at Sea* (New York: William Sloane, 1950), 104–114.

4. Finney, in general, chose not to use the correct names of the enlisted men he wrote about and instead used composite descriptions. Finney wrote that the last communication he had with Smith was in 1938 and did not know the fate of the retired soldier. Finney, *Old China Hands*, 252–257.

5. *The Walla Walla* (Shanghai), (16 August 1930): 5; (30 September 1930): 5; and other issues for marines leaving the service and remaining in Shanghai. Military men have not ceased to remain in the Orient, and many of the reasons for remaining far from home are still the same as for the old China hands. A popular work on the subject is: Mike Sager, "Thailand's Home for Wayward Vets," *Rolling Stone*, (May 10, 1984), 27–28, 33–34, 36–37, 72.

6. The major exception to this generalization is Col. David D. Barrett, who spent twenty-three years in China during a career that spanned thirty-five years. John N. Hart, *The Making of an Army "Old China Hand:" A Memoir of Colonel David D. Barrett* (Berkeley, Ca.: Institute of East Asian Studies,1985), xi.

7. Finney, *Old China Hands*, 255.

8. William S. Simms to Pee Gee, 21 August 1901, "Personal Correspondence, July–November 1901," Papers of William S. Simms, Manuscript Division, Library of Congress, Washington, D.C.; Worton interview, 96, MCOH, MCHC.

9. LGEN James P. Berkeley interview by Benis P. Frank, (1971), 89–90, MCOH, MCHC.

10. Berkeley interview, 78. The officer that gave the information on the Chinese temple and the treatment of the missionaries to his landing party wishes to remain anonymous. His China service questionnaire remains in the possession of Dennis L. Noble.

11. Peffer, *The Far East*, 114. The standard work on missionaries in China is: Kenneth Scott Latourette, *A History of Christian Missions in China* (London: Society for Promoting Christian Knowledge, 1929). Another very useful work is, Paul A. Varig, *Missionaries, Chinese, and Diplomats: The American Protestant Missionary Movement in China, 1890–1952* (Princeton: Princeton University Press, 1958).

12. Unless otherwise noted, all material on the ascent of the Min by Howell is contained within, Glenn Howell, "Ascent of the Min," U. S. Naval Institute *Proceedings*, 65 (May 1939): 709–713.

The Diary

MAY 25, 1921—SIXTY MILES ABOVE WOOSANG [WUSONG].

We unmoored at five [A.M.] and sailed for Chungking with a deckload of coal ... [and we were later struck by heavy weather, with severe rolling.]

We passed a sinking junk some half mile distance, but we did not see her until we were past her. I was strongly tempted to take a chance and turn, but it meant of a certainty loosing my masts and my deck-load of coal and possibly the ship herself, nor could I have lowered a boat. So I stood on with a heavy heart, for the poor wretches were frantically waving an improvised signal of distress. However, I presently saw a junk standing toward them, and I have no doubt they were picked. up.

MAY 26, 1921—TEN MILES BELOW CHUNGKING. The mate, both doctors, and myself sat out on the fo'c'sle for an hour before dinner enjoying the sunset. That is the part of the day I love on this river—that and the early morning. I certainly am in love with China. It never fails to interest me keenly in all its phases. However, I shall be glad to start home in September, for I don't want to become a confirmed Easterner.

There is some difference now in the ship. I have put through many alternations that she needed—new pumps, new blowers, new anchor gear, and other things. I really think she is in better shape now than at any other period since her commissioning in 1914.

I like the looks of our new crew. They are a younger lot than the bunch we got rid of, but they are amenable to discipline and anxious to learn, and that goes a long way.

"...we moored to the bank one mile above ... a little city surrounded by a wall." This 1921 photograph is representative of such a walled city along the river. (Photograph courtesy of U.S. Naval Institute.)

MAY 28, 1921—ABOVE WEHU [WEIHU]. I gave the firemen a rest this morning, for they are green and I don't want to push them too hard right now. My practically new crew is a good one—or will be when I get it in ... shape, and I believe that we are going to have a happy summer.

JUNE 3, 1921—HANKOW. I called officially on everyone this morning—H.I.J.M.S. *Uji* and *Sagu* H.M.S. *Matu*, and the American British Consul Generals.

The *Uji* is a gunboat, the *Sagu* a cruiser. Their captains were polite as usual; we drank sake and whiskey. I have no difficulty in getting along with the Japs, but I certainly hate them. There is no doubt they reciprocate our feeling. Every wellposted American or Britisher out here with whom I have discussed the subject is convinced that war with Japan is not very remote now and that it will come within five years.

JUNE 5, 1921—CHENGLIN. [Howell receives orders for temporary duty on staff of Admiral Strauss.]

JUNE 6, 1921—OFF LOW POINT YANGTZE KIANG. The *Tangting*, a China Merchant's steamer, arrived this morning from Ichang bringing word of rioting there night before last just as she sailed. I hope that there will be something left to straighten out when we arrive.

JUNE 9, 1921—FIFTY MILES BELOW ICHANG. A Japanese merchant steamer gave us a chase all forenoon, and just a mile below Shasi [Shaxi] came up abeam of us. But they never got further than abeam. Though the fires were badly dirty, my brave firemen hurled coal into the teapots, with the agreeable results that we stepped away from our friend. How we love that flag!

JUNE 11, 1921—ICHANG. In the evening I landed a machine gun and two bluejackets at Carney's to protect the Bund, and I told him to be sure to see that the news of their being there got thoroughly spread abroad.

JUNE 12, 1921—FORTY MILES ABOVE ICHANG GORGE. I sparmoored at six in the evening forty miles above Ichang, having burned twenty tons of coal. Twice during the day I had to sparmoor to clean fires. And twice the ship was in serious danger due to the inability of the firemen to keep steam up. We got over two bad rapids by sending down the old men, though the kids did their level best.... At this rate, it will be impossible for me to make Kweichowfue [Kweichoufu], 110 miles up, and the first place we can obtain coal

...I decided to return to Ichang tomorrow morning and telegraph the Patrol Commander for more firemen with experience.

JUNE 13, 1921—ICHANG. We sailed at six, went merrily down the Gorges averaging 17 knots over the ground, and anchored at Ichang before nine o'clock. I immediately sent the Patrol Commander a telegram demanding trained firemen.

...[Everyone] is sure there will be more looting.... To all inquiries I announced that if looting began I would land and protect Americans.

[At a conference between Japanese and British gunboat commanders,] the British wanted to land at sunset and tell the General to remove his soldiers from the foreign settlement as landing parties from the gunboats would guard it during the night. I refused to agree to this for two reasons: it relieved the General of all responsibility and invited looting; it is contrary to international law. In the end they all came around to my way of thinking [to land only if disturbances broke out], and we divided the foreign settlement into three districts—the Japs taking the upriver section, the *Palos* the downriver part, and the British in the Central Part. I was careful to pad the British between the Japs and my gobbies for obvious reasons. We arranged a searchlight watch to be kept by each ship in turn, agreed to land at the first indication of trouble from the beach, and the conference ended.

[Nothing happens.]

JUNE 16, 1921—ICHANG. Cooper tiffined with the General. Six of the Sinbin were brought in just before tiffin, having been captured by the soldiers that morning. They were defiant, impassive. One of them was an important leader. The General chopped off his hands and gouged his eyes out, beheaded the rest, and then ordered tiffin.

And this is the Twentieth Century!

At eight I went on board the Japanese steamer *Taoyen* for passage to Chenglin. [Howell is to perform temporary duty as aide to Admiral Strauss.]

JUNE 17, 1921—CHENGLIN. The *Taoyen* being a Japanese steamer, I found the passengers stupid....

JUNE 20, 1921—CHANGSHA. I went on board the *Wilmington* [the flagship of the fleet] in the Customs' sampan and reported to Captain Wood, the Commander of the Yangtze Patrol, and to Admiral Strauss.... The Admiral took me below to the cabin, and I told him and Captain Wood about the Ichang looting in detail. My action afterward the Admiral thoroughly approved.

We arrived at Yochow [Yochow], and the Admiral sent me ashore in the ship's dinghy with Sue [Su][an interpreter], ... with orders to take a look-see at the city, find out the cause of the fire, and observe conditions. I had to walk the length of the town to find the fire: it had been occasioned by somebody upsetting a kerosene lamp, and ten houses had been burned. There were no more than the usual soldiers about the streets and everything was tranquil. So I went back on board and reported, and the *Wilmington* upanchored and headed up the Tangting Lake for the Seang River and Changsha.

I suppose that I answered a thousand questions today. I am apparently the first man the Admiral has run into who has made any effort to study the Yangtze and its towns....

I tiffened with Captain Wood and the Admiral. All is not well between them, and I believe I know the reason. Captain Wood has been on the river since January, but until this trip he has never been above Nanking. The consequence is—to put it baldly—he knows nothing about the locale of his job, and the Admiral has discovered it.[1] The Admiral flatly disapproves [of Wood] ... permitting _____ to put armed gobs on Chinese-owned junks chartered by American firms. So do I.

We arrived at Changsha at four o'clock in the afternoon.... Directly [after] we anchored, I took the Admiral ashore for a walk through the native city and then back along the Malu. He was keenly interested in the shops and the little details of Chinese life.

JUNE 21, 1921—AT SEA YANTZE KIANG. In the evening the Admiral and I had another long talk. I like him enormously, and we think alike on a great many subjects. He told me many of his experiences in command of the North Sea Mine Barrage. We discussed the prevailing discontent in the Navy, bolshevism, the unsolvable mess here in China, the future of the Navy, disarmament, missionaries, and religion. He is very well read, and we got off onto the subject of books, upon which he has very pronounced tastes. I enjoy my talks with him very much, and I believe that he likes me.

JUNE 24, 1921—AT SEA YANTZE KIANG. Another long day cruising. It seems strange not to have to be forever stopping and cleaning fires the way I do all the time.

JUNE 26, 1921—FORTY MILES ABOVE ICHANG. The Admiral and Buchanan came on board at six [A.M.], we broke his four starred flag, and the USS *Palos*, flagship of the Asiatic Fleet, got underway and stood upriver into the Gorges.

The ship made the best run I have ever seen her make. We had specially imported a horribly expensive coal from Chungking for the occasion, and we slid over the rapids with the greatest of ease. No accidents occurred at all.

Admiral Strauss is the first Commander-in-Chief of our fleet who has come up the Gorges and I think that today's trip has accomplished a good deal for the future of the *Palos* and the *Monocacy*. He has seen the necessity of putting good men and officers on these ships, of keeping them in excellent repair. He has grasped the difficulties under which we labor. I should not be surprised to be ultimately relieved by a Commander, for the duty up here really requires a man of more experience than people around my time have.

JUNE 27, 1921—ICHANG. [Admiral returns and Howell's temporary duty ends. Howell visits a temple at Santung [Santong] and is amazed to find initials and dates of Westerners who had been there in 1849.]

JUNE 28, 1921. [In Howell's absence, a junk rammed the *Palos*, drifted off, and then capsized. Then a sampan, filled with missionaries from Szechwan, capsized.] Our gobs were very quick. Smiley got one of the boys as he floated past. They manned the [*Palos'*] sampan, dashed after the overturned sampan, righted it and got the other boy out from underneath it, and then rowed madly to Mrs. Hooker and pulled her in. It was very excellent work, and all Ichang is talking about it. Mr. Squire was rescued by a Chinese sampan, but Mr. Hooker was drowned. Neither of the boys could swim; so the feat of their being saved was all the more remarkable.

JULY 2, 1921—FORTY-EIGHT MILES ABOVE ICHANG. [After waiting for the river,] got underway at 5:00 [A.M.] and stood up the Ichang Gorge. The morning proved bad going—a very stiff current all the way, though we had no particularly bad trouble getting over the rapids.... We did better during the afternoon and I sparmoored at half past six above the Yeh Tan, [Tetan] now but a harmless race, though a devil at lower water.

JULY 3, 1921—KWEICHOWFU. I will admit that I am profoundly relieved to arrive here all right. This is the most dangerous cruising in the world, and the Ichang-Kweichowfu stretch is the worse.

JULY 4, 1921—KWEICHOWFU. Next Fourth of July I want to be in the mountains or at the seashore. I have suddenly decided I want to go home.

JULY 5, 1921—SIX MILES ABOVE KWEICHOWFU. We started gaily enough, but one boiler began priming. So at 5:30 [A.M.] I anchored, we pumped out the boiler, filled it with fresh water and got underway again. Fifteen minutes later a tube burst in the same boiler. Fortunately, there was a place at hand where we managed to sparmoor and just in time too, for the stream was dropping rapidly. Darn this ship! Everytime I think I have her fixed up, she has to go and pull a new one on me....

JULY 9, 1921—FOUCHOW [FOUCHOU]. I almost lost the ship twice today—once in the last rapid below Fouchow—but to begin with the F'oumientan [Foumiantan].

We got underway at 5:00 [A.M.] and reached F'oumientan at 5:40. It is a nasty rapid and right on top of it is the Kwanyintan [Kuanyintan], another bad one, with hardly a breathing spell in between. However, we weathered those and breezed along until 8:30, at which time having made good 16 miles we anchored on account of our miserable coal and cleaned fires.

We got underway again at 10:30, had good going for a bit, and then hit more rapids and races. The N'oukeitan [Nougeitan] was vicious, but the last one—but two or three miles from Fouchow was the worse of the lot. The stream was low, in spite of having our best firemen on watch, and we got stuck in the rapid. We could gain nothing, and below us was a nasty heap of rocks. For about five minutes it was touch and go, but finally by extraordinary efforts the firemen got enough steam up to shove her over. Even old Lee, the Number One pilot, confessed afterward that he was frightened.

We anchored two miles above Fouchow at two o'clock with 3½ tons of coal left in the bunkers.... We were anchored in five fathoms of water close to the bank and a wire out to stakes on the beach. There was little current in so close; so everything being secure, I had my cot put up on the bridge, and I turned in at four for a nap.

At six a big junk passed between the ship and the bank, pulled the wire loose, and jerked the ship ahead. And as she settled back with the current the anchor broke ground. I awoke just as the ship began to drag. Once started, she went fast. I let go the other anchor, but away we dragged into the river, the *Palos* gathering sternway every moment. We could hear the anchors scraping and bumping over the rocks underneath, and I expected the anchor chains to part at any moment.

[The engineers] got up steam in a marvelously—and dangerously— short interval, and presently we got the engines going just fast enough to hold the ship where she was in midstream. I held her there for an hour until we had a full head of steam up.

Then began the fight to get the anchors up. The starboard one argued the matter for ten minutes, but we finally got him as he bounded loose from a rock. But the port one refused to budge. At 7:30 it grew totally dark, but I hated to give up that anchor and 30 fathoms of chain. We steamed ahead on it, to starboard and to port, stopped the ship and let the current pull her back until the chain straightened with a jerk that shook the ship. Six times we broke her loose from the rocks only to have her catch again. Fathom by fathom we cinched up on her. The cogs slipped once, and we lost ten preciously earned fathoms. At half past eight, we finally got her, though her stock was horribly bent. Very cautiously, we stood over to the beach. We anchored, and then as soon as possible we got three lines to the beach, up through a cornfield, and around a big tree. It was a quarter to ten before we finally got the refractory *Palos* tied up so she couldn't break loose again.

Then the old Chinese gentleman who owned the cornfield and tree screamed out through the night for us to go away. So just to make sure that somebody didn't cast off our lines during the night, I had the Mate put an armed guard over the tree. I was secretly amused at the stern air which two of my newly caught gobbies buckled on revolvers and canteens, looked to their ammunition, and set off to the beach for the cornfield and the tree....

The water is rising fast, and Lee tells me that we shall probably have trouble with the rapids tomorrow.

What a day!

JULY 10, 1921—SHENGTUO. Another merry day!

We got underway at five [in the morning] ... and stood upriver. The Yangtze is rising rapidly, and as a result we bucked one rapids after another. It was a constant battle with the river.

About a mile below Hwang Tsao [Huang Cao] (Yellow Flower) Gorge, we sparmoored to the bank and cleaned fires in order to have the best possible steam through the Gorge. At 10:00, we got underway again and a bit later approached the rapid at the entrance to the Gorge. It was shooting out of the confined Gorge with a deafening roar, and I felt from the moment I saw it that we could not make it at this water. However, we went right ahead and smashed full tilt into it. We might as well tried to steam up Niagara. When the steam dropped to 100 lbs., I stopped, dropped back, waited a bit until [the engineers] got steam up to the popping point, and tried once again.

It was entirely useless, for the current is now stronger than the best possible speed of the ship—13¼ knots. The coal is good, my best firemen were on watch, and I had to give up. We edged over to the bank and sparmoored in quiet water alongside a steep bank covered with corn.

The river is undoubtedly on the rampage, so I tied the ship up with wires to sturdy trees, painted watermarks on a rock on the beach, and prepared to wait until the Yangtze decided to behave. At a quarter to twelve, Lee reported that water was coming into the forward hold.

"What next?" I groaned at Julian.

Neither of us was unduly alarmed, for the leak was not unexpected when one considered the frightful strain to which the bow was subjected to last night. However, we investigated the forward hold only to discover that the water was leaking in from the paint locker. Then we opened the paint locker amidst some excitement to discover a horrible mess. It was nearly full of a combination ... made up of river water, various and diverse paints, cement, oil, and the clothes of Ferguson, the gallant center of the *Palos* Pilons.[The ship's football team.]

We pumped it out and found that two small holes had been punched in the bow by the flukes of the port anchor, which investigation developed to have been snarled up with the wires last night. It was a simple matter to patch the holes....

What a situation! An American war vessel in full commission tied up to trees on the edge of a cornfield near a tiny Chinese hamlet. We may be hung up here for a week. Coal was my only concern, and since we can get that [at the nearby village] there is nothing to worry about. The country folk will supply us with eggs, chickens, ducks, geese, and corn. Marooned we are, but no one gives a whoop. We are forty-five miles from Chungking, the river is rising rapidly. Let her rise!

It is very interesting business this getting over a rapid. You sneak your ship on it with safety values popping. Now you are in the very edge of it. Then you go full speed and smash into it. There is a grand smother of foam; the water pours over your fo'c'sle; the ship buries her nose; she vibrates all over; the fireman stoke furiously; her bow edges up into the tongue of the rapid, shaking off the water; there is a tremendous roar; the pilot is at the wheel—old Chinese, serenely edges the ship a little to starboard, a bit to port; you keep your eyes on the beach; inch by inch the ship gains; she stops, steaming frantically at that vicious, overwhelming sweep and rush of water; she is making no headway. This is the critical moment. You give a command. The crew rush forward into the bow. The stern comes up; the bow goes down; very slowly the ship begins to forge ahead again. Of a sudden, as if hidden chains were slipped, the ship lurches ahead, rolling. You are over the rapid; you slow to standard speed. The banks guide by as usual; the crew disperses aft. Astern the roar dies to a murmur. You rarely look back.

JULY 11, 1921—SHENGTUO. We lay here quietly tied up to the trees in our cornfield all day. I spent most of the daylight hours on the

"What a situation! An American war vessel ... tied up to trees on the edge of a cornfield." (Photograph by Glenn F. Howell, located in his diary.)

bridge, which in port I convert into a combination study and bedroom....

Dunbar, my radioman[,] who is also the commissary steward, set off with Joe [Howell's Chinese steward] at six and returned with chickens, eggs, and pork all of which he obtained from a village four miles from here.

Then, too, the peasants of the countryside come bearing their little store of eggs and fowls and beans down on the bank abreast the ship and wait patiently there until someone comes out and buys their produce. Eggs cost practically nothing. A good chicken sells for 200 cash, which is 10 [cents in] American money.

In the afternoon, I permitted fifteen of the crew to go hiking into the country, and they had a great walk. The Doctor and I went for a brief stroll at sunset, but it was a brief one.

The peasantry about are a simple, primitive people. Their huts are of mud, thatched, near bamboo groves, and overrun with children and fowls and dogs and pigs. I see but few cats in China. Here are also white goats, a fair breed of cattle, and an occasional water buffalo.

Their farming is primitive. Their method of preparing the soil is to stir it with sharp sticks. A plow would be practically useless on account of the rocks and also the tiny size of the fields, which are tucked away in every nook and corner of the mountains. They grow corn, rice, beans, some tobacco, pumpkins, squashes, and the tree from which wood oil is obtained. (I am going to study botany before I come out to China a third time.)

These people seem to be contented with their simple life. They do not recognize silver coins: their mode of exchange is cash, 200 cash making one Mexican dollar or 50 [cents] American money. Were it not for the soldiers and robbers, they would be one of the happy peoples of the world—if any such exist.

JULY 12, 1921—SHENGTUO. In the afternoon, I set off shortly after tiffining with Red Evans and Polly to buy some chickens and to look the countryside over.... At about an hour from the ship, we passed a fair sized farm house, and upon Polly inquiring if they had chickens for sale and their affirmative reply we entered the courtyard, stepping over a baby water buffalo in order to get in.

The entire family eased out into the courtyard to see us. I counted eighteen persons, but I suppose there were some bedridden souls who couldn't come out. A bench was fetched, we sat down, and the bargaining began.

The house was built of mud, the roof was thatched, and the windows were simple gratings. The courtyard was muddy: a huge water buffalo near the entrance gate stood guard over its baby. Two pigs, one cat, and a few chickens loafed comfortably about.

Most of the family had gathered near us on the step just outside the door of the house. There were four babies, the littlest held by Grandpa, who deigned not to come outside but blinked at us from the interior. There were six women and girls—all with bowed feet, and seven men and boys—everybody dirty and wearing the inevitable blue cotton garments of different shades of fading—or, one might say, fades of shading.

After much conversation shading all the way from discussion to argument in which all hands took part, it was finally agreed to sell us chickens at 280 cash per catty. We accepted the terms.

There was a mad scramble after the chickens. One of the ladies went in and brought out a primitive cutty scale. One of the men fetched a pipe, crammed fresh tobacco leaves in it, and offered it.

The lady weighed each chicken with a knowing air, but it soon developed that neither she nor anyone else around there could read the scale with any surety. Polly in the end had to be in charge and straighten them out. As each chicken was weighed, its legs were tied with strands of twisted straw and it was unceremoniously dumped into a basket. Then they were forever flopping loose and getting out again and being chased and fetched back. Finally we accumulated six. Then the real calculating of the day began—the sum that should be paid in dollars for we had no cash. The entire family gathered around the counting frame, and the uproar speedily became deafening. They finally figured out that they wanted 4400 cash, or 2 dollars and 200 cash. We gave them 3 dollars, and they went into the house and presently returned with the change—1900 cash—strung on straw strings and weighing more than the six chickens. We hired one of the men to carry the cash and the chickens back to the ship and departed, leaving the family in high good humor.

The transaction had consumed an hour and a half. Yet not a soul around the place had done anything resembling work during that time. Yet they are miserably poor. Time means nothing to the Chinese. To be sure, today is today, but there is always tomorrow and mas que anyway....

I left Red and Polly to buy what eggs and poultry they could and came back on board the ship, took a bath, and then read Henry Van Dyke.

JULY 13, 1921—SHENGTUO. ...I rather like this being marooned, for one gets through a vast amount of work done, and it is such a relief nowadays to be out of touch with the world ... We pick up an occasional bit of news by radio, something no other ship has ever done up this far, for the mountains usually raise the dickens with radio. We cannot send, of course, but we can receive from the *Elcano* at Ichang and the *Wilmington* at Hankow. We get a bit from Cavite [the Philippines], too, but only occasionally.

JULY 15, 1921—SHENGTUO. During the night the water stopped rising, hesitated, and began to fall. We therefore laid our plans to leave tomorrow, though it is doubtful if we can make it. The river rose at this point 32 feet from the time we tied up at the bank. It will probably drop as much within the next five days. Small floods may be caused by local rains, but a really big ... [rise] comes usually from the very sources of the Yangtze, 1,000 miles above Chungking and is apparently due to the snow melting in the Himalayas.

JULY 16, 1921—SHENGTUO. I thought it worth while to take a chance at the rapid this morning, for the water is steadily falling. I made three attempts to get over and spent an hour altogether in the rapid, but it is still too much for us. Everybody was highly disgusted, but the *Palos* is not designed for sustained high speed, and I had to give up and ease the ship over the bank and moor her as before....

The *Monocacy* arrived in Ichang yesterday—(we picked it up by radio)—but she will wait until we can get our pilots and some good coal down to her. I think I shall send the Mate down to help and advise Hanson, for they are all new on there, and at this season of the year they will have a hard job getting up to relieve us.

JULY 17, 1921—SHENGTUO. I sent Dunbar to Chang-chou [Zhang Zhou?]—a twelve mile hike—with a telegram to the Patrol Commander, telling of our predicament and stating that I would try again as soon as the river fell some more.

JULY 18, 1921—CHUNGKING. We shoved off from our cornfield, and after a twenty minute-inch-by-inch, erg-by-erg struggle with the Loowater or Palostan, as we have dubbed our friend the rapid, we finally got over with no leeway at all. Yells of joy arose when the devoted vessel finally got over the damned thing, and I passed around cigars amongst the pilots and the firemen.

It was hard going all day long, for this amazing river is on the rise again. Had we waited till noon, the Palostan would have been thrown back again....

The Gorge ten miles below Chungking proved bad going, but we fought our way up it and presently came to the great golden Buddha, which sits in it twenty foot high majesty serenely by the riverside. As we passed the god, the pilots fired off a string of firecrackers and the entire ship's company solemnly chinchinned to the sacred one.[2]

So we came to Chungking. We passed my old Jap friend, the *Toba*, well below the city, ran across the corner between the Yangtze and Kialing Rivers, followed the waterfront, crossed the river again, passed H.M.S. *Cockchafer*, which got up [the river] but can't get down, and came to our moorings. I have rarely experienced the sense of relief I felt when I stopped the engines and the riding chain took up the strain. Here at last was the end of my fourteen hundred miles of journeying from Shanghai.

Sidney Harris was the first of the old gang on board. He offered me his bungalow for the summer, and I thankfully accepted it. I suspect that it will be a sort of bachelor's hangout while we are here.

Breezy Windham, Sidney Harris, Julian, the Doctor, and I ran over to the *Cockchafer* before dinner for a cocktail and brought back St. Aubyns, the First Lieutenant (Captain Thurstfield is up in the hills.) They left early for all hands were tired.

I think I will like Chungking as well this summer as I did last year.

JULY 19, 1921—CHUNGKING. I rose at six and dawdled away two hours at my oldtime occupation of watching the early morning procession of funerals, weddings, and marketers passing the ship. At ten thirty I left the ship in my chair, ... crossed the river, and called upon the Consul. I found him to be a very nice youngster named Howard Bucknell, Junior, about twenty-five, a student interpreter who has just finished a marvelous trip through the edge of Tibet with Major Magruder, our Military Attache in Peking. He is temporarily filling in until a regular Consul comes. I arranged to hold the investigation into the shooting of a Chinese soldier by sailors from the *Monocacy* last March tomorrow on board the *Palos*....

JULY 20, 1921—CHUNGKING. [On the day of the investigation, we] waited until eleven to see if the Chinese would send any representatives, but since they failed to appear I went ahead at eleven and held

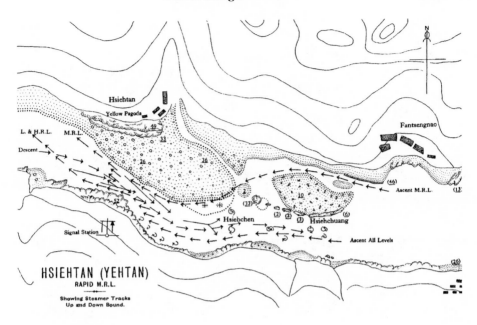

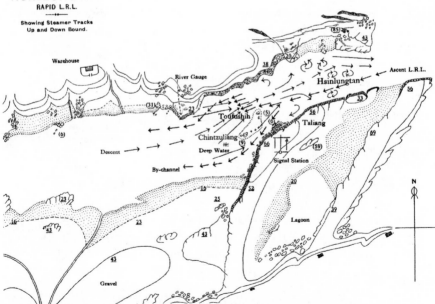

Top: **The Hsiehtan rapids.** *Bottom:* **The Hsinlungtan rapids. (From:** *A Handbook for the Guidance of Shipmasters on the Ichang-Chungking Section of the Yangtze River,* **1931.)**

the darn thing and found that the soldiers fired first upon the sailors in their junk. Hence the blame rests with the Chinese....

I have been somewhat worried about Captain Wood, (the Commander of the Yangtze Patrol) and a gang of Navy women he is bringing up here. They are due on the *Alice Dollar*, and I must confess that I don't know what to do with them. I had made up my mind, however, that under no conditions would I ask people up here to look out for them. There has been quite enough of that sort of thing going on. But Breezy Windham stepped in quite on his own accord and offered to take them in. I warned him, and then I thankfully and gratefully accepted his offer.

JULY 21, 1921—CHUNGKING. At four thirty [P.M.] the *Alice Dollar* arrived. I hastily dressed and dashed via my chair for the noble vessel. I found on board her Captain Wood, his mother, his wife, Mrs. Baum (the wife of the Captain of the *Wilmington*) and Mrs. Hanson (the wife of the Captain of the *Monocacy*). These ladies and Captain Wood accepted with eclat the invitation of Breezy.

I suppose it would be appropriate if I explained right here that I dislike nineteen out of twenty of the Navy women I meet out here. They are almost without exception eager to take all they can get, provided it is free. They will be anybody's guest indefinitely—so long as it is free. They go running all over the Orient, confidently throwing themselves on the mercy of strangers. They all like cocktails and "a good time," provided someone else pays for it.

Mrs. Hanson has a legitimate excuse for coming up here: Yen will be here all winter. The others calmly accepted Breezy's proposal with the handwaving of royalty. None of the women is the twentieth woman.

Captain Wood plans to remain here two weeks, but the women will probably go away in the next trip of the *Robert Dollar*. The present plot is that as soon as the *Monocacy* arrives here, the *Palos* will take the Patrol Commander down to Hankow and thence proceed to Shanghai for repairs and liberty. I had hoped to stay longer up here, but it doesn't make much difference for it is now merely a question of weeks as to when I shall be relieved and start home.

JULY 22, 1921—CHUNGKING. At 10:00 [A.M.] General Wang, the Adjutant of the First Army of Szechwan, called in regard to the shooting of the soldier, and I spent two hours diplomatically assisting him to save face. He in the end was quite frank and pathetic about it.

He told me he knew that the whole business was the fault of the soldiers, but that he could not go back empty handed to them for they would be very angry and might mutiny. He finally ended the thing by requesting me to discuss the matter with the Commissioner of Foreign Affairs, and I agreed to that.

I was amused at one thing tonight. It appears that the only telephones in Chungking are connecting Bollard's house with Reid's. But alas! Mrs. Bollard and Mrs. Reid have quarreled and are not speaking to each other.

[Some of the navy women depart on this day, with the remaining women of the party departing on July 26.]

JULY 27, 1921—CHUNGKING. At ten [A.M.] there came on board the American Consul and the Chinese Commissioner of Foreign Affairs to reopen the investigation into the shooting of the soldier by the *Monocacy* sailors. I think that I have finally scotched that affair for good, though it took an enormous effort to accomplish it.

JULY 28, 1921—CHUNGKING. Julian and I got back on board at nine [from the bungalow]—somewhat to the disgust of Captain Wood, whom I have grown heartily to dislike. I think it annoys him that I refuse to stick around to amuse him.

JULY 30, 1921—CHUNGKING. ...Julian met me with a telegram containing news that affects us strongly. The *Monocacy* sailed from Ichang for Chungking day before yesterday.... She limped back to Ichang ... the next morning, having cracked her starboard high pressure cylinder. This is a serious accident. The ship must go to Hankow, and under the most favorable conditions cannot arrive in Chungking before the middle of September. Nothing would please me better than to stay in the Upper Yangtze until I am relieved.

AUGUST 1, 1921—CHUNGKING. August!—my tour of duty on the Asiatic Station is rapidly nearing its close. I am glad, but I am sorry—but mostly glad....

[Went to tiffin with the Consul, Sidney Harris, the Postal Commissioner, and Captain Wood].... In the middle ... [of tiffin], Sidney gave a great start and a cry.

"What is the trouble, Mr. Harris?" asked our host politely, and all hands looked in surprise upon the flushed Sidney.

"Captain Howell pinched me," said Sidney, haltingly.

A shocked silence followed, but I broke it by seriously remarking that it began to look as if it were high time Sidney left drink alone if it affected him like that. Sidney was in a shocking rage the rest of the meal, but being dignified and British it was probably good for his soul. I don't know what Captain Wood thought of the proceeding.

I went up to the bungalow in the afternoon and then walked over to the Second Range [of hills] to call on Statler. Instead of that, I blundered in upon a lair of missionaries playing at tennis. They were very nice—too nice, in fact—and I sat down in the midst and radiated the Good Time I was having.

It's no use: missionaries and I simply don't mix, and my motto is to stay clear of them. All that I ask is that they leave me alone. But every once in awhile some intrusive reforming soul gets too close to the bat— and bing!

Amongst those present at the missionary tennis tea was one Miss Lindblad, a missionary lady with thin hair and a face like the rejected design of a gargoyle, who is probably very good and certainly very sour. She wrote a most unpleasant letter to the Consul last fall about my crew's bungalow, waiting however, until the *Palos* was clear of Chungking before she wrote it. She received a reply that must have offended her, for she, though present at tea, made no sign of recognition to me— nay, her countenance drooped like the tail shaft of a ship that has been running all summer up and down the Gorges....

AUGUST 4, 1921—CHUNGKING. Captain Wood and I went over to the city this morning, for he wanted to buy some silk. I never go over there unless it is absolutely necessary, for Chungking is the dirtiest city I have ever seen, and I do not like the misery and squalor and horrible sights of dying people one always sees....

We found out this morning that our pilots will arrive tomorrow in the *Robert Dollar*. If they do, Captain Wood will go in the *Dollar* and we shall sail day after tomorrow for Kiating [Jiating]. I am particularly desirous of making that trip, for the *Palos* has never been above Suifu. I have, however, been afraid that I couldn't get rid of the Patrol Commander soon enough.

AUGUST 5, 1921—CHUNGKING. Much joy and also bliss! Ships poured in this afternoon—the *Shuhun* and then both *Dollars*.

At five, Captain Wood and I left the ship for the *Robert Dollar*, and

I was glad to have his pennant flutter down and mine go up again. He made himself a nuisance. He—However, there's no use to knock a guy when he's down, for Captain Wood has been passed over three times for permanent Captain and this last selection finishes him. He is to be relieved by Rear Admiral W. H. Bollard next month, an appointment I do not yet understand, for he is one of the upper admirals. At any rate, I delivered Captain Wood on board the *Robert Dollar*, we had several drinks, and then I said farewell and went with deep content back to the *Palos*.

AUGUST 6, 1921—SOME TEN MILES ABOVE CHUNGKING. At
ten I shoved off ... and stood upriver, bound at last on my long cherished trip to Kiating, the headwaters of steam navigation. For a time all went merrily, but just after everything got settled down and we had been underway an hour or so, there came a frightful thump in the engineroom, and Jimmy McDonald headed for the beach and anchored—(fortunately we were out of sight of Chungking.)

Investigation developed the fact that exactly the same accident had happened to us that happened to the *Monocacy*. In her case, the nut on the crosshead of her starboard high pressure backed off. Ours had sheared off. Our men must have been quicker than her's to shut off the steam, or her's may have happened on the upstroke and our's on the downstroke, or else we simply had luck. At any rate, I don't think that any permanent damage has been done, though we have to be here until tomorrow to fix everything up. I expected something to go flooey, and I'm glad it's nothing fatal.

It seemed very natural—this spending the day abreast a cornfield....

Sixty miles above Chungking.

We tested out the starboard engine at seven and found it all right. We had planned to get underway at eight, but a thick fog held us up until ten minutes to nine....

The river up here is swift, but not difficult. We went through two easy rapids and one small gorge.

AUGUST 9, 1921—SIAO SIN KI [XIAOXINQIL?]. The current
[en route to this location] is swift, and we had to go full speed three or four times to get over rapids. The river is as wide as ever, but it is much shoaler, and the rapids are caused by shoals rather than by constrictions of the banks. We anchored a bit before dark at Siao Sin Ki, a village twelve miles above Luchow, where we shall coal again.

Lee tells me that the *Palos* and some soldiers argued with guns here during 1918.

AUGUST 10, 1921—LUCHOW. I learned quite accidentally that the war was over between the United States and Germany and Austria on July 2. Rather an absurd way for us to end the thing! Woody is to be thanked as usual.—I suppose history will record him as a great man. Never will I admit it—not to my dying day plus—of course, my opinion makes a lot of difference.

AUGUST 11, 1921—LITCHANG [LICHANG]. A majority of the natives go entirely nude up here—an odd fact, for I do not believe that any other people in the world, even the Aborigines of Africa, wear absolutely no clothes.

We excite the liveliest interest as we go along: it is evident that gunboats are an unfamiliar sight up here.

We anchored for the night abreast Litchang, a walled town. Every town of importance in this region has a high stone wall surrounding it—with the gates securely closed before sunset. Back to primeval times!

AUGUST 12, 1921—SUIFU. The annals of Suifu date from 134 BC when it was established the capital of a principality by Emperor Kien Yuen [Jian Yuan]. It is built on a rocky promontory between the Min and Yangtze....

The coal will not come tomorrow, so at half past two I left ... and walked some five miles up the bank of the Kinsha [Ginsha]. I saw quite enough to convince me that I have no desire to take the ship up the Kinsha. Shoals, rocks, sandbars abound and I see no reason—nothing to be gained by risking the ship....

AUGUST 13, 1921—SUIFU. Dr. C. E. Thompkins and Mr. Moncrief called this morning and breakfasted with us.[3] They are of the better type of missionary and proved of much assistance to us with information on coal, Kiating, and Chengtu....

AUGUST 14, 1921—THIRTY MILES ABOVE MIN RIVER. We sailed at the crack o'dawn and made heavy steaming all day, anchoring at ten and again at four on account of dirty fires, the coal not being any too good. The Min is narrow, and the current averaged eight knots. So all we could make good was thirty miles—about a third of the distance to Kiating.

The Yellow Dragon Gorge is composed of red sandstone cliffs on either side and is beautiful....

We cruised for an hour this afternoon with less that two feet under our bottom, a circumstance that doesn't worry me at all any more....

AUGUST 15, 1921—KIEN WI HIEN.

A very good run today, considering the coal ... I anchored first at nine to clean fires—on a sandy beach which was populated ten minutes after the Killick went down by most of my gobbies in the scantiest of garbs—playing ball, swimming and running races. Fully one hundred natives rushed to the spot from all directions, and a large audience was ours until we sailed.

An occasional gunboat—one or two a year—is the only craft other than junks or sampans they see. The *Monocacy* was here in 1914. The *Palos* has never been here before. I can't understand why not—with all this fascinating country crying to be explored.

At two thirty we came to Kien Wi Hien, a walled city 68 miles above Suifu and anchored for the rest of the day to coal.

AUGUST 16, 1921—SIPA [XIPA].

We had a horrible run today, making good but 21 miles, 13 of which we made this morning and the river shoaled so that the steaming is becoming more and more difficult. The current runs between 8 and 9 knots, and at about noon we struck a rapid ... that nearly proved our Waterloo. We got in it, went ahead full speed, and then stuck. It was one of those places where you cannot turn around, cannot go ahead, and dare not go downstream stern first, for had we done so, we would have smashed against cliff or grounded on the shoals. After thirty five minutes—and rather anxious minutes—we got over it.

An audience of 200 watched us anchor at the little village of Sipa. The current is so strong that we not only had one anchor down, but it was necessary to put out two wires to trees and sparmoor, also.

There soon gathered a crowd of 500 people which shifted in personnel, but not in numbers until well into the night. It is one of the few occasions they have ever seen a steam vessel, and it is the first time one has ever anchored here.

I went for a short walk at dusk, and was amused to see ... the thrifty housewives near the ship ... had set out in front of ... [their] house[s] small tables on which were arranged with mathematical exactness wee piles of peanuts, each containing five, so that the spectators on the bank could refresh themselves as required and stove off the pangs of hunger at one cash per pile ($\frac{1}{21}$ of an American cent).

AUGUST 17, 1921—KIATING. I had several doubts this morning as to whether we could make it. Cruising resolved itself into one constant scrap with the river. We were underway at five, but we ran into a fog at seven and had to anchor for an hour. At a bit past eight we went on—struggles on would be a better way to put it. The river [en route] is running most[ly] ... at 9 or 10 knots, and it was a fight all the way. Once we spent an hour in one rapid, going full speed for 20 minutes straight—a feat for the *Palos*.

Kiating appeared in view. We struggled on. One last full speed bell at the river off the corner of the city where the Yaho[Yahou] River roars into the Min, one last set of horrible soundings of five and six feet over a rocky bottom, and we crossed to the bank just above the city and anchored in 12 feet of water and 30 fathoms of chain. We put out three wires to trees against a freshet, and I left the bridge with a great sigh of relief. I have brought the ship up as far as she can possibly go, for the present cruising end of the Min is one mile above our anchorage, and I am satisfied. We are 1635 miles from Shanghai....

We got any number of 5 feet soundings today, and at one horrible place I cruised for 20 yards in four feet of water, the ship drawing 3 feet 9 inches.

Doctor Barter and Bollard called at half past two. Barter is an Illinois medical missionary who has been here four years and in China thirteen.[4] He, Julian, and eight of my men arranged to leave for Mt. Omei [Mt. Emei] tomorrow morning.

Bollard is on leave from Chungking. He and Mrs. Bollard leave here day after tomorrow for Chengtu by boat, and Doctor Carll arranged to go with them....

AUGUST 18, 1921—KIATING. I left the ship at half past two and walked four or five miles upstream along the bank. At a point one mile above our anchorage it is impossible at this height of water to navigate the *Palos* due to the narrowness and shallowness of the stream. However, I don't want to take the ship any higher up. C'est suffisante—as we say in French. (The idea of this casual remark is to annoy anyone who reads this log without my permission.)

Above Kiating, the Min narrows and divides into numerous shallow channels between little islands. The borders of its banks are flat, and truck gardening appears to be the main occupation. Indeed, I could almost fancy myself in the States in some places, but about the time I could convince myself that the terrain looked exactly like a country landscape at home I was sure to turn a corner and come upon a widow's arch or a roadside joss.

We took on board 7 tons of coal today, rotten—but the best to be had here—for which I paid at the rate of 10 cash per catty or about $8 Mex ($4 American currency) per ton. By the time one translates catties into pounds and piculs into tons and cash into dollars and Mexican dollars into gold dollars it is apposite to call a policeman and arrest the madman.[5]

AUGUST 19, 1921—KIATING. I inspected the holds this afternoon and then turned to straightening out my desk—a staggering job.

At four I crossed the Min River ... and had a delightful climb to a point abreast the head of—I believe—the largest Buddha in China. From the village at the base of the red sandstone cliff which contains the Buddha leads a broad stone stair carved out of the cliff itself. It is a dim, green stair, flanked on the one side by the red cliff and a multitude of small Buddhas sitting in niches and on the other by a thick vegetation through which one can see the river directly beneath. The steps are worn by the feet on countless thousands. The giant Buddha is two hundred feet in height from the base to the top of the head. it has been accurately carved out of the solid rock in a recess facing the juncture of the Min and the Yaho and its base is washed by the rapid which results from this meeting of the rivers. The body has been left to a green old age, but the features have been covered with a cement and then painted. The solemnity of a close view is ruined, however, but the fact that shrubs pushing their persistent way through a crack in the upper lip give one an instant impression of the straggling evidences of manhood of a youth of eighteen.[6]

There are temples and other images on this delectable cliff, which I shall investigate at my leisure.

There was an execution some two hundred yards from the ship this afternoon, which two of my gobs saw. The victim was bound, made to kneel down, and was shot in the back by two hundred soldiers. I wonder what the poor wretch had done.

AUGUST 20, 1921—KIATING. Rain and a high wind last night. The river consequently began rising this morning, a fact that relieves my mind a bit, for there is only 11 feet depth in this plaguey river and my cruise would come to a dreadful end if I allowed the *Palos* to get caught up here for the winter. However, if you don't take a chance occasionally in this world, you don't get very far. I fear, though, that I shall have to send the *Palos* back to Chungking under the command of the Mate when I leave for my intelligence trip to Chengtu via Mt. Omei.

I called upon General Chen, the District Commander, at two this afternoon, going in state in my chair and accompanied by the post-master as my interpreter. The poor postmaster had to get out of his chair at the gate of the yamen, but I was permitted to ride in state through the several courtyards to the very door of the General's office.

We were received by the Chief of Staff in plain clothes, i.e., a long silk gown, and immediately the General entered—also in a long, dark, silk gown. He was, I suppose, a man of forty, not illfavored, with more of a beard than most Chinese have. He wore a Panama [hat] which he kept on during the entire interview. He was very cordial, told me he disliked Europeans, but liked Americans because of their attitude toward China, and invited me to a feast....

The postmaster told me today that the big Buddha is over two thousand years old, and I can well believe that statement.

AUGUST 21, 1921—KIATING. [Attends the banquet given by General Chen.]

...I found that the General is really well educated, and his talk showed a surprising knowledge of American and European affairs. We discussed the Lolos, ... and he insisted upon comparing the Chinese Lolo problem with our negro problem.[7] Then I used three of my cards showing him the organization of an American Army and explaining the different ranks to him. Fortunately, he did not ask for the corresponding Naval ranks, for I regard myself as ranking with generals in China.

After the tiffin, the General took me over to a school for officers he has just started and which is evidently his pride. We went all over it. I was surprised to find it beautifully clean and everything in perfect order. I saw the textbooks and notebooks and recognized several old friends of Naval Academy days, particularly problems relative to danger space and angles. At five I left and returned on board, not feeling quite as low as I anticipated....

...It seems a big scrap is going on between Ichang and Hankow, geographically speaking. Just who is fighting who is not known, but one side has set up a battery on Sunday Island and is peppering all steamers who attempt to pass. Hence no mail....

I forgot to mention that during the tiffin when I was engaged in a frightful struggle with my chopsticks there mysteriously appeared at my side a silver fork and spoon. Quite by accident, I learned that the faithful postmaster had dispatched a messenger to the *Palos* for them and had thusly and thereby saved my life.

AUGUST 23, 1921—KIATING. I had General Chen, three of his staff, and the postmaster to tiffin today, and it was a grand success.... [T]he protestations of friendships between China and America were very fluent.... The General really looked quite well. He had shaved and was not under the influence of opium. We had tiffin, during which the Army officers kept their hats on, a polite tribute, but a hot one. After tiffin, I took them all over the *Palos* from bridge to bottom, and they really enjoyed it. The General is very keen about anything pertaining to gunnery, but everything about the ship interested him. Then he gave me his photograph, and I gave him mine, and then I took some pictures of the party with my camera.

They left about four, and I considered the day well spent. With a little effort one can gain the good will of these wild, outlying people. It is neglect of one's duty not to put forth that duty. Besides, it is fun to do it.

I leave tomorrow for Omei, and the *Palos* will start for Chungking under my trusty Mate in two or three days.

AUGUST 24, 1921—FORTY MILES FROM SHINKAISIH [SINGAISIH]. At ten minutes to eight I said au revoir to Julian, bade him be careful of the ship ... and went ashore ... [to begin the expedition. Stopped forty miles later at a missionary summer resort.]

AUGUST 25, 1921—SHINKAISIH. ...Foster and Johnson arrived at ten, and I like both of them. Foster is a big rawboned, farmer-looking geologist, [and] sincere ... I accepted his offer to take us up Omei with enthusiasm, though I usually like to lead my own exploring expeditions. Jenson is a solid missionary from Yachow, four days to the northwest of here, engaged in educational work, and a fine American....

About 1900, a missionary obtained permission from the Omei priests to build a bungalow here on Monkey Mountain[,] which is a spur of Omei, upon the payment of an annual rental. The ice broken, other missionaries built bungalows, until now there is a population of about one hundred and fifty Americans, Canadians, and Britishers who come annually here for their three month's vacation. The bungalows are scattered all along the mountainside over a mile, rude affairs but comfortable and well adopted for their purpose. A committee runs a small cooperative store, the upkeep of the Chapel and five tennis courts, and the transportation. Everything seems to be working efficiently except their transportation, which in my opinion is at present hopeless. Of course, none of them have too much money and they have to keep the cost of the coolies down to a minimum, but it seems unreasonable to suppose that with a whole country full of coolies only forty or fifty are available to carry people's junk around.

...[H]ere ... [the missionaries] live during the summer three thousand feet above the city, drinking tea, worshipping frequently, and playing tennis every dry afternoon. After their isolated existence during the other nine months of the year, their getting together during the summer suits them, and most of them appear to be entirely satisfied with life and themselves, for are they not sure of the harp and the crown? They are.

I met many of them during the day, but of the lot I like the Fosters, the Jensons, and the Humphreys. Mrs. Foster is an efficient young lady with four beautiful children and an amazing fund of common sense. The Hensons are fine solid Americans, and Doctor and Mrs. Humphrey are real Americans of an excellent type from Philadelphia. I also like Soper, a Newfoundlander who is an enthusiast on photography and manual training.

[Rain delays departure.]

I am so glad that no one asks me to ask the blessing at the meals— I suppose that in a pinch I might mumble it the way Uncle Fletcher did when I was a kid—only I have no moustache to talk confidently to.

AUGUST 26, 1921—WAN NIEN SIH [WANNIANSUI] OMEI.

...It develops that there will be barely enough coolies to carry a minimum amount of bedding and food; we shall have to walk. I don't mind walking but this hopeless inefficiency regarding coolies is annoying....

The trail first went down some two thousand feet. We ascended to a pass and then descended again and presently found ourselves on the stone road traveled by all pilgrims to Omei.... At a spring ... we refilled our canteens, the first time in China that I have dared drink unboiled water. The same spring supplies the Tah O sih just above where we stopped [for a rest at Holy Water Temple] and the water is supposed to have curative powers, childless women pray to the josses in this temple.

On we went ten li ... to Flying Bridges, a beautiful bridge between two mountain streams dashing between high canyon walls. The sides of the canyon were of the smoothest basaltes, rich, fringed with over-hanging green, and the ancient stone bridge with their mossy arches fitted into the beauty of the picture.

There are two ways to make the ascent of Omei from Flying Bridges—it is here that the real ascent of the mountain begins—: one up through the temple and off to the left; the other to the right and very steep. Due to the report that the first route is impassable on account of heavy rains, we chose the more difficult of the two roads and began to climb.[8]

The stone road immediately became a stone stair and we climbed steadily upward into a dense mist that gave one a lovely grey view ten feet in any direction

...It was a steep and long climb, but we came to Wan Nien Sih (The Temple of Ten Thousand Years) a good half hour before dark and decided to spend the night here.

I must relate such fragments of the history and traditions of Omei as I have been able to pick up in order that reference to them may be made as I proceed. It seems that a holy man named Riuskien came from India in the early part of the sixteen hundreds riding an elephant and bearing the sacred books of Buddha. Riuskien was probably a Chinese who had gone to India and studied Buddhism there, but he may have been an Indian. In any event, in crossing a river near Omei he dropped his sacred books. Some of them he recovered, and he dried them by spreading them out on Washan, a mountain one hundred miles by trail southwest of Omei. The others were swallowed by the fishes, and the only way the precious wisdom could be obtained was by beating the heads of the fishes, the fishes bleating out a word for every swipe. Hence, every temple on Omei contains a hollow, wooden fish head, the beating of which is part of every ceremony.

Since Riuskien made Omei his resting place, the mountain became one of the four sacred mountains of China. Hundreds of thousands of pilgrims visit it every season. Old men save their pitiful earnings year upon year to make the pilgrimage. It is one of the great centers of Buddhism. The usual pilgrimage months are June, July, and early August. The peasants are too busy now with the rice harvest, and its of course too cold in the winter and early spring.

We ran into Mrs. Wellwood in the entrance to [the Temple of Ten Thousand years]. She has been missionarying in China for many years and, though she has lived in about Kiating since 1900, she has never climbed Omei before, though she spent two weeks at Flying Bridge twenty years ago while her husband climbed the mountain....

Her husband was home on furlough when the United States declared war on Germany, and he, though well along in years, went to France as a Y.M.C.A. man on duty with the Chinese Labor Corps. One night the hut in which he was sleeping was blown to fragments by bomb dropped from a German aeroplane. She came back to China: there was nothing else for her to do. She is sad, broken, old; and China is not the country for the sad, the broken, and the old.[9]

At dusk we entered the temple proper. Where sits Riuskien upon his bronze elephant. It was impressive—the great, bronze elephant dimly gathering in the vague light of the yellow lamp swung high above us; the mighty Riuskien sitting in golden state, his placid face expressing a peace and dignity not of modern times; the golden canopy hardly visible above the gathering darkness; the slow-burning, mysterious incense; the three chanting priests at their evening worship; the rhythm of great bells, sweet gongs, and booming drums.

There was a real reverence on the part of the priests and their acolytes, and we Westerners stood there very quietly. It was beautiful.

There broke in upon the party one Mr. Graham, the husband of the lady missionary with whom I tiffined today. I disliked him even before I turned round to see who had no better sense of the fitness of things than to break in upon religious worship with loud conversation about the butterflies he had been chasing all day enroute to the mountain. He very effectively broke the spell, and the chanting priests became merely a lot of dirty Chinese worshipping idols, and we drifted away to meet the newcomer and prepare for supper in another section of the temple....

The missionaries always annoy me by referring to beautiful things like Riuskien upon his elephant as "idols" ... I am not at all convinced that it is not best to leave the Chinese worshipping a definite deity through the medium of beautiful statues rather than force Christianity upon them in the ugly way it is presented by the missionaries. It is absurd to assume that they will be damned if they are not converted: to assume that is obviously a supposition contrary to the principles of Christianity.

AUGUST 27, 1921. [The party proceeds upward in a heavy mist and stops within a thousand feet of the summit.]

I sounded Foster out on the missionary question today, and he

made the rather astonishing statement that it would be better for China
if all the missionaries left the country. He said the Chinese could and
would work out their own salvation. I suspect that he gets heartily tired
of having to live with them all the time.

I feel rather bummish to be forever criticizing these missionaries
after I have accepted their hospitality. But—I did my best to dodge
them, but they forced it down my throat. At any rate, I may as well be
frank.

AUGUST 28, 1921. [Attains the summit and visits the temple of
The Everlasting Peace of Omei.] The temple is built on the very edge
of a sheer cliff a mile long. I peered over—and looked directly down
five thousand feet. I suspect that I am not the first person who looked
and drew hastily back and made sure of his foothold before he looked
a second time....

I cannot understand these missionaries who come year after year
to Shinkaisih and spend three months loafing and playing lah-de-dah
tennis on good afternoons, when there is a whole horizon full of wonderful, unexplored mountains. Many of them never even climbed Omei
but once in their lives—If I keep on, I feel that I shall get to hating these
soulcatchers—But as I have said before . . in my log, it's no use: missionaries and me simply don't mix....

[After visiting the temples and exploring the area, the party begins
the descent on August 29, and arrives in Shinkaisih at four in the morning. One member of the party from the *Palos*, Red Evans, becomes sick
and the party proceeds to a hospital near Suchi [Suqi]. They find two
sailors from the *Palos* recovering from illness.]

[Howell plans on striking across country to Chengtu.]

AUGUST 31, 1921. I ... sent my card to the magistrate and
informed him of my impeding departure for Chengtu. I shall have to
take a guard of four soldiers, because there is too much danger of rows
with robbers if I don't. To be sure, we have our guns and can take ample
care of ourselves, but in this way the responsibility is on the shoulders
of the Chinese. A guard is also necessary on account of face pidgin.

The Doctor ... took me to visit the various mission compounds, all
very comfortable homes.... I was primarily interested in the efforts of
these Kiating missionaries to introduce new breeds [of animals] and to
improve others. Regardless of one's opinion about their major work,
one must admire their efforts in this direction. Justin, by dint of his

personal exertions, brought up to Kiating last fall three foreign cattle, the first to enter Szechwan. Soper has a Swiss goat, which he brought in last year. Both Justin and Barter have introduced the White Leghorn. Quentin is breeding a Tibetan duck, larger than any duck I have seen, and Barter says that it is excellent eating. Barter has a herd of picked native cattle.[10] They are introducing better vegetables and grains and foreign flowers. Here is certainly a very concrete good they are accomplishing.

[September 1, 1921, Howell departs by junk on the Min River. Arrives Chengtu on September 6.]

...The *Alice Dollar* sank some junks containing soldiers in the Gorges. Hence, both Dollar boats are boycotted and are being fired upon in the Gorges. Our machine guns are defending them. It seems to be rather a nice mess all around.

SEPTEMBER 7, 1921—CHENGTU. There was waiting for me at the Post Office a telegram containing grand news from Julian. There have arrived at Chungking my relief, Lieutenant Commander Ralph Sampson, the son of Admiral Sampson of Spanish War fame, and Lieutenant Warlich, Julian's relief. Doctor Carll has been detached and ordered to the Philippines. The *Monocacy* is due to arrive at Chungking on the twelfth. The *Palos* will then proceed to Shanghai under my command. Upon arrival there, Julian and I will turn the craft over to Sampson and Warlich, and then—India, Egypt, Europe, and home. Will I return to Chungking without delay? I'll say I will.[11]

...I sat down [at dinner] as the guest of honor of one of the worse gangs of cutthroats in the world. Here were the men who control a province containing more that half as many people as the United States of America boast—not only control it, but have the power of life and death over that part of the population they can reach. Here sat the men who defy Peking, who laugh at the efforts of the embryo South China Republic to enlist their aid.[12] Here sat the men whose motto is "Szechwan for the Szechwanese!," but whose ambition is wealth. My host—his own capital menaced by outrageous bands of bandits daily growing stronger—whose borders contain stubborn, unsubjugated tribe people who cannot be subdued, hemmed in on all sides by enemy states, sends an army against her neighbor to the north and then another upon a treacherous errand against Hupeh. Here as I sat as the guest of honor of the man whose soldiers and American gobbies are engaged in guerilla warfare....

We had a very gay feast.... The affair broke up sometime after three, and I went back to Smith's Yamen and spent the remainder of the afternoon buying Mandarin coats and tapestries....

I am eager to reach Shanghai.

SEPTEMBER 8, 1921. It is [Hewlett, the British Consul's] opinion, and mine coincides with it, that after Szechwan settles her present initial turbulence the foreigners will be expelled from the province—certainly from Chengtu. There is no way that foreigners above Kiating can be protected. Our gunboats cannot go higher—except possibly a few miles—than Kiating, and not above Suifu for more than three months of the year. A relief expedition is not to be thought of: it would take thousands of men, and difficulties of transportation in the event would be almost insurmountable.

Several circumstances lead to this belief that an antiforeign uprising will occur within five years viz:

1. The fact that Szechwan is entirely self-supporting and self-sufficient.
2. The "Szechwan for the Szechwanese" movement.
3. Bolshevist propaganda.
4. Anti-foreign attitude and propaganda of the press.
5. Tactlessness of the missionaries, who of course have but one point of view.
6. The realization by the Szchwanese of the extreme difficulty of punishing them.
7. Their exaggerated idea of their own importance and power.
8. The rows in the Gorges between gunboat and merchant vessels on the one side and soldiers and bandits on the other....
9. The return of the "students" sent to France. In the meantime, their letters—.

(This relates to an extraordinary affair of which I have not previously learned. Some organization in France arranged with the French in Chengtu two years ago to send them 300 students per month from Szechwan, the idea being that light work would be provided for these Chinese, which would support them while they received education and learned French. This organization shipped students regularly to France for a year and a half[,] number[s] unknown. What caused the scheme to collapse I could not discover, but what actually occurred is that these Chinese are left stranded in France, doing the most menial labor. They

have joined the bolsivik labor organizations there, and their letters to
Chengtu—they are published frequently—are most violently
anti–French and antiforeign. Their letters are bad enough, but when
they return!)

10. The increasing irritation of the Chinese at the immunity of for-
    eigners during riots and revolutions. Wealthy Chinese must
    flee into the homes of foreigners for protection in time of trou-
    ble.
11. Secret societies—all anti-foreign.
12. Alleged misrule of the French in Annam....
13. The Tibetian boundary question.
14. Recent small outrages against foreigners....

Chengdu is surrounded by an enormous wall five miles long and
pierced with but four gates which are religiously and carefully closed
and strongly barred every night at sunset.... [O]nly by the express command of the Governor can those be opened at night.

[Howell leaves at midnight, but the governor promises to have the
gates open.]

Through the silent streets we went to the gate. There was scarcely
a delay—a card, a bit of cumshaw, a command, and presently the great
doors swung wide.... It was almost medieval—the great wall looming up
in the darkness, the clang as the huge gates boomed shut behind me,
with my high sedan chair with its four white great decorated lantern,
the silent blackness ahead....

[En route to Kiating.]

SEPTEMBER 12, 1921—SIHMAN [SIMAN]. I must admit that I
have no solution to offer to straighten out the horrible mess in China,
where every province is in the hands of unprincipled thieves and mur-
derers, where the tendency is more and more toward complete anarchy. I can see but two solutions: (1) Leave China alone and let her work
out her own salvation, passing down into the depths of black anarchy
and building up again on the ruins; (2) let the foreign powers step in,
straighten out the country, and run it until the Chinese can handle it
themselves....

SEPTEMBER 13, 1921—CHUNGKING. At one o'clock I returned
on board my little white gunboat, tanned healthy and glad to be back
... I found Sampson on board, ill from dysentery and quite fed up with

life. His orders are to relieve me upon the arrival of the ship at Shanghai, for they wish to give him this opportunity to observe the river.

[Departs Chungking September 16, 1921. Discovers 1,075 pounds of opium aboard the *Palos* and throws it overboard.]

SEPTEMBER 18, 1921—ICHANG. A thrilling day.

At 7:00 [A.M.] we got underway from Kweichowfu, and within ten minutes were shooting down the Windbox Gorge between its towering walls. A bit later, we entered Washan Gorge, 24 miles long and running a millrace.... Never shall I forget that dash. The Gorge was full of great whirlpools which picked up the *Palos* with ease and flung her from side to side. The junks were in groups—a fatal arrangement on the dangerous, narrow passage—and as many as four of them would be helplessly locked together, whirling helplessly, totally beyond control.

Old Lee early relinquished the wheel to Number Three, and then stood there directing him with marvelous canniness. Time and again, I threw the engine telegraphs to full speed to dash through a dangerous squeeze. The towering walls of rock on either side, the tortured boiling water, the junks helplessly turning as we bore down upon them—then the cargo of soldiers shouting in terror as we dashed straight for them only to swerve at the last moment, the roar of our passage— we made good 22 knots an hour in all[,] an impressive time.

Once it looked as if we were certain to smash into a junk or the cliff. We had ten feet to spare on either hand.

Once Number Three lost his head, and gave the wheel a spin that must have nearly torn the steering engine from its foundations. Red was the quartermaster on watch, we heard a peculiar noise from down below, and we both turned pale and looked at each other. Had the slightest thing gone wrong with any bit of the operating machinery of the *Palos* it meant her loss with all on board. But whatever the noise was, it was not the steering engine, and on we went to dodge the next group of junks.

In the midst of the mess, a shot rang out from the cliff over our heads and a bullet pinged into the water abreast of the ship. I rang the General Alarm and went to General Quarters, the crew flying to the machine guns and six pounders. I cautioned Red on no account to take his eyes away from Number Three at the wheel. I was tempted to let go a round at the unseen bandit or soldier on the cliff, but I verily believe that had I done so all hell would have been let loose in the Gorge. One shot would have set the soldiers in the junks to firing at each other, at us, at the cliff, and bedlam would have ensued. So I wisely contented myself with keeping everybody under cover for a few moments. Then, no further shots being fired, I secured from General Quarters. Fifteen more nervewracking moments, and we were out of the Gorges at last. The remainder of the day proved easier going, though we passed about five thousand troops in junks during the day.

About noon we passed the *Doudart de Lagrie*, laid up in a creek repairing her wounds sufficiently to allow her proceeding to Shanghai. A bit below the *Doudart*, we passed a small, upbound Chinese steamer, the Captain of which shrieked at us as we passed and told us that no ships were permitted to go to Ichang and that we should be fired upon if we did not turn back. We laughed and went on through the Metan Gorge, the Crooked River, and at last into the Ichang Gorge for the last time, still making 20 knots over the ground. I went again to General Quarters before we left the Ichang Gorge, for I wasn't sure what was ahead of us.

We shot out into the calm river below the Gorge—the last of the Upper River—and I heaved a sigh of relief and turned to the business ahead. At San Ye Tong, ... were gathered a thousand soldiers—Szechwanese—straggling over the back of the city, carrying stretchers and rifles. The city of Ichang was disappointingly quiet as we passed it, and I rounded to and anchored without incident in my old anchorage below the Standard Oil barge.

Doughtry from the *Villalobos*, Hawkins, and some other people called and told us the story of the siege of Ichang.[13] About the tenth of this month ... the attack by the Szechwanese began in earnest, though they had been coming down the Gorge for three weeks prior to that time. The situation is now a draw, with the Hupeh troops under Wu Pei-Fu holding the city, but the Szechwanese in possession of the hills across the river and the terrain back of the river and the city. Night before last the Szechwanese actually entered Ichang, but Wu Pei-Fu drove them out.[14] To date there have been a thousand killed altogether in this odd warfare. The *Villalobos* was fired upon two days ago when she steamed up to relieve the *Elcano*, and Doughtry returned the fire with machine guns. The *Robert Dollar* started up the Gorges this morning, but over three thousand shots were fired at her by the Szechwanese troops from the time she got underway until she entered the Ichang Gorge, and she was compelled to turn back after having been struck forty times. The British *Anlan* started up also but was fired heavily upon and returned to Ichang. Wu Pei-Fu has seized the *Shuhun* on the ground that she has been performing unneutral service, and she will be sent to Hankow. It is a beautiful mess.

Doughtry and I shoved off at five and went over and called upon my old friend Carney, who went with us to the Club, still open in spite of the row. We had a drink, a little music, a game of pool, and then hustled back before dark, for with the setting of the sun a steady senseless sniping began on the city from the hills across the way. Sampson, Wheeler, Warlick, and I had dinner at the accompaniment of a regular pinging. Needless to say, the bulletproof doors and port on the starboard side of the ship were closed.

I was approached during the late afternoon by the Foreign Committee of Defence, who wanted to have the *Palos* carry them up the Gorges to Nat'o for a conference with the Szechwanese General. This I refused to do: first, I am under orders to proceed with all speed to Hankow; second, I approve of neither of the Committee of Defence nor of their Wilsonian methods. Conferences mean nothing ... [to the] Szechwanese, and I decline to be a party to any such foolishness.

I was aroused five or six times during the night by heavy bursts of firing, but none of the bullets hit the ship though they splashed all around us. However, I managed to obtain a fair amount of sleep.

SEPTEMBER 19, 1921—HOSUCH [HOSU?]. Various steamers and junks arriving during the night were the occasions for the bursts of firing, but desultory firing kept up until ten o'clock this morning ... I have really quite a drag around here on account of the action I took last June when everyone was hesitating.

I learned that Peanuts, the crew's mess boy for years, who left us a few months ago, has been waiting for the ship at Ichang for two weeks. Day before yesterday he drowned in a sampan upset.

At a bit past eleven I went to General Quarters, got underway, and stood down river. I hoped that the troops on the hills would give us an excuse to open up on them, but they kept a complete silence, and we said farewell to Ichang without incident.

SEPTEMBER 22, 1921—HANKOW. I still felt rotten this morning; so Julian got her underway and took her to Hankow, anchoring a bit before noon inboard the *Wilmington*.

Sampson and I immediately went over and reported to the Patrol

Commander, and I received my orders home via merchant conveyance to the West Coast of the United States and permission to turn
over the command to Sampson tomorrow morning. Heigho, the last
day!

Sampson went back to the *Palos* for tiffin, but I stayed for lunch
with Captain Wood, who was kind enough to express his pleasure at
my summer's work.

I spent the afternoon in frenzied packing as did Julian, and I
finished by dinnertime, though I was very tired. Ulen called in the evening, and then I went up to the bridge and turned in there for the last
time, Red fixing the lights as always. It was moonlight, and I didn't
sleep very much.

SEPTEMBER 23, 1921—HANKOW. The grand day—my detach-
ment. From the bridge I watched my last Hankow sunrise, while I drank
the delectable coffee Joe fetched me.

There was a final, frenzied packing. Then Julian and I shoved off.
George Smiley, Brej Ferguson, and Jack Carnova, whom I am sending
home, ... [went] in a sampan with our luggage and instructions to put
it aboard the *Hanyang* and await us there.

I turned over the confidential papers and the money to Sampson.

We held quarters. The crew were mustered on the fo'c'sle. I stepped
out and read my orders and then turned to Sampson and said, "I am
ready to be relieved, sir."

...[Sampson] read his orders and then turned. We both saluted. "I
relieve you, sir," he said.

I was no longer the Commanding Officer of the *Palos*. No more
would I have to worry about the steam, the anchorage, the machinery.

The motor sampan came alongside. Julian and I shook hands all
around. We passed four sideboys into the boat, Goofy Ayers, the
coxswain, Eddie McLeavey the engineer. We shoved off, the crew waving and smiling at us.

I wonder how many of them I shall see again—Stevenson, Pope,
Harris, Perry, Pat O'Grady, my good, little quarterback, Knight. Erick-
son, English, little Ski, and good, old Red Evans, my standby in everything.[15]

I hate to leave my little white ship, but I am homeward bound on
a high bow wave. So peace be to La Palouse. May her way ever be easy,
and her bones never rest beneath the sea.[16]

Notes

1. Tolley, however, writes that Wood, "before his relief ..., had immersed himself with enthusiasm in riverine affairs." Captain Wood recommended six World War I patrol type craft, known as Eagle boats, augment the patrol. "Then he wrote a very complete, knowledgeable report on what was up the Yangtze." Tolley confirms that Admiral Strauss was "furious" over the placing of armed guards on junks flying the American flag. Tolley, *Yangtze Patrol*, 98–99.

2. "Just below Chungking, on the south bank, an immense gilded Buddha, Tofussu, sits contemplating a Yangtze which at highest flood washes his lap. For the junkmen, this the end of danger. Here, they chin-chin to Tofussu in thanks for their safe passage, for their victory over their hereditary enemy, the Ta Ho, the Great River and its dragon children. More affluent ones set off strings of firecrackers to emphasize their appreciation. It was not the custom for gunboaters to chin-chin. For one thing, the Chinese would have laughed at such presumption. For another, the missionaries hearing of it instantly, would have taken even a dimmer view of a group they felt were at best not on too sound terms with Heaven." Tolley, *Yangtze Patrol*, 233–234.

3. C. E. Thompkins not found in *China Recorder Index*; Mr. Moncrief may be Jessie Edwin Moncrief of the American Baptist Foreign Missionary Society who arrived in China in 1915. He served on the staff of the West China Union University, *China Recorder Index*, 339.

4. Dr. Barter not found in *China Recorder Index*.

5. 1 pictul equals 100 catties, or 133⅓ pounds, or 60.453 kilograms. 1 catty equals 1½ pounds, or 604.53 grams. Hsu, *Modern China*, xxxiii.

6. This may be the Buddha near the present Leshan described as "supposedly he largest in the world. It was cut into the face of a sandstone cliff by a team of workers under the supervision of a Buddhist monk called Haitong. Work began in A.D. 713, and the project took 90 years to complete. "The Buddha is 234 feet high, with shoulders that are 92 feet wide; the head is 48 feet high, while each of the ears is 23 feet long. Records suggest that the Buddha was carved to protect boatmen from drowning in the swift currents in the river below. The Great Buddha or Da Fu Temple itself is located above the right shoulder of the statue." Summerfield, *Fodor's China*, 318.

7. In a book contemporary with Howell, George Babcock Cressey writes: "The 'barbarians,' as they are often termed by the Chinese, include more than two hundred tribes or divisions. The chief races are Miao, Lolo, and Chungchia, with Tibetan and Burmese stocks in the extreme west. Each group has its own language or dialect and leads a semi-independent political existence. These people are simple and ignorant but cheerful and kindly. Most of them live in the mountains where they eke out a simple living as herdsmen, hunters, and primitive farmers. The people are strong and energetic and the women have never bound their feet. These tribes have a common quality in their hatred for the Chinese. Many districts have never been conquered and form virtually independent states, so indicated on many maps. Chinese authority extends only as far into the mountains as military control is effective, and there has been frequent guerrilla warfare." George Babcock Cressey, *China's Geographic Foundations: Survey of the land and Its People* (New York: McGraw-Hill, 1934), 371.

8. On page 3,500 of the diary, Howell notes the altitudes of the main points: Mount Omei: 11,000 feet; flying bridges: 3,500 feet; and the temple: 5,000 feet.

9. The Chinese Labor Corps was a British idea to import labor for use in Europe and, of course, to free men for combat. Close to 100,000 were sent and about 2,000 died from various causes while serving. Michael Summerskill, *China on the Western Front: Britain's Chinese Work Force in the First World War* (Norwich, Great Britain: Michael Summerskill, 1982).

10. There is no listing for Justin or Barter in the *Chinese Recorder Index*. There is a

listing for A.P. Quentin, Rev., whose affiliations were with the American Methodist Episcopal Mission and the Chekiang Mission. Reverend Quentin served in a number of locations, including Hunan, Kiangsi and Szechwan Provinces and Shanghai. His wife was Carol Winifred and he was from Canada. *China Recorder Index*, 395.

11. Howell was mistaken about Sampson's first name. He was relieved by Lieut. Comdr. George W. Sampson, born October 18, 1885, in New York. Class of 1907 and ranked 59 in a class of 207. Retired as a Comdr. on December 1, 1933, and died on February 3, 1934. *Register of Alumni Graduates*, 197. The *Register of Commissioned Officers* for 1921 indicates Lieut. (j.g.) James Monroe Connally, born April 9, 1896, in Missouri and appointed from Missouri in 1918, as the new second in command of the *Palos, Register of Officers, 1921*, 88–89.

12. The "South China Republic" Howell refers to is the government set up by Sun Yat-sen at Canton that planned on defeating the warlords and unite China under the Nationalists Party.

13. Doughtry appears to be: Robin B. Daughtry, born April 20, 1890, in Georgia and appointed from Georgia. Class of 1913 and ranked 27 in a class of 139. Retired as a Comdr. on April 21, 1925, and died November 1960. *Register of Alumni Graduates*, 184.

14. Wu P'ei-fu (22 April 1874–4 December 1939) was a warlord and leader of the Chili (Hopei Province) military faction who became the dominant military leader in north China in 1922. Although his control was broken by another warlord in 1924, he continued to control the Honan-Hupeh-Hunan area until defeated by the Northern Expedition forces under Chiang Kai-shek in 1926.

Wu was noted for his disagreement of uniting China by force and his resistance to the influence of the Japanese in China's affairs. Later, he would eventually change his views about the use of military force in uniting China, but he consistently resisted Japanese influence in his country. Wu, after suffering a series of military defeats, announced his retirement from public affairs in 1926 and took up the study of the Buddhist canon and the Confucian classics. In 1931 he moved to Beijing.

After the Japanese occupation of Manchuria, the Japanese began to make attempts to persuade Wu to head a Japanese-controlled autonomous government in north China. Wu began to express alarm over the spread of communism in Nanking, the capital of the Nationalist government of Chiang Kai-shek. He then expressed interest in listening to the Japanese. In 1938, the Japanese again approached Wu P'ei-fu. His price for cooperating was "a free hand in mobilizing a Chinese anti–Communist army of 500,000 men, supplied and equipped by Japan," and the gradual withdrawal of all Japanese troops from China. The Japanese refused. Late in 1939, while under heavy pressure from the Japanese, Wu died of blood-poisoning. He received an elaborate funeral, with the Nationalist Government honoring him for his refusal to serve the Japanese. "At war's end, Wu's remains were disinterred and reburied in a state ceremony. Although his overbearing manner and fierce temper had antagonized many of his military colleagues and subordinates, his personal honesty and his indifference to wealth and high political office had won the admiration of many contemporaries, both Chinese and foreign." Howard L. Boorman, ed., Richard C. Howard, ed., *Biographical Dictionary of Republican China*, Vol. III (New York: Columbia University Press, 1970), 444–450.

15. In 1925, Howell on his third tour in Asia, while serving aboard the flagship of the Yangtze Patrol, notes in his diary that "a delegation from the Pigeon consisting of Smiley and Harris came over … to present their respects of the four or five old Palos men now in the Pigeon. Pope is also on board that ship, as are one or two others." Howell also records a revealing insight during the conversations between the former shipmates. "I asked Harris what he meant by coming back again and again to the River and he said that it is the only place in the world where he feels really comfortable. It is interesting to see how these old stagers return again and again to River. There is no doubt about its fascination."

16. Kemp Tolley writes that the *Palos* was decommissioned in 1937 at Chungking. She was sold to the Ming Sen Industrial Commission and became a hulk for the storage of wood oil. The hulk was still afloat in 1939, "a sad reminder of what once had been … If spirits of Old River Rats can return, … they must have shed a tear for the inglorious end of a once glamorous lady." Tolley, *Yangtze Patrol*, 236–237.

EPILOGUE

The diary of Glenn F. Howell while commanding the gunboat *Palos* is interesting reading for anyone. The journal is valuable for a number of specific reasons. As brought out earlier, very few Americans realize their armed forces had regular stations and ships homeported in China. Richard McKenna's successful novel, *The Sand Pebbles*, introduced the Yangtze Patrol to a wider audience. McKenna placed his fictional gunboat, the *San Pablo*, in the time period of the 1920s. Howell's diary provides either a counterpoint to the views offered in the novel, or, in some cases, confirms what McKenna portrayed. The commanding officer of the *San Pablo*, Lieutenant Collins, for example, sees the military as the thin line protecting the American way of life and he is, perhaps, a little too willing to use force. In a speech to the crew he announces: "We serve the flag. The trade we all follow is the give and take of death. It is for that purpose that the American people maintain us. Any one of us who believes he has a job like any other, for which he draws a money wage, is a thief of the food he eats and a trespasser in the bunk in which he lies down to sleep."[1] If one adds this portrayal with the stereotypical view of military officers having no political views, but if they do they are a bit conservative, we then have the conception most civilians have of the leaders of the United States military. How does the commanding officer of the *Palos*, Glenn F. Howell, measure up to this picture many Americans carry of the military?

There is no doubt that Glenn F. Howell is very strongly American. When a Japanese ship tries to pass the *Palos* on the Yangtze River, his firemen work extra hard so the gunboat will not be overtaken. Howell's entry, "How we love that flag," is indicative of the feelings of many officers of the period.

When Howell is en route to settle "bandit" problems in the Gorges of the Yangtze River, his diary entries indicates that he is anxious for action, thus at first seeming to fit into the niche created by McKenna's character. Yet, as the *Palos* is transiting the Wushan Gorge, the gunboat is fired upon. Howell puts his crew at battle stations, but then records: "I was tempted to let go a round at the unseen bandit or soldier on the cliff, but I verily believe that had I done so all hell would have been let loose in the Gorge. One shot would have set the soldiers in the junks to firing at each other, at us, at the cliff, and bedlam would have ensued." At another time, during unrest at Ichang, the captains of British and Japanese gunboats want Howell to join them in putting landing parties ashore to inform the Chinese general to remove his soldiers from the settlement. The sailors from all three gunboats would provide the protection for the international settlement during the night. Howell writes that he refused to do this as "it relieved the General of all responsibility and invited looting ... [and] it is contrary to international law." Howell records, however, that he would put a landing party ashore if disturbances actually broke out and Americans were threatened. These actions indicate that, no matter what the naval officer wrote about hoping for action, Howell's responses to explosive events was to think out the consequences and not rush head-long into combat. This is hardly the view of the impetuous officer, which suggests that perhaps other captains of U.S. gunboats reacted in a similar manner.

Howell's diary reveals there is no question he is a member of the Republican party: his comments on Woodrow ("Woody") Wilson and, especially Secretary of the Navy Josephus Daniels, are amusing, but does give an indication that the naval officer is thinking about the political process. In fact, given the isolation of China duty, Howell is well informed on those running for elected office in the United States. Howell may not have been a political pundit of the first order, but the important thing to realize is that the diary indicates at least some naval officers were making an attempt to keep themselves informed about the political scene in their country despite being thousands of miles from home and in an area of poor communications.

In the 1920s, the navy felt their greatest threat came from Japan. While many in the United States had only a vague notion of where Japan was located, Howell's comments reflect the views of many who served in Asia. "I have no difficulty in getting along with the Japs, but I certainly hate them. There is no doubt they reciprocate our feeling. Every well-posted American or Britisher out here with whom I have discussed the subject is convinced that war with Japan is not very remote now and that it will come within five years." Richard McKenna, however, in a nonfiction

article recorded many enlisted sailors liked Japan and, completely breaking the stereotype of the old China sailor, wished to retire there instead
of China.[2]

Howell's diary shows the love-hate relationship with China and the
Chinese that most military men in the Middle Kingdom experienced.
Howell could be almost lyrical in his description of the countryside and
describe the Chinese very sympathetically, only to make a racist remark
later in his writings. While the duty in the Celestrial Kingdom was looked
upon as good, and the China station gained almost mythical status among
servicemen, still many did not care for the Chinese. As explained earlier,
this is due to not understanding the language, which in turn meant not
understanding the culture. Howell is symbolic of the majority of the military men who served in China prior to World War II: they found a fascinating country, but one they could not understand. Two caveats must
be placed on this observation, however. There were a minority of servicemen in China who did learn the language and the culture and grew
to love China and the Chinese. This included both officers and enlisted
men. Howell, unlike many of his brother officers, tried to travel in China
and I believe this opened his mind more to the country. Howell, however, appears not to have tried to learn the language, thus denying himself a chance for a better understanding of his surroundings.

In a similar vein, most military personnel took very little notice of
what was taking place around them. This may seem somewhat strange to
people today, but one must remember that very few Americans understood the language, so how could one expect them to grasp the com-
plexities of a nation in the throes of a major political upheaval? To most
military men the Chinese were simply a backdrop in the area they happened to be stationed. McKenna, who served on a gunboat in the 1930s,
later recalled he failed to notice what took place in China. Howell, to his
credit, does seem to grasp some of the major happenings by at least
quizzing many people, usually Westerners. Of course, this method would
elicit only a Western view of the events.

In *The Sand Pebbles*, McKenna introduces the subject of missionaries in China and their dislike of the gunboats within the first twenty pages
of the novel and thus the reader becomes aware of the friction between
the two groups of Westerners. Indicating that McKenna realized the dis-
cord, many parts of Howell's diary expresses his dislike of missionaries.
Like other military personnel serving in China, the naval officer had a
definite hierarchical classification of missionaries. He saw nothing wrong
with medical missionaries, or those trying to bring new agricultural methods to the Chinese. He also respected Catholic missionaries, as they were

more educated. He saved his wrath for what would today be called Fundamentalist. As indicated earlier, the missionaries were put into a very difficult position. McKenna used this difficulty to great effect near the end of his novel when a missionary decides to place himself under Chinese law, despite a landing party from the *San Pablo* making a running fight to rescue the people at the mission. The conflict between missionaries and the military in China was never resolved and Howell's observations are an excellent example of the viewpoint of the military.

There have been very few nonfiction books on the U.S. military in peacetime and only one that includes all of the American military in China in peacetime.³ If there are any observations on the armed forces, it usually centers around the officer corps. The publishing of Howell's diary gives readers the best daily description of the peacetime navy in China. Furthermore, as discussed earlier in this book, the diary shows something of enlisted men and their relationships with those who led them. Like the love-hate relationship with China, Howell's diary shows that many officers could not shake off their training and education to really understand the enlisted force. On the other hand, because of their lack of education and economic status, it is doubtful that the enlisted force could ever comprehend officers.

The People's Republic of China has launched the building of the Three Gorges dam on the Yangtze River. When finished, this huge barrier will displace millions of people and flood out an area where Howell and many ship captains did battle with the mighty Yangtze River. Because so few Westerners traveled to this remote region in the 1920s, the diary of an articulate observer becomes even more valuable, as almost everything, if not all, that Howell observed will be beneath water once the Three Gorges dam is completed. The way of life of the peasants described by the naval officer when the *Palos* remained moored to a tree awaiting the river to fall will truly be finished forever after the completion of the dam.

Because he possessed a good eye for detail and because he wanted to be a writer, Howell leaves us glimpses of some of the Westerners who populated China when most of their countrymen in the United States would see the Middle Kingdom as remote as the moon. One myth about the Westerners who lived in China prior to World War II is they were a fascinating lot, but a bit eccentric. The diary does a wonderful job of bringing out some of these whimsical, but interesting people. Some are a bit sad, others a bit strange. Mrs. Wellwood, the widow missionary who Howell met on his foray to Mt. Omei, will now be known, as will her husband's exploits in the Chinese Labor Corps. Very few readers will be able to forget the gallant stand of Corporal Watson on the *Palos*. There is also the interesting short biography of an enlisted crewman who Howell identifies only as "Ski."

The value of Glenn F. Howell's diary while serving as the commanding officer of the gunboat *Palos* on the Yangtze River during the period 1920–1921 is that it provides readers with an articulate look at a long vanished naval life. It also gives a view of a remote area of the world that will soon be lost because of modern technology, and it provides a very informative example of how one culture interacts with a far different society. If the United States continues to send its troops to regions of the world where the culture is far different than its own, then Howell's diaries can help illuminate some of the pitfalls of such undertakings. Lastly, Glenn F. Howell's diaries can help people of today uncover Westerners that contributed to the story of China that would normally receive very little attention. The study of Glenn F. Howell's period of time on the mighty Yangtze River can lead to the saga of S. Cornell Plant and G. R. G. Worcester, two Englishmen who fell under the spell of the *Chang Jiang*. Plant continues to help Chinese ship masters over seventy years after his death. Once the Three Gorges dam is completed, his damaged memorial will rest beneath the water and he will probably slip behind the veil of history. Worcester, through his monumental work on junks, sampans and the people who worked them, continues to help those interested in maritime history understand the contributions of the Chinese to the maritime world.

All of these views and people are once again brought to life because of the articulate and insightful views of Glenn F. Howell.

Notes

1. McKenna, *Sand Pebbles*, 81.
2. Richard McKenna, "Life Aboard the USS *Gold Star*," in *The Left-Handed Monkey Wrench: Stories and Essays by Richard McKenna*, ed. Robert Shenk (Annapolis, Md.: Naval Institute Press, 1986), 107–140. This essay gives one of the best nonfiction accounts of enlisted sailors in the peacetime navy in the Pacific.
3. Dennis L. Noble, *Eagle and the Dragon: The U.S. Military in China, 1901–1937* (Westport, Ct.: Greenwood Press, 1990).

Appendix 1:
The Last Cruise
of the *Palos*

by Vice Admiral T. G. W. Settle,
U.S. Navy (Retired)

The weather had made up blustery from the nor'nor'west on the afternoon of the first of October, 1934 when the U.S.S. Palos dropped her Shanghai pilot at Woosung and rounded up into the Yangtze. She was starting her last cruise up that mighty river which had been her habitat throughout her twenty years' lifetime. The old gunboat had just been overhauled in the Chinese Navy's British-run Kiangnan Dockyard in Shanghai and was replete with new stacks, new boiler tubes, green crew, and orders to take over the job of permanent station ship at Chungking in Szecuan Province some 1300 miles above Woosung.

As Woosung faded astern the *Palos* rolled heavily in the trough of the muddy seas. Our native Woosung-to-Hankow pilot rushed off the bridge to be politely seasick over the lee main deck rail and some of our less polite crew didn't quit a lee rail. After our sampans at their davit heads began slapping into the water, we zigzagged upstream, keeping the seas alternately on the starboard bow and quarter to ease her.

All afternoon the engines had to be stopped, one at a time, to blow debris out of the main injections and to look for vacuum, of which the Chief was somewhat shy. His compound reciprocating engines had been rated at 400 H.P. in 1914—they leaned outboard eight degrees from the vertical to make the cylinder heads fit in under the engineroom overhead structure. Through the long years of battling *Old Man Yangtze* the structure and all machinery had accumulated a high degree of lost motion and flexibility. A look into her engineroom underway would have sent a big-ship engineer balmy. Every piece of apparatus vibrated, oscillated, and danced; each with its own period and orbit, independently of its fellows.

As dusk came on, the steering engine jammed. We shifted to the hand gear and anchored for the night, having made good 25 miles from Woosung. During the next ten days, the *Palos* plodded along by day, utilizing all slow waters, back currents close in to the muddy banks and anchoring occasionally to clean fires while practicing the hand steering gear each day. We anchored, or moored to a pontoon, nightly and coaled ship every day or day and a half.

We pulled into Hankow, 600 miles up from the coast, on 11 October and secured at the Hamburg-Amerika pontoon with the *Panay*. This was our last foreign-style city—the last Russian ballerinas, numerous in the French Concession "dumps"—the last piped plumbing and ice in our drinks.

The Middle Yangtze is a superlative example of a meandering river. One may have the curious experience of passing a steamer, say 1,000 yards abeam on opposite headings; the steamer apparently gliding along on the rice paddies, both ships bound up-river and five or ten miles from each other along the river. In flood seasons the intervening peninsulas are submerged, along with the navigational beacons. Ships have gotten lost and cruised for hours over the flooded countryside, dodging hillocks, temples, and clumps of trees, hunting for the river. When you finally find it you may have to steam along on the wrong side of a dike for miles until you come to an aperture big enough to let you through back into the stream.

On a sultry Saturday afternoon, 20 October, the *Oahu*, station ship in Ichang, noted a pillar of dense black smoke rising high into the air to the eastward. It was the *Palos*, distant some ten miles air line, probably eighteen by river, chugging along hoping her stokers would hold up and her stacks not melt down before she made the haven which Ichang promised to be. About four hours later, the "smoke column" with its gunboat fastened at its base moored to the Socony pontoon and the *Oahu*'s crew piloted our parched liberty party to "Cock-eye's" for resuscitation.

While the *Palos* drew her breath in Ichang and the mate rigged her and drilled the crew for heaving rapids, spar mooring and such like, the Captain made a round trip to Chungking in the Jardine-Matheson ship *Kiawo* (pronounced jaw-woe), to familiarize himself (as much as one can in one such trip) with the Upper River. The *Kiawo* was commanded by Captain Taffy Hughes, a Welshman who had been a blue water master mariner before coming to the river. He and his *Kiawo* had figured in major roles in the famous 1926 Battle of Wanhsien between a British naval force and the Szechuanese General Yang Sen. Hughes is one of the few foreigners who have personally piloted vessels in the Upper Yangtze. He was assiduous in giving the greenhorn *Palos* skipper information on anchorages, rapids and all manner of river lore. He had an English mate, the inevitable Scotch engineer, and a crew of assorted brands of Chinese.

In our first gorge above Ichang Hughes blew his siren to warn a deep-laden junk ahead. The blast echoed back and forth across the narrow gorge in a staccato most startling to the newcomer. Taffy explained that in the large gorges one must be easy on the siren, for a blast reverberates for hours sometimes with little diminished vigor, to the confusion of subsequently passing shipping. He had once made a prolong blast at a stubborn junk and was surprised, upon returning past the spot three days later, to hear it still echoing away in the gorge.

When the Skipper got back to Ichang the water mark was several feet below the *Palos'* optimum level and still falling, so no time was to be lost in starting up-river. Late on 29 October we got our pilots, the Chow brothers, on board. With their native quartermasters, stove, goods, opium and a "makee-learn" boy, they were stowed away in the forward boatswain's hold.

So at dawn the next day we unmoored from our good Socony pontoon, eased into the stream, and turned over the conn to the elder Chow. His native quartermaster took the wheel. His conning was not verbal but by wiggly-finger. He rested a hand on the pilot house window forward of the wheel and wiggled the index finger as necessary; movement to the right (or left) meant "Bring her to starboard (or port)." A sort of come-on sign meant "Steady as you go." Speed of ruddering was dictated by emphasis of the fingering, supplemented by the steerman's independent judgment of the situation.

We got through the Ichang Gorge without incident and to our first rapid, the Paitungzu, mild at that level. In it our evil friend, the steering engine, failed. We shifted to hand steering, got through the Tanungtan, also mild, and approached our first hot spot, the Kunglingtan. This one was bad, not so much because of excessive water velocity, although it was fast enough, but rather by placement of rocks. There is a big rock in midstream and the southern channel was impassable for steamers at that time. Flanking the main rock and little down stream from it in the north channel are several small but wicked rocks known as the "Pearls." The up-passage procedure at this level for a long, low-powered ship was to give her full gun, head directly for the central rock (working up to good ground speed in the relatively slack water in its lee) and a few yards below it rudder her smartly into the fast water to starboard, hoping the stern will clear the lower "Pearl" which will be directly astern when the ship is straightened out. Then all we had to do was squeeze onto our steam pressure while we crept up the fast water to the head of the rapid.

The next day was a memorable one for the Palosians. We stood up through the three sections of the Hsintan ("New Rapid"—formed by slides only some 150 years ago), moderate at our level, and towards midday approached the Hsintan running at its full strength. Several miles below it we slowed; cleaned fires; broke out heaving gear; sent a fresh fireroom crew below; took up all slack in our belts and started through. In a few hundred yards distance we would have to climb the ship about five feet vertically and the tongue of the rapid was flowing at 14 knots or more. After a few preliminary skirmishes at the foot of the rapid we eased up in a back current in lee of a projecting cape of the southern foreshore. Then we gave her an energetic "full" on the engine telegraphs, rounded the cape and steamed into the edge of the main flow. We had been making probably twelve knots over the ground in the back current and when her bow was thrown into the swelling edge of the tongue the *Palos* had a momentary water speed of around twenty knots. The fo'c's'l was flooded and the ship decelerated like a ferry hitting a piling in a ferry slip. Our momentum was soon dissipated and we crawled up the edge of the tongue into ever faster water, so close to the rocks that had we had a grassy bottom it would surely have been close-cropped on the inboard side.

A couple of ships' lengths and we were "stuck." The current equaled our ten knots thru the water and our ground speed was zero. The customary bandit-coolies were waiting expectantly abreast us on the foreshore. We passed them the end of a ⅞" steel cable, hung on in the current while they hauled ahead 150 fathoms of it, made the end fast to a boulder at the head of the rapid and threw the bight clear of the rocks into the water. This wire came into the ship through a fairlead block at the break of the fo'c's'l, then forward to the capstan. Our fo'c's'l crew threw it around the capstan, took out the slack, then heaved us ahead, the engines all the while putting out all the turns that the sweating and furiously shoveling stokers could send them steam for. The capstan heaved us ahead a ship length or so then it stuck—could heave no more with its full head of steam. So the final maneuver in heaving a rapid was in order, sheering. The pilot ruddered her gently out from the foreshore into the stream, springing her ahead on the cable in so doing; then eased her back inshore while the capstan took in the resultant slack in the wire. This out-and-in sheering is repeated until the ship is over the top of the rapid, but on this occasion the third out-sheering was a little too rank or there was a weakness in the cable—anyway, it parted. Our fires and firemen still being in reasonable good shape we only dropped astern a little and held her close in to the foreshore while we broke out the ¾" wire and passed it to the trackers. This time on the second out-sheer it parted at an old sharp-nip weakness. Our fires were clinkering now and our fireroom crew pooped. Nothing to do but back her down the rapid and start all over again. We slowed to steerage-way, eased into the middle of the tongue and let the current carry her astern (head up-stream, of course).

It is axiomatic on the Yangtze that whenever one is in an uncomfortable spot a heavily laden junk comes along to further complicate matters and the old river didn't favor us this time. When the second wire parted a huge junk loaded to vanishing freeboard, appeared at the top of the rapid, turning and sheering rankly in the turbulent water. Likewise a standard attribute of all junks is that they appear bent upon collision with a ship. One may not merely steer to clear them; one must actively dodge them. Among the vortices at the foot of the tongue this junk threw herself athwart the stream, across our bows. It took drastic use of engines and rudders to clear her and her howling crew by a "dragon's breath." We anchored in a precarious spot a mile down-stream where passing swirls dragged about in spite of our engines, one or both of which kept turning over slowly. Fires were cleaned, tiffin served to all hands, the stokers given a good blow on deck, and the last wire, a ⅝" one, broken out.

Then, with as much trumped up determination as we could muster we started up roaring old Hsintan again. Old Chow steered her gingerly and the Skipper was certain he would hear the zing of the wire parting on each out-sheer. Each time it held he was sure its margin of strength was used up and it would certainly fail next time. But at last a tender sheer, with engines and capstan straining with every BTU in their steam and the crew sallied forward to the fo'c's'l, put her over the top. The *Palos* slithered ahead into the glassy water above, the capstan reeling exuberantly, taking in the slack of the wire and keeping it out of our propellers.

The battle with the rapid was over. Now came the usual battle of words with the tracker-brigands. We hove to at low engine speed and a sampan came alongside with the tracker headman, our first tow wires, and a howling crew of natives. The headman was brought to the forward gun deck for the bargaining. The Number Two pilot was spokesman; the Engineer Officer put on his Special Disbursing Agent beard and stood by with a mess attendant as "interpreter for the defense." The tracker started negotiations by demanding 850 silver "head" dollars, not an immoderate opening bid under the circumstances (being only three or four times the proper figure). In fifteen minutes they were really warmed up, with shaking of fists under noses and threats of the tracker to shove off with our wires. After a half hour their drama was played out and a figure only about twice the correct amount was agreed upon.

That afternoon we had to heave another rapid, the Niukoutan but did so without incident and anchored at Patung 60 miles above Ichang where that night's coal junk was awaiting us.

Next morning we came upon Chinchupiao, a low-level rapid as yet running only mildly. We should have steamed up it without difficulty, but insufficient "power insight" brought us to with falling steam part of the way up it. So we yelled with the siren for the trackers and heaved it.

Then in the afternoon we got stuck in a fast race in Wushan Gorge. There was no anchorage for many miles astern and turning a 160-foot ship at that place in the narrow gorge was out of the question. On the precipitous rocks abreast the ship was a fisherman plying his net (one never sees these fishermen catch a fish). Our pilot shouted to him to take our lines for spar-mooring but he complacently ignored us and went on with his fish-netting. One of our native boatmen was stripping to swim the few feet ashore when a soft spot in the race, a swirl, came along and let us ease ahead the few yards necessary to clear the fastest water. And so we huffed and puffed our weary way through the rest of the gorge and to this night's coal junk at Tamato, just above the town of Wushan.

Next day we heaved the Hsiamatan (which we undoubtedly should have steamed) and about midday came to the Paotzutan, a mid-level rapid still running lustily. But by carefully conserving our BTUs until we could see the "white of his tongue" we steamed over this one. Though we would not have believed it at the time, Hsiamatan had been the last rapid we were to have to heave. We had found the real reason for our needless heavings. Whenever the Chief shaved we had to heave a rapid, but when he had a lusty stubble of beard we bowled over the rapids and thru races as in the days of the *Palos'* youth. We considered offering up his razor to the next riverside Buddha; but as Buddha is usually portrayed as beardless we thought better of it and merely promised the Chief a general court if he shaved again.

On 3 November the Chief's stubble was gratifyingly hobo-like and we steamed over two low-level and a mid-level rapid, all running fairly strongly. But the Chungking water mark had started rising. When we anchored at Kulino we sent the carpenter ashore, as usual, to paint water marks a foot apart on rocks abreast the ship so we could keep track of the local level during the night. The rise reached us during the night and our level started up. It was the worst level for the rapid just ahead of us, the

Miaochitsu, and in the morning it was booming along extra strongly because of the rising tendency. It appeared as strong as Hsintan had been, and to heave this one we would need two hundred fathoms of wire. We did not have that much ⅞" left, and all our wire had been overworked. So the [U.S. gunboat] *Tutuila* in Chungking was asked by radio to send us another reel in the *Kiawo*. And we settled down to wait for a steadying water mark, keeping the Chief's razor under hack. All hands got some needed rest.

The evening of the second day Chungking reported falling water and Number One Chow thought "maybe can do" tomorrow. The local water mark steadied during the night and in the early morning showed a down tendency. The new *Tutuila*'s wire had not arrived but the Chief's whiskers were bristling with virility, so we shoved off for a try at old Miaochitsu who had been thumbing his nose at us these two and a half days. We sneaked up on him, and at the moment of getting his tongue over our fo'c's'l gave her four bells and all the jingles in our repertoire. The *Palos* climbed the edge of the tongue, slowing despairingly; all hands were shoving her ahead with their hands and will power. She worked herself slowly to the top, hung there an agonizing minute, then wiggled herself clear and over. The Chief went below and shaved off his praiseworthy whiskers, but he was premature, for we almost got stuck in an inoffensive little rapid (at that level), the Tungyangtzu, a few miles up.

Next day the *Palos* pulled up to the city of Wanhsien, mileage 173, half-way from Ichang to Chungking, and anchored off the Socony installation in company with the Standard-Vacuum ship *Meiping*.

The heaving rapids were astern of us and our main worries now were the daily searches for coal junks and hoping the *Palos* would hold together until we could sneak her thru to Chungking.

But "Old Man River" had one more tussle for us in his bag of tricks. At a place called Lochi, our last anchorage before Chungking, we had a hard time finding holding ground. A strong freshet from heavy rains was setting in and had washed out most of the sand patches (upon which it was customary to anchor at this level) leaving the underlying shingle (gravel) through which our anchors dragged easily. We finally found a small sand patch a mile above the town and anchored in it, putting out several preventer spring wires to the shingle foreshore. During the night the local water mark rose some six feet and the velocity increased ominously, even close in to our shingly bank. An hour before dawn we started warming up as usual and got our lines in from the foreshore. Then suddenly the anchors broke out and started dragging heavily through the shingle. The freshet had scoured away our sand patch from under our anchors. One engine was warm enough to get turning over and steam was gotten on the steering engine in a hurry. The problem was to use the engines to minimize dragging but keeping enough load on the chains to keep her headed up, ruddering to hold her 20 to 50 feet off the foreshore. Flashlights attempted to keep the foreshore in sight thru the cold wind-driven rain. The current was probably seven knots past the ship. The minutes passed interminably slowly with ... [visions] of almost piling up on the foreshore or dragging our anchors off the steep shingle bank into deep water, riding ahead to slack chains or dragging astern uncomfortably rapidly as slow or fast spots in the swirling current passing the ship. When we were about down to the town when our precarious would have become still more precarious, the horizon began to lighten up faintly, enough to make out topographical features. With deep relief we heaved up the anchors and stood up against the evil-intentioned muddy torrent.

In mid-afternoon of that day, 12 November, the long trek all but completed, we passed the large gilded Buddha called Tofussu on the south bank just below Chungking. Up-bound junk men "chin-chin" to Tofussu in thanks for their safe passage thru the gorges; affluent ones set strings of firecrackers to emphasize their thankfulness. I had hoped for the opportunity to so propitiate him and had invested five *mex* dollars in firecrackers at Wanhsien, so we slowed and gave old Tofussu a sincere bang-up show.

A couple of hours later the gallant old *Palos* was making fast to the American gunboat moorings off the Navy Club in Lungmenhao Lagoon, Chungking.

APPENDIX 2:
THE CREW OF THE PALOS
JUNE 1920

LCDR Glenn F. Howell
LT Thaddeus A. Hoppe
LT(MC) Reuben Barker

A.L. Andus	MM2cT	A.C. McGuire	S2c
S. Atkielski	S2c	C.H. Newlin	F2cT
E.R. Ayers	S2c	J.H. Newsome	F3cT
J.A. Carnova	S2c	W.T. Noble	E1c(r)T
J.W. Cloer	F2c	P.T. O'Grady	F2c
R.L. Clowes	F3cT	J.F. Pedigo	F2cT
E. Conley	F3cT	W.T. Petterson	S2cT
J. Crown	F1cT	F.X. Pillert	CJMT
E.W. Doyle	MM1cT	J.J. Portis	CoxT
A. Dupont	Eng2cT	O.P. Prather	F3cT
J.C.W. Evans	S2c	F.B. Pzybysz	F3cT
C.A. Furguson	S2c	W.W. Roland	CW2
B.L. Franklin	Eng2cT	W.H. Saul	SeaT
H.C. Gibson	Sea	M.R. Selby	CyT
G.E. Grun	S2c	Ah Sing	Cabin Cook
N. Harris	Eng1c	J.H. Slaughter	JM3cT
R.J. _____	CBMT	G.E. Smiley	S2c
C.G. Hoy	BM1cT	C.D. Smith	F3cT
W. En Huston	SeaT	L.H. Smith	E1c(g)
R.E. Johnson	Yeo3cT	Ah Soon	SC1c
J.L. Knight	Sea	H.G. Taylor	GM1cT
J.E. Lewis	S2cT	U.M. Walker	BM1cT
O.H. Merwin	F2c	C.C. Winfrey	F1cT
L. Mitchem	F1cT	Yong Ki	WrStd
A.J. McAllister	Pm2cT		

APPENDIX 3: PUBLISHED WRITINGS OF GLENN F. HOWELL

Books

Howell, Glenn. *Medals of Honor: Hero Tales of the American Navy*. New York: Dial Press, 1931.

Articles

Howell, Glenn. "The Battle of Wanhsien," U.S. Naval Institute *Proceedings*, 53 (May 1927): 527–533.

_____. "Operations of the United States Navy on the Yangtze River—September, 1926, to June, 1927," U.S. Naval Institute *Proceedings*, 54 (April 1928): 273–286.

_____. "Captain Plant," U.S. Naval Institute *Proceedings*, 55 (March 1929): 206–208.

_____. "Hwan Tsao," U.S. Naval Institute *Proceedings*, 64 (August 1938): 1151–1155.

_____. "Chungking to Ichang," U.S. Naval Institute *Proceedings*, 64 (September 1938): 1312–1316.

_____. "Army-Navy Game: Or, No Rules of the Road." U.S. Naval Institute *Proceedings*, 64 (October 1938): 1435–1438.

_____. "Opium Obligato." U.S. Naval Institute *Proceedings*, 64 (December 1938): 1729–1735.

BIBLIOGRAPHY

Archival Material

Berkeley, LGEN James Phillips. Interview by Benis M. Frank, 1971, Oral History Program. U.S. Marine Corps Historical Center. Washington, D.C.

Moriarty, Brig. Gen. James F. (USMC), Papers of. China Repository. Naval Oprerational Archives. U.S. Naval Historical Center. Washington, D.C.

Simms, William S., Papers of. Manuscript Division. Library of Congress. Washington, D.C.

Thomas, Charles W. "The United States Army Troops in China, 1912–1937" History Term Paper, Sanford University, June 1937. U.S. Army Military Institute. Carlisle Barracks, Pennysylvania.

Books

Alden, Carroll Stores. *Lawrence Kearny: Sailor Diplomat.* Princeton: Princeton University Press, 1936.

Bonavia, Judy. *The Yangzi River.* Lincolnwood, Il.: Passport Books, 1997.

Boorman, Howard L., Howard, Richard C., eds. *Biographical Dictionary of Republican China.* Vol. III. New York: Columbia University Press, 1970.

Braisted, William Reynolds. *The United States Navy in the Pacific, 1897–1909.* Austin: University of Texas Press, 1958.

_____. *The United States Navy in the Pacific, 1909–1922.* Austin: University of Texas Press, 1971.

Cooling, Benjamin Franklin. *Benjamin Franklin Tracy: Father of the Modern American Fighting Navy.* Hamden, Ct.: Archon Books, 1979.

Ellsworth, Harry Allansen. *One Hundred Eighty Landings of United States Marines, 1800–1834* (Washington: History and Museum Division, Headquarters, U.S. Marine Corps, 1935.

Finney, Charles G. *The Old China Hands.* Garden City, NY: Doubleday, 1961; reprint, Westport, Ct.: Greenwood Press, 1973.

Flint, Roy K. "The United States Army on the Pacific Frontier, 1899–1939," in

179

The American Military and the Far East: Proceedings of the Ninth Military History Symposium, United States Air Force Academy, 1–3 October 1980, ed. Joe C. Dixon. Washington: Government Printing Officer, 1980.

Garraty, John., ed. *Encyclopedia of American Biography*. New York: Harper & Row, 1974.

Grover, David H. *American Merchant Ships on the Yangtze, 1920–1941*. Westport, Ct.: Prager, 1992.

Hart, John. *The Making of an Army "Old China Hand": A Memoir of Colonel David D. Barrett*. Berkeley, Ca.: Institute of East Asian Studies, 1985.

Henson, Charles T., Jr. *Commissioners and Commodores: The East Asian Squadron and American Diplomacy in China*. University of Alabama: University of Alabama Press, 1982.

Hoyt, Edwin P. *The Lonely Ships: The Life and Death of the U.S Asiatic Fleet*. New York: David McKay, 1976.

Hsu, Immanuel C.Y. *The Rise of Modern China*. 3rd ed. New York: Oxford University Press, 1983.

Hurd, David. *The Arrow War: An Anglo-American Confusion*. New York: Macmillian, 1968.

Karsten, Peter. *The Naval Arsitocracy: The Golden Age of Annapolis and the Emergence of Modern Navalism*. New York: Free Press, 1972.

Kierman, Frank A., Jr., "Ironies of Chinese-American Military Conflict," in *The American Military and the Far East: Proceedings of the Ninth Military History Symposium, United States Air Force Academy, 1–3 October 1980*, ed. Joe C. Dixon. Washington: Government Printing Officer, 1980.

Knox, Dudley. *A History of the United States Navy*. New York: Oxford University Press, 1948.

Johnson, Robert E. *Thence Around Cape Horn: The Story of the United States Naval Forces on Pacific Station*. Annapolis, Md.: Naval Institute Press, 1963.

_____. *Far China Station: The U.S. Navy in Asian Waters*. Annapolis, Md.: Naval Institute Press, 1979.

Knox, Dudley. *A History of the United States Navy*. New York: Putnam, 1948.

Leaderer, William. *All the Ships at Sea*. New York: William Sloane, 1950.

Lodwick, Kathleen. *The Chinese Recorder Index: A Guide to Christian Missions in Asia, 1867–1941*. 2 vols. Wilmington: De.: Scholrarly Resources, Inc., 1986.

Lovette, Leland P. *Naval Customs, Traditions, and Usage*. Annapolis, Md.: Naval Institute Press, 1934.

Maclay, Edgar Standton. *Reminiscences of the Old Navy: From the Journals and Private Papers of Captain Edward Trenchard and Rear Admiral Stephen Decatur Trenchard*. New York: Putnam, 1898.

McKenna, Eva Grice and Shirley Graves Cochrane. *New Eyes for Old: Nonfiction Writings by Richard McKenna*. Winston-Salem, NC: John F. Blair, 1972.

McKenna, Richard. *The Sand Pebbles*. New York: Harper's, 1962.

_____. "Life Aboard the U.S.S. Goldstar," in *The Left-Handed Monkey Wrench: Stories and Essays by Richard McKenna*. ed. Robert Shenk. Annapolis, Md.: Naval Institute Press, 1986.

Millett, Allen R. *Semper Fidelis: The History of the United States Marine Corps*. New York: Macmillian, 1980.

Noble, Dennis L. *The Eagle and the Dragon: The United States Military in China, 1901–1937*. Westport, Ct.: Greenwood Press, 1990.

Noel, John V., Jr. and Edward L. Beach, eds. *Naval Terms Dictionary*. 5th ed. Annapolis, Md.: Naval Institute Press, 1988.

Offutt, Milton. *The Protection of Citizens Abroad by the Armed Forces of the United States*. Baltimore: Johns Hopkins University Press, 1928.

Peffer, Nathaniel. *The Far East: A Modern History*. Ann Arbor: University of Michigan Press, 1958.

Plant, Cornell [Samuel]. *Glimpses of the Yangtze Gorges*. Shanghai: Kelly & Walsh, Limited, 1921. Second edition, 1936. *Register of Alumni Graduates and Former Naval Cadets and Midshipmen*. Annapolis, Md.: U.S. Naval Academy Alumni Association, 1982.

Seager, Robert, II. *Alfred Thayer Mahan*. Annapolis, Md.: Naval Institute Press, 1977.

Shoup, David. *The Marines in China, 1922–1927: The China Expedition which turned out to be the China Exhibition: A Contemporaneous Journal by David M. Shoup, USMC*. Hamden, Ct.: Archon Books, 1987.

Summerskill, Michael. *China on the Western Front: Britain's Chinese Work Force in the First World War*. Norwich, Great Britain: Michael Summerskill, 1982.

Swisher, Earl. *China's Management of the American Barbarians: A Study of Sino-American Relations, 1841–1861, With Documents*. New York: Octogon Books, 1972.

Teng, Ssu-Yu. *The Taiping Rebellion and the Western Powers: A Comprehensive Survey*. London: Oxford University Press, 1971.

Tolley, Kemp. *Yangtze Patrol: The U.S. Navy in China*. Annapolis, Md.: Naval Institute Press, 1971; second printing, 1984.

U.S. Department of State. *Papers Relating to the Foreign Relations of the United States, 1901 and 1912*. Washington: Government Printing Office, 1920.

Van Slyke, Lyman P. *Yangtze: Nature, History, and the River*. New York: Addison-Wesley Publishing Company, 1988.

Who's Who for Idaho. Portland, Or.: Capital Publishing Company, 1950.

Williams, William A. *The Old Corps: A Portrait of the U.S. Marine Corps Between the Wars*. Annapolis, Md.: Naval Institute Press, 1982.

Winchester, Simon. *The River at the Center of the World: A Journey Up the Yangtze, and Back in Chinese Time*. New York: Henry Holt and Company, 1996.

Worcester, G. R. G. *The Junks and Sampans of the Yangtze*. Annapolis, Md.: Naval Institute Press, 1971.

Articles

Albion, Robert Greenhalgh. "Distant Stations," U.S. Naval Institute *Proceedings*, 80 (March 1954): 265–273.

Curtis, E.R. "Blood is Thicker Than Water." *American Neptune*, 27 (July 1967): 157–176.

Hoh, Erling. "The Long River's Journey Ends." *Natural History*, 105, No. 7 (July 1996):

Merrill, James M. "The Asiatic Squadron: 1835–1907." *American Neptune*, 29 (April 1969): 106–117.

Morton, Louis. "Army and Marines on the China Station: A Study in Military and Political Rivalry." *Pacific Historical Review*, 29 (February 1960): 221–245.

Settle, T.G.W. "The Last Cruise of the *Palos*." *Shipmates*: U.S. Naval Academy
     Alumni Association, 24, No. 4 (April 1961): 2–6.
Tate, E. Mowbray. "American Merchant and Naval Contacts with China, 1874–
     1850." *American Neptune*, 30 (July 1971): 171–191.
Tolley, Kemp. "Three Piecie and Other Dollars Mex." *Shipmates*: U.S. Naval
     Academy Alumni Association, 28, No. 10 (December 1965): 8–10.
Ware, Bruce R., Jr. "Winning the Engineering White E." U.S. Naval Institute
     Proceedings (April 1919): 593–621.

EDITOR'S MILITARY HISTORY

Dennis L. Noble retired from the U.S. Coast Guard in 1978 as a Senior Chief Marine Science Technician (E-8). He served at a number of shore stations and cutters, making two trips to the Antarctic and six to the Arctic and other locations between these extremes. After retirement, Noble returned to school, earning a Ph.D. in U.S. history from Purdue University. He is the author of ten books, including two on the U.S. military in Asia: *The Eagle and the Dragon: The United States Military in China, 1901–1937* and *Forgotten Warriors: Combat Art from Vietnam*. The author now writes full time and lives in Sequim, Washington, with his wife, Loren, and a strange dog and an even stranger cat.